ROUTEMASTER

First published 1991
Second edition 1995

ISBN 185414 178 3

Published by Capital Transport Publishing
38 Long Elmes, Harrow Weald, Middlesex

Printed by Bath Midway Press
Midlands Industrial Estate, Holt, Wiltshire

Above RM 1 at an aluminium exhibition on the South Bank in June 1955, showing the 'Saunders RT' style offside route number arrangement originally fitted. *Bruce Jenkins*

Opposite RM 1 in Vauxhall Bridge Road while at work from Cricklewood garage in May 1956. *Bruce Jenkins*

Contents pages RM 2 in its original green livery and early production RM 113. *LT Museum*

Front cover RM 1122 in Surbiton on its first day in service, 9th May 1962, the day after London said goodbye to its last trolleybus. *Geoff Rixon*

Back cover RML 2429 at Uxbridge in June 1966. *Capital Transport*

ROUTEMASTER

KEN BLACKER

VOLUME ONE
1954-1969

Capital Transport

CHAPTER ONE
RM 1   10

CHAPTER TWO
RM 2   28

CHAPTER THREE
RML 3   32

CHAPTER FOUR
CRL 4   36

CHAPTER FIVE
THE SLAVE RIGS   41

CHAPTER SIX
THE RM IN PRODUCTION   42

CHAPTER SEVEN
BUILDING THE RM   56

CHAPTER EIGHT
TRIALS AND TRIBULATIONS   58

CHAPTER NINE
LEYLAND ENGINES   62

CHAPTER TEN
RM 664 – THE SILVER LADY   64

CHAPTER ELEVEN
THE TROLLEYBUS CONVERSION YEARS   68

CHAPTER TWELVE
THE FIRST THIRTY-FOOTERS   80

CHAPTER THIRTEEN
RMF 1254   84

CHAPTER FOURTEEN
THE RMCs   88

CHAPTER FIFTEEN
TOWARDS STANDARDISATION   96

CHAPTER SIXTEEN
THE RCLs   104

CHAPTER SEVENTEEN
THE MAIN RML BATCH   108

CHAPTER EIGHTEEN
MID-SIXTIES AND RESHAPING   112

CHAPTER NINETEEN
NORTHERN GENERAL   122

CHAPTER TWENTY
AIRPORT ROUTEMASTERS   126

CHAPTER TWENTY ONE
ALDENHAM AND THE ROUTEMASTERS   130

CHAPTER TWENTY TWO
QUIETENING THE ROUTEMASTER   132

CHAPTER TWENTY THREE
THE FRM   134

CHAPTER TWENTY FOUR
AMBASSADORS ABROAD   140

AUTHOR'S NOTE

The history of the Routemaster is an ongoing one which hopefully will not be concluded for many years to come. This first volume outlines the complex story of London's most famous bus from its inception and takes it up to the end of 1969, at which point the Country Area operations and vehicles were transferred to London Country Bus Services Ltd and the Central Area operations came under the control of the Greater London Council.

In a volume of this nature there are limitations on the amount of detail that can be included. Where technical matters are concerned I have endeavoured to cover all major points without going into such a wealth of small detail as to make the narrative uninteresting to all except a small minority of readers. For space reasons it has not been possible to list the routeings or termini of services referred to, or every intermediate alteration or withdrawal; this information can be obtained elsewhere. Nor has it been possible to document within the text all of the many weekend variations from the standard Monday to Friday patterns of operation. Wherever withdrawal dates are quoted these relate, unless otherwise stated, to the first date the vehicle or service referred to is non-operational, it having worked for the last time on the previous day.

Every effort has been made to make this history as accurate as possible but it is an unfortunate fact that, no matter how careful the author may be or how assiduously the finished draft is checked by others, a few mistakes are likely to creep in undetected. A work such as this consists essentially of thousands of facts strung together in what, hopefully, forms a readable story, and it is almost impossible to avoid missing out or misinterpreting the odd one. A particular difficulty arises when even information from official sources proves contradictory, as it sometimes does.

I am indebted to many people who have assisted in one way or another in the preparation of this volume, generally by providing information or by checking the text. I am especially grateful to Lawrie Bowles, Colin Curtis, Ken Glazier, Jim Jordan, Peter Nichols, Alan Nightingale, Bob Pennyfather, Douglas Scott, Colin Stannard, David Stewart, Reg Westgate and Bob Williamson, but particularly to the late Ron Lunn who was my colleague over many years in collating London bus history and whose notes I have referred to frequently when writing the text. My thanks, too, to the many photographers whose work I have used; it is their photographs which bring the story to life.

London, December 1990   KEN BLACKER

Top RM 588 at Holloway in August 1961 during the brief period of RMs running alongside trolleybuses on route 609 on Sundays. *Gerald Mead*

Centre The Green Line coach version of the standard RM, represented by RMC 1509 in Kensington High Street in 1964. *Fred Ivey*

Right KGJ605D was one of 65 Routemaster coaches built for British European Airways following trials with RMF 1254. *Geoff Morant*

INTRODUCTION

In the annals of public transport history it is rare to encounter a vehicle which has become a legend in its own time, but such is the case with London's famous Routemaster. Conceived as an idea shortly after the second world war, created in prototype form in 1954 and put into production in 1959, the Routemaster should, by all normal criteria, now be a thing of the past. Yet it lives on, and although its numbers are now greatly diminished, the Routemaster story is by no means at an end.

Well before the Routemaster came on the scene, London Transport had already demonstrated its commitment to the achievement of a standardised double-deck fleet of its own design with the famous RT. The harsh operating conditions which prevailed throughout much of London had long since convinced the Company's engineers that vehicles had to be specially designed which were capable of coping with those conditions, whilst standardisation paid big dividends in slashing unit costs and cutting down-time. However there was a price to be paid, as better than average vehicles could only be obtained at a cost, and London Transport was frequently criticised for purchasing more expensive buses than its provincial counterparts. The Routemaster was indeed dearer to produce than its contemporaries, not only because of its technically advanced specification but also because of heavy development and tooling costs which had to be offset against it. Back in 1956 it was hoped that a production run of at least 4,000 Routemasters would be achieved, giving a very wide spread of overheads, but this was not to be. However at a premium of about ten per cent above other double deckers the Routemaster was not really expensive when its potential for very long life was taken into account.

Events were to dictate that the Routemaster would be London's last standardised bus. Large scale standardisation on a specialist vehicle involves a lengthy gestation period followed by a long production run over many years to achieve the required numbers as well as to spread manufacturing costs as widely as possible. There is the danger that it can lead to stagnation in design and a loss of forward thinking, with a risk of obsolescence in the later years of manufacture as outside trends catch up with and then overtake it. To an extent this is what happened to the Routemaster. In 1954 when the first prototype was built the front-engined double decker with open rear platform was the norm for town work everywhere and served many country districts too, but manufacture of the Routemaster was brought to a halt in 1968 because the rear-engined, front entrance bus suitable for one man operation had begun to prevail. And though a splendid rear-engined Routemaster, full of potential, was eventually designed and built, it came too late.

The Routemaster was launched into a transport scene vastly different from that of today. London's trams had been finally banished only two years before the first prototype was built, and the final remnants of the STL and STD classes were still in service along with the last remaining Guy double decker. New RTs and RTLs were still being delivered, although the end of their production run was nigh. And the massive trolleybus network was still almost intact, providing the Routemaster with its first major task which was to eliminate electric traction from the streets of London. This was an era of uncertainty for public transport operators with a permanent downturn in trade now apparent. A portent for the future came with the publication in February 1955 of a Ministry of Transport Enquiry under S.P. Chambers into the conduct of London Transport which, whilst concluding that the undertaking was conducted efficiently and with due regard to economy, suggested measures which included the use of standee buses to meet heavy traffic surges. Even before the first prototype had entered service, the first rumblings of the debate which were later prematurely to end Routemaster production were beginning to be heard.

The claim was made, with perfect justification, that the Routemaster was the most advanced integral and chassisless double-deck bus anywhere in the world. Over the long years which have since passed, the faith held by its designers in its unique construction has been amply justified, and fears that the integral design would prove more vulnerable to mishaps proved totally unfounded. The Routemaster confounded all its critics and, despite early engineering problems, has proved its worth many times over to become longer lasting than any other urban bus.

CHAPTER ONE

RM 1

Above **The London of the days when the Routemaster was first conceived was a city run down in the aftermath of war and struggling to improve despite early post-war austerity and shortages. The bus, tram and trolleybus fleet had received only minimum maintenance in the war and keeping it running on a day to day basis was a problem. The supply of new vehicles was strictly controlled and totally inadequate. In these inauspicious circumstances it needed real vision to look as far into the future as the life of the Routemaster would be required to extend and to design a vehicle of such quality. This view at Gardiners Corner, Aldgate, typifies the 1947 London scene with a mixture of buses (LT, STL and 'utility' Guy) and trolleybuses which was a far cry from the standardisation which the LPTB craved. All was to be swept away, even the buildings in this photograph, in the brave new era in which the Routemaster dream was to reach fulfilment.**

In October 1947, less than three months before its abolition under the nationalisation plans of the Socialist government of the time, the London Passenger Transport Board's chairman, Lord Ashfield, gave authority to start development of a chassisless double deck bus design of aluminium construction. From this far-sighted decision sprang the famous Routemaster which, in terms of economy of operation, longevity, and suitability for its task, can almost certainly be regarded as the most successful motor bus ever designed.

The Routemaster was a fusion of concepts, many of which had been applied only sparingly to the construction of road passenger vehicles, if at all. The ultimate production design represented the combined labours of many design staff and engineers working in teams at London Transport's Chiswick works, at the AEC plant at Southall and at Park Royal. Co-ordinating all, and the main source of inspiration for the entire project, was A.A.M. Durrant CBE, C Eng, FIMechE, FCIT, FRSA. As Chief Mechanical Engineer (Road Services) of London Transport for more than three decades, 'Bill' Durrant was at the forefront of his profession and highly respected throughout the industry. He guided the work of the mechanical design teams and was the

main instigator of many new concepts which were tried out. Detail work on the famous Routemaster body, with which we are all so familiar, progressed through frequent meetings at Chiswick led by J.W. Wicks, the works manager, who was in charge of the body design team. Other major contributors were the chief draughtsman, Phil Lunghi, who had earlier been deeply involved in creating the RT, and Arthur Sainsbury, the highly competent foreman of the Chiswick body shop. Assisting them was external consultant Douglas Scott who had earlier designed the bodywork and exterior of the RF single decker and was largely responsible for the shape and decor of the Routemaster.

Right from the start, the main design theme envisaged a chassisless vehicle employing a box section body of extremely rigid construction built of aluminium alloy. The crux of the concept was to achieve lightness of weight in order to maximise passenger carrying capacity within legal constraints, coupled to an operating performance superior to that so far achieved. Key features had to include its suitability for jig-built production on a mass scale, the standardisation of units, and rigid control of the manufacturing process to achieve the very maximum of parts inter-

changeability and minimum of downtime, together with the highest possible level of passenger and crew comfort, all combined in a vehicle with a guaranteed long life span.

At the outset, certain major features, including the size of the vehicle, the position of the engine, and the siting of the passenger entrance and staircase, were not established. Indeed, although the original concept was based on a double decker, even this was questioned in the early design stage. Neither was the use of a diesel engine always a foregone conclusion as the pro-trolleybus lobby was strong at the time, and prudence dictated that the new design should be suitable for electric operation as an alternative to diesel should the former be decided upon.

In the sphere of chassisless construction for road passenger vehicles, London Transport had already led the field in 1939/40 with the fleet of 175 trolleybuses built for it by the MCW organisation. These had operated with complete success throughout the war in some of the most difficult and war-ravaged operating territory, playing a strategic role in serving the docks and factories of London's East End and in linking the commercial heart of the City with the northern and eastern suburbs. Many of the major thoroughfares

Left Construction of road vehicles in aluminium alloy represented an almost unknown quantity at the Routemaster's conception. The main previous exponent of the art had been Short Brothers, whose experience in building the first British all metal aeroplanes and flying boats using light alloys led from 1926 onwards to the construction at Rochester of alloy bus bodies. Lighter but admittedly more costly than wooden bodies with steel strengtheners, they gained comparatively little popularity and most of Short's extensive output continued to employ conventional construction. Just one aluminium double decker had been tried out by a London Transport forerunner, a 46-seater on a Tilling Stevens B10A2 chassis delivered experimentally to East Surrey in December 1928 and purchased by them in April 1929. PK 4244 spent most of its time at Swanley on route 407 and was sold in 1935.

Above Right The suitability of chassisless construction for passenger road vehicles was doubted by many in the industry. Fears were held that the resultant structure would be found too rigid to withstand constant road stresses or, alternatively, insufficiently strong because of the lack of a solid backbone which the conventional chassis provided. A demonstration of faith was needed to sway the sceptics and this was provided on an impressive scale by London Transport itself with its large fleet of MCW chassisless trolleybuses which proved in every way to be at least as good as the conventional chassis plus body combination. The comparatively insignificant Dartford firm of John C. Beadle (Coachbuilders) Ltd had a vision ahead of their time when, in 1939, they took out several patents with a view to going into production of chassisless or integral buses and coaches. The war intervened but four prototype 33-seat single deckers were built afterwards, three of which were alloy framed. Their 1946 patent specification was for a vehicle capable of receiving any suitable type of engine or transmission without adaptation of the standard body. More than 500 vehicles were built from 1948 onwards, many of the earlier ones like EFU855 using reconditioned pre-war running units where new ones were impossible to obtain. Manufacture ceased in 1957 just before production of the next chassisless alloy bus, the RM, got under way.

over which they operated still had granite sett surfaces, often very uneven, but the constant pounding which these caused had done nothing to reduce the rigidity of the body structures.

Aluminium alloy construction was another matter altogether. It had been very little favoured by the bus industry before the war and the few efforts made to propagate it, principally by Short Bros Ltd (who, in addition to being bus builders, also had aircraft manufacturing interests) proved unsuccessful. However, the rapid development in aluminium alloy construction, forced on aircraft manufacturers by war needs, impressed a number of people whose peacetime preoccupation lay in motorbus construction. One of these was A.A.M. Durrant who, though himself seconded to the Ministry of Defence as Director of Tank Design, was able to learn from London Transport's experience in aluminium alloy technology in another military sphere, that of aircraft manufacture, gained through the Board's position at the head of the London Aircraft Production consortium based at Aldenham and, later, Leavesden. Steel framework could be adapted to secure a high degree of weight saving but, the more thinly the structure was gauged, the more quickly it

would be prone to failure through corrosion. Aluminium alloy could suffer from its own type of corrosion problems but the structure, being inherently lighter than steel, could be built to more substantial dimensions within the same weight limits.

A proposition mooted as early as July 1947 to collaborate with Leyland Motors Ltd (as body manufacturers) and Imperial Chemical Industries Ltd (producers of aluminium alloy) in the design and construction of 25 chassisless light alloy buses got nowhere, but London Transport engineers kept a close eye on developments elsewhere in the bus industry which, as it happened, were very few. John C Beadle (Coachbuilders) Ltd of Dartford had patented a form of body construction manufactured entirely in aluminium alloy which they claimed could result in a 40% reduction in weight compared with a standard body, and four single deck chassisless prototypes were built in 1947. The Board's engineers inspected these under construction, and Beadle was asked to submit a design for the construction of a double decker embodying the same principles. No further co-operation with the Dartford company stemmed from this, but the operating performance of their product continued to be observed from a distance.

Meanwhile, contact with ICI (who were also Beadle's suppliers of aluminium alloy) was maintained, ICI having a close interest in developments in Switzerland in the use of aluminium alloy for road vehicle and railway rolling stock construction. The Beadle chassisless single decker later went into full production, initially incorporating running units salvaged from older vehicles as new ones were not available. Several Tilling group companies purchased the distinctive looking bus version and coaches were also built later, for which BET companies were often customers. Although they gave quite good service, many, particularly those built earlier in the production run, were never entirely satisfactory, often developing a crab-wise gait, probably through lack of rigidity. In the view of G Verdon-Roe, Managing Director of Saunders Engineering & Shipyard Ltd of Beaumaris, Anglesey (who in addition to building RT bodies for London Transport also shared their interest in, and discussed with them, aluminium body design) some manufacturers of alloy bodies failed to understand the principle that design should be for equal stiffness rather than equal strength when replacing steel. With the Routemaster, London Transport's designers made no such error of judgement.

By the early 1950s, design work was well advanced in many respects. When the conversion plan was approved by the Minister in 1954, the goal was now set as producing a vehicle to commence replacement of the existing trolleybus fleet from 1st January 1958 onwards. A finite time lay ahead for building and testing prototypes and for establishing a production line from which delivery would commence in August 1957. Already the basic formula had fallen into shape. In 1951 came the decision that the vehicle should be no larger in size than a 65 seater. A bigger, 70 seat vehicle had been considered and rejected, despite the totally successful operation of a large fleet of 70 seat trolleybuses. The grounds of rejection were that a bus approximately 30 feet long would cause difficulty in congested London streets and would experience accommodation problems at terminal points and in garages. It was decreed that, from an operational point of view, any vehicle with seating capacity in excess of 65 would be slow at stops and would lead to inefficient fare collection. The feasibility of building a two-axle bus with 64 seats (plus five standing passengers) within existing construction and use regulations had already been demonstrated by the design staff and it was on this basis that the design work for the Routemaster proceeded.

The in-depth review of passenger carrying capacity which resulted in the adoption of a 64 seater was part of a complete reappraisal of all operating requirements in order to establish the form which the new vehicle should take. In A.A.M. Durrant's own words, "We asked the Operating Managers to try to erase from their minds all past features they had specified, to think out their requirements from rock bottom and ignore for the time being any restrictions that hitherto may have had any influence upon them, such as Ministry regulations, the aim being to get down to the ideal bus from their point of view; if necessary we could go into the question of seeking some relaxation or other in the regulations later on". Much operational research was employed to establish the optimum platform width and position, stanchion positioning etc. In due course, the single rear entrance was chosen after considering front, centre or even a combination of entrances; similarly, since this precluded a rear engine and an underfloor unit would have made the bus too high, the conventional front engine position was chosen.

On the basic question of double versus single deck, the latter was ruled out because equal carrying capacity would be achievable only in standee conditions, and experience in the United States was already showing that

passengers forced to accept cattle truck conditions for peak period journeys were liable to forsake bus travel in off-peaks even though seats would be available, and it is the buoyancy of off-peak travel that is essential to the bus operator from a financial standpoint.

High performance, especially in acceleration and braking, was accepted as a basic requisite of the new design right from the start, since this meant a job done more efficiently and cheaply using fewer vehicles. An early preference by the design team for a full-fronted double-decker was ruled out after objections from two quarters. The Transport & General Workers Union protested on the grounds that driving and maintenance would be made harder. The management side's less credible objection, voiced by a member of the Executive, A.B.B. Valentine, was that at stops shared by trolley and diesel buses heading for different destinations, elderly or poor-sighted people might mistake one for the other.

The few people who gained access to the experimental shop at Chiswick in the closing months of 1952 saw a mock-up of the front and nearside of the proposed body design, which by now had been almost finalised. Minor modifications continued, principally in the bonnet and grille areas, and the design for RM 1 took final shape during 1953.

Facing Page **The Routemaster-to-be gradually took shape over a period of time. The box dimensions of the body were dictated by existing construction and use regulations and seating capacity requirements, but detail features were settled by the design team, sometimes using trial and error as the means for arriving at a satisfactory conclusion. A pre-prototype model was constructed during 1952 in plasticine on a wooden frame at a scale of 1:5. It is seen here with the first type of half-cab front proposed after the original plan for a full width cab had been abandoned. A family similarity to the pre-war TF class and the post-war Green Line coach RTC 1 was readily apparent in the bonnet design. The vertical dividing strip in the opening segment of the upper deck windows is of interest but it is not known if sliding ventilators (as favoured by most provincial operators) were being considered or if this was, perhaps, just a careless feature included by the model-maker which signified nothing. Note the neat way in which the lower side panels were extended downwards to incorporate the lifeguard.**

Left **Following quickly upon the heels of the plasticine model, a full-size mock-up was constructed in the experimental shop based on a timber framework with aluminium panelling. The design features of the 1:5 model were reproduced remarkably closely, including the RT-style indicator layout.**

Facing Page **The impracticability of the original bonnet arrangement led, in the latter part of 1952, to a substantial redesign resulting from which the smooth frontal contour was broken by a bulging bonnet front. A vertical radiator was obviously under consideration at this stage, and the mock-up now demonstrates the inferior front and nearside destination displays now intended for the Routemaster.**

Above **1953, and the mock-up now closely resembles the design finally adopted for RM 1. Examination of the interior rear bulkhead shows the upper part of the window surrounds in a light colour, a decor feature employed on later members of the RF class but not used on the Routemaster.**

It had been accepted from the outset that a major share of the manufacturing work would go to AEC with whom London Transport had a contractual agreement dating back to 1933 to purchase a minimum of 75% of its bus requirements in any given year. Since bodywork construction was crucial to the chassisless design, it was inevitable that AEC's associate company, Park Royal Vehicles, would take a leading role in this respect. However, London Transport had demonstrated with the RT family that it did not wish to single-source any major contract and, from as early as 1952, discussions were held with Leyland Motors Ltd over the Integrally Mounted (or IM) project, as this new bus was then known. In November of that year, C.B. Nixon, Leyland's Chairman and Henry Spurrier, his able assistant, who as Sir Henry, later led Leyland through one of the high points of the company's history, discussed with London Transport's Chairman, Lord Latham, the role which Leyland might play in supplying buses to the new design. At the time there was still internal debate as to whether the new fleet would be motor or trolleybuses but Leyland was prepared to co-operate in the design and production of either. Well before the 1954 decision to replace trolleybuses with motor buses the designers had accurately anticipated this outcome and finalised their plans for the first prototypes to be powered by diesel engines.

In due course, four prototypes were authorised. Two were to be constructed by the established combination of London Transport, AEC and Park Royal, and the actual manufacture of both commenced at Chiswick in 1953 using parts and expertise supplied by the other two partners. Supervising their construction was Arthur Sainsbury who had already earned his place in the annals of London bus history with a technically advanced body, designed by and named after him, which had been fitted to STL 2477 in May 1950. For the further two prototypes, London Transport turned to other suppliers, Leyland being the contractor for all mechanical equipment on both of them. Two separate builders were invited to supply the bodies. The choice of MCW was an obvious one. This concern had not only supplied the chassisless trolleybus fleet, which had been built at the Metro-Cammell works in Birmingham, but it was also currently heavily committed to the construction of chassisless single deckers, mostly for export, albeit of steel rather than alloy construction. Furthermore, MCW was heavily involved with London Transport in the RT construction programme, then drawing to a close, having supplied bodies from both the Metro-Cammell plant at Elmdon and Weymann's at Addlestone. It was at Addlestone that the new prototype bus was to be built. The other choice of supplier was, on the face of it, a little more surprising. Eastern Coach Works Ltd of Lowestoft was not an established supplier to London Transport, nor had it accumulated any substantial expertise in the construction of chassisless vehicles, although it was one of the very few bus builders at the time to standardise on aluminium alloy construction rather than steel. However ECW was, like London Transport, a unit of the state owned British Transport Commission whose subsidiaries were always required to consider placing orders within the group rather than outside and, in effect, to give first refusal to Bristol and/or ECW. By virtue of its contractual obligations to AEC and the sheer volume of its new bus requirements, London Transport was able to steer clear of the standard Bristol/ECW combination imposed wherever possible on other state owned concerns, the ECW bodied RFW and GS classes of single decker being gestures towards group solidarity as, presumably, was the ordering of a Routemaster prototype.

The public announcement by London Transport that all trolleybuses with the exception of seven routes in south-west London were to be replaced by diesel buses starting in about three years' time was made on 28th April 1954. The same occasion was used to break the news that the replacement bus would be of a lightweight type with 8ft wide aluminium body which would carry 64 passengers and yet weigh no more when fully loaded than the 56 seat RT. Greatly improved suspension and transmission would give the smoothest possible ride. Two prototypes would be under test by the end of the year. Well before this announcement, rumour had been rife that a new type of London bus was on the way; many now looked forward eagerly to seeing what it would be like.

RM 1 poses for its first official photograph. Construction is not complete at this stage as the front trafficators have still to be fitted, but it is roadworthy. The original front end treatment of bonnet and wings presents a bulbous and slightly fussy appearance, and the symbolic dummy registration number LTE 1954 is noteworthy. The lack of tumble-home on the lower body sides produces a boxiness which sits uneasily with the otherwise gently curved appearance of the vehicle when viewed from this angle.
LT Museum

Side on, the Routemaster's appearance suffered from the unaccustomed uprightness of its front profile. Such squareness had not been seen since the Bluebird LTs and the original STLs, both produced more than two decades earlier. As with the RM, the upright front of these two earlier designs was influenced by a desire to achieve maximum seating capacity. LT Museum

RM 1 was unveiled on AEC's stand at the Earl's Court Commercial Motor Exhibition on 24th September 1954. A gathering of trade representatives at Chiswick had been afforded the privilege of inspecting the vehicle at an official press day shortly beforehand. The new bus which stood before them was an impressively well conceived and well built forerunner of a model which would clearly be costly to produce and probably economically feasible only to London Transport with its vast purchasing power. In technical specification, it was undeniably at the very forefront of passenger vehicle design, upholding the London Transport tradition of being ahead of the field in terms of technology and quality. Few would have realised, way back in September 1954, the huge impact which the Routemaster would have on the London bus scene in years to come and the tremendous longevity it was to achieve. Few, too, would have believed this vehicle was to mark the end of the road for London Transport's independent vehicle design and that purchases following on from it would be 'off the shelf' models.

Admist all the gloss and glamour of the new vehicles at Earl's Court that September the Routemaster was, without doubt, the star of the show because of all the innovations which it embodied. For the technically minded, it presented an exciting insight into a host of new developments even if some of these may perhaps have seemed foolhardily complex, or expensive beyond the reach of the smaller operator; but, for all its newness, there was also a slight pang of disappointment for many in the Routemaster. After being promised a revolutionary new vehicle, its general similarity in layout and shape to any other conventional double decker came as a mild surprise, especially as it was rather box-like in shape compared with the curvaceous RT, much less bright and airy internally, and definitely lacking in destination display which had taken a 25 year step backwards to the standards of the LTs and STs of 1929/30.

Appearances, however, were deceptive and behind what many regarded at the time as an uninspired exterior lay a design which was revolutionary in so many ways. "This Bus Is Years Ahead" proclaimed London Transport's house magazine and, in many respects, this was true. Technically, the Routemaster was unsurpassed and yet, within a decade, it was to present an enigma. Who could have foreseen the great and rapid changes within the industry which would so quickly render the front engine-rear entrance configuration obsolete for most operating applications?

To one group within the industry, the Routemaster's design features came as no surprise. Those who had attended the International Union of Public Transport's congress at Munich in July 1953 would have heard a paper given by A.A.M. Durrant which unveiled many of his ideas on bus design, including the weight-saving advantages of chassisless construction, particularly when applied to double deckers. The practicality of his ideas on suspension systems and transmissions, voiced at the congress, was also demonstrated to the extent that they were all incorporated in the new bus which everybody with any interest in passenger vehicle design was keen to examine at first hand.

RM 1 was the very embodiment of the principle that weight saving was of paramount importance. The adoption of an integral structure of high duty aluminium alloy to serve as the main load-carrying unit was at the heart of the design in eliminating the heavy conventional chassis frame and substituting two much lighter subframes upon which to mount the mechanical units front and rear. In order to produce greater passenger accommodation than on the RT, the overall length had been increased from 26ft to 27ft (the maximum then permitted on two axles) with an increase in wheelbase from 16ft 4ins to 16ft 9ins. The loading platform had been slightly reduced in length, the front bulkhead had been moved forward (giving a shallower cab), and the upper deck front had been made almost vertical. The effect of boxiness which the latter expedient produced was a source of regret to the design team especially as previous vehicles up to the RT series had featured a sweeping front end which, in design parlance, contributed to the humanity and acceptance of the big vehicle in London streets. A tapering-in of the front was adopted to help lighten the contour, and the problem was further mitigated to an extent by giving a more sloped rear than on the RT. Within a box dimension of 27ft by 8ft, the Routemaster seating capacity was increased over the RT by two on the lower deck to 28 and by six on the upper deck to 36 but with no increase in gross weight and no great loss of comfort. Like the RT, RM 1 was legally permitted to carry eight standing passengers under the PSV Seating Capacity Regulations of 1954 but, by agreement with the Transport & General Workers' Union, a maximum of only five was enforced. The seat spacing on the lower deck was only one quarter of an inch less per seat than on an RT although the upper deck was slightly more cramped with a loss of one and a quarter inches per seat. The original unladen weight of RM 1 was remarkably low at 6tons 14cwt 2qrs. Fully laden with 64 passengers it tipped the scales at just 11tons compared with 11tons 5cwt for a loaded 56 seater RT.

The extremely rigid box structure was formed by joining together the underframe and floor, the sides, the roof, and the front and rear bulkheads, with additional stiffness provided by the intermediate floor and its supports. The driver's cab and nearside front wing assembly were carried by the front bulkhead while the rear platform and staircase were supported by the upper saloon. Deep crossbearers corresponding in position to the pillar sections formed the main members of the underframe, transferring the load to the body sides and thus dispensing with the need for conventional chassis frame longitudinals. On the lower saloon body sides, interior stress panels extended from skirt to waist, sandwiched between the crossbearer and pillar joints, and were solid riveted to the pillar flanges. The main crossbearers, of considerable strength, were fabricated from I-shaped high duty alloy, while the pillars were of H-section, bolted to the crossbearers with angle-brackets. The waist and cant rails, which were not critically load bearing, were simple channels riveted to the pillars in bay lengths to support the panelling and window pans. Intermediate floor bearers were also of I-configuration, forming supports for the upper saloon pillars which were again H-section but of lighter material. The roof framing was of square section aluminium alloy tube to which overlapping external panels were riveted in bay lengths. Elsewhere, the panels were bolt-jointed and blind-riveted to the frame without the addition of cover strips.

A particularly interesting feature of the Routemaster body was the rear end design which, owing to the density of London traffic and the propensity for rear-end collisions, was of unit construction. It was built up of four separate units: the vertical section incorporating the rear window, the lower portion of the staircase up to and including the fourth tread, the upper half of the staircase, and the platform flooring. The farsighted concept that, on production vehicles, these items could quickly be removed and replaced by new ones from stock, was amply justified time and time again in the years that ensued.

Almost every aspect of the Routemaster's mechanical specification was of interest, not least the means by which the various units were hung from the chassisless body. Two main subframes, one each at front and rear and called the A and B frame respectively, were responsible for supporting most of the running gear although certain items were attached directly to the underside of the body, notably the gearbox and the 25 gallon fuel tank. The A frame, which could easily be detached and pulled out in wheelbarrow fashion, consisted of two pressed steel channel section longitudinal members joined by crossbearers, including a substantial box section under the centre of the engine carrying the main engine mountings and those of the front suspension units; a further channel section member joining the front end of the longitudinals supported the front of the engine. The subframe was wide at the rear to anchor on to the body sides at the number 2 crossbearer, but tapered at the front to normal chassis frame width.

The Routemaster's unusually large lower rear window was clearly influenced by RT design, although the upper one, in its glass fibre frame, was not. Neither the rather fussy horizontal direction indicators nor the curious mounting of the nearside rear light within the grab handle were features which were retained into the production era.
LT Museum

The engine fitted to RM 1, though only as a temporary expedient, was an AEC A204 type 9.6 litre unit as used on the RT except for variations necessary to accommodate the Routemaster's unusual form of three point rubber mounting designed to isolate engine vibrations from the bus itself, especially when idling. Modifications were also made to the oil filler and dipstick which were moved to be forward facing for access from the front to suit the bonnet lid which was unusual in lifting up alligator jaw style from hinges in the bulkhead. In the long term, it was intended to use a new engine then under development at Southall, but this was not yet available. The conventional fluid flywheel was a bolt-on unit capable of being changed without disturbing the engine. A very unusual feature was the fitment of an underfloor radiator in a slightly inclined position behind the engine and served by a chain driven fan. This arrangement was necessary to release the maximum body space for passengers; within the 27ft maximum length permissible at the time, siting the radiator and fan ahead of the engine in the conventional position would have prevented the achievement of a 64-seat capacity. The front end layout, including bonnet and wings, was the idea of A.B.B. Valentine. It superseded a much neater version by Douglas Scott which had itself replaced the original full front concept, but was no longer suitable because engine and pump modifications now required a higher bonnet with larger forward projection than the Scott design provided for. Its bulbous effect clashed with the overall body styling and the design team were far from happy with its appearance, whilst from a practical point of view the wide bonnet caused visibility to the nearside to be much less satisfactory than on the RT. As there was no radiator at the front, there was no need for a grille, the front panel carrying instead a prominently displayed large bullseye, modified by an elongated central bar, and seven downward 'spikes' to the centrally placed number plate.

The suspension marked a big step forward. Instead of conventional leaf springs, coils were used (with shock absorbers to control them) to give a softer ride which, besides lessening bumps and vibrations for passengers, was intended to reduce the stresses and strains imposed on the body structure and give it a

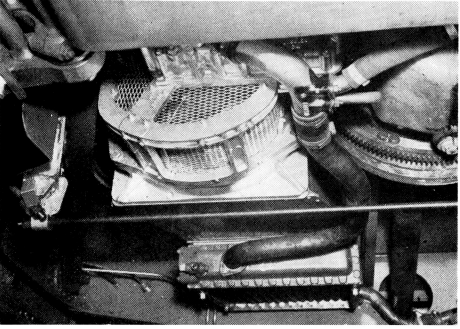

Above Right **The 'alligator jaw' style of bonnet lid permitted engine oil checking and topping up to be done from the front rather than reaching over the wing. However the wing panel itself could be quickly lifted off if required by undoing a pair of lock nuts. The front grille was also easy to remove, and in its absence the front end of the frame and lack of a conventional upright radiator can be clearly seen.** LT Museum

Right **Looking rearward at the underside of the bus behind the front boat, the wire mesh containing the fan can be seen mounted as a sub-unit with the water pump ahead of the radiator. The latter, which was inclined upwards towards the rear, received air from the fan blowing, through ducting, onto the heater exchange element. This quickly proved to be a totally unsatisfactory feature of early Routemaster design.**

longer life. At the front, the suspension was independent for each wheel in a manner by then in common use on private cars but previously used in a standard PSV application only by Midland Red, and then only on single deckers. This eliminated the need for a normal axle and relieved the front end bulkhead of high racking stresses, permitting lighter construction at this point than would be practicable in conventional bodies. Radius arms in the form of wishbones were employed to resist acceleration and braking torques. The front suspension member, bolted to the outside of the A frame side members was officially referred to as the front 'boat'. At the rear, the suspension was not independent so an orthodox style of axle was used. However, the same system of coil springs and shock absorbers was used, the tops of the coils bearing upon a specially strengthened wheel arch structure built into the side of the bus. The big advantage of coil springs at the rear was that they could be placed further out to the edge of the bus than leaf springs, thereby improving stability and freedom from bumps. So stable was the Routemaster than it could tilt safely to 32 degrees with only the top deck fully loaded, whereas the RT only just met the 28 degrees requirement in the same circumstances.

The rear, B, frame, which was also quickly detachable, was pivoted to the body structure just behind the midships mounted gearbox and supported the axle. The drive and differential assembly was offset to the left to correspond with the position of the engine and produce a straight transmission line, reducing protrusion in the lower deck gangway. The engine was set a little to one side to provide greater width in the driver's cab. An unusual feature of the rear axle was the employment of a spiral bevel drive instead of the well proven worm and wheel type which was in almost universal use because of its reliability, the almost unknown (at least in a PSV application) spiral bevel design being chosen in order to reduce friction loss. The rear axle ratio was 5.22:1.

The transmission and braking systems on the Routemaster were both largely untried on PSVs except that experiments had been carried out in extensive service trials on a number of RTs. The Wilson type epicyclic gearbox, a long time London Transport favourite, was retained, but the principle of preselection of gears was abandoned in favour of direct gear changes made by electro-hydraulic valves controlled by the familiar column-mounted gear lever, the gear brake bands being individually operated by direct hydraulic pressure from an oil pump within the body-mounted gearbox. This type of hydraulically operated gearbox, first proposed by Self Changing Gears Ltd of Coventry, had already been tried out on four RTs at Turnham Green (RT 778, 2207, 2208, 2273), these being the forerunners of 'two pedal' control, no clutch or operating pedal being necessary with this type of transmission. When changing upwards, the driver merely had to keep the throttle open and, at the appropriate moment, move the selector lever from one gear to the next.

A power hydraulic system was also used for Routemaster braking instead of the full air system previously favoured by London Trans-

port. Once again, Midland Red had been at the forefront in adopting hydraulics as a standard concept and the Daimler CD650 double decker built a few years earlier had also featured a hydraulic braking system, but the great majority of operators remained very sceptical. Another Turnham Green bus, RT 902, had already been fitted with Lockheed hydraulics devised by Automotive Products Ltd of Leamington Spa, using technology derived by AP from its aircraft experience. The hydraulic system offered several apparent advantages, not least of which was a saving of some 112lbs in weight over a comparable air system. Reaction to a brake application was reckoned to be faster and smoother than with air and,

because of the use of a mineral oil, corrosion within the system should not occur, nor should freezing. The pump for the Lockheed constant flow system was mounted on and driven from the gearbox, the brake fluid container and two pressure accumulators being located under the floor on the offside. All four brake drums, of 15.5ins diameter with conventional leading and trailing shoes, were operated by S-shaped cams in conjunction with worm and worm-wheel type slack adjusters. The handbrake, mechanically connected only to the rear wheels, was mounted to the left of the driver instead of to the right, as had previously been the normal practice, so as to give unimpeded access to the cab.

The rear platform design, with its cubby hole where the conductor could stand without impeding passenger movement, was excellent. The glass-fronted faretable case was in a much more accessible position than on the RT; the small open compartment above it was for the time card and the conductor's waybill. Just visible is the wheelarch seat with a capacity for four, one more than on the RT, which was how the additional seating for two in the lower saloon was achieved. LT Museum

Steering was through the conventional AEC worm and nut gear which was well tried and ensured a long trouble-free life. Power assistance was not thought possible at this stage without a complete redesign of the linkage which was not easy within the restricted space available. Although the driver was not given power steering, he was provided with a comfortable cab, the design of which, including the seat, was the result of a comprehensive review of the ergonomic principles involved, the study of such being all the rage at the time. The only problem was that the cab appears to have been designed around drivers of average size, making it difficult or impossible for very short or very tall people to cope with.

Inside the Routemaster body, both floors were made of a corrugated alloy material sandwiched between flat sheets, a hard-wearing rubber and cork composition mat covering the upper side, with bevelled slats in the gangways. The floor cove panels on both decks were of chequered aluminium and the ceiling panels of sheet aluminium which, though cut in bay lengths, extended from one cant rail to the other, the normal separate cove panels being eliminated. To save weight, resin-bodied fibreglass was used for the bonnet top, wing valances and rear emergency window frame, and also, unusually, for the backs of the seat squabs. The seat cushion and squab fillings employed a resilient foam plastic material saving some 7.5lbs per seat compared with those in use on the RT. Timber was almost totally eliminated except for some hand rail and stanchion fixings, the platform sillbar and staircase treads.

In its internal decor, the RM broke away totally from the RT tradition by employing throughout colours which were generally much darker than Londoners were used to. The main side panels and window surrounds were rexine covered in damask red which would have given a very drab overall effect had it not been relieved by polished aluminium window surrounds. Above the windows ran a horizontal aluminium strip with a white plastic insert, and the ceilings were in sung yellow which helped, on the upper deck, to disguise nicotine stains.

The Holdsworth seating moquette was in a new and very attractive tartan style of mainly red but with yellow vertical lines to keep the design bright. This pattern, designed by Douglas Scott, was later adopted as standard for the production run and has now lasted in use for over three decades without becoming dated in style. Red hide seat edges were provided and seat backs were in a mid-grey, officially Chinese green, leathercloth. The seat frames were of the familiar RT type in polished alloy.

The platform and staircase stanchions and handrails, together with their brackets and fixings, were of stainless steel while those fitted in the upper and lower saloons were of polished alloy. The platform itself was well designed, particularly from the point of view of the conductor who was provided with a recess below the stairs, likened officially at the time to a sentrybox, where he could stand without impeding passenger flow. He had his own capacious locker, including a full-height compartment for his overcoat, and on the front of the locker door facing out onto the platform the farechart was displayed in a glass fronted container. Also under the stairs were the batteries in a cradle removable from the outside but topped up via a hinged flap inside the bus.

The saloon side windows were rubber glazed in alloy pans, there being four opening windows in the lower saloon and six upstairs. All were the same as those of the RF single decker, being of the Hallam Sleigh & Cheston winding quarter-drop type omitting a bar at the lower edge of the opening section to improve visibility. The two front windows of the upper deck and the nearside bulkhead window on the lower deck also contained quarter-drop windows and these were lockable to prevent opening in cold weather. At the rear, the very large platform window, deeper than the side windows with its top at a higher level, was inherited from the RT but the upper deck emergency window was smaller than on the RT and a little out of proportion with the one below.

No heating system was fitted but two slot type intake ventilators were provided at the front of each saloon, controlled by the conductor. Internal lighting was of the normal RT type. Fluorescent lights had been considered which would have been fitted in panels flush with the ceiling, but cost militated against their use while traditionalists preferred screw-in tungsten bulbs as being easier for

The interior saloon of RM 1 in its original condition demonstrates the one-piece ceiling panels and the stylish new moquette. Standards of comfort and finish have not been compromised in the quest for weight saving as happened on many provincial buses of the time. Before entering service the flat front bulkhead was substantially revamped with the installation of heater ducting and the removal of the ventilators and quarter drop nearside window. LT Museum

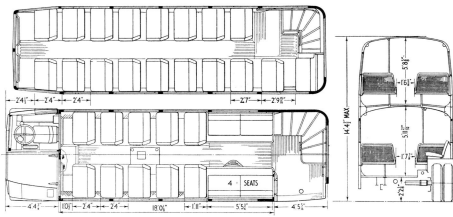

Above **Looking rearwards in the upper saloon, most of the familiar RM design features are already apparent although the ceiling construction and seat frames were revised for the production run. The rear seat armrest adjacent to the stairwell was perpetuated in earlier production vehicles but later discontinued.** LT Museum

A 1954 seating plan of RM 1 showing the principal dimensions and a contemporary diagram from *Bus & Coach* showing the layout of the front and rear (A and B) frames and the components which they support. These frames are shaded, and their points of attachment to the body shell can be clearly seen.

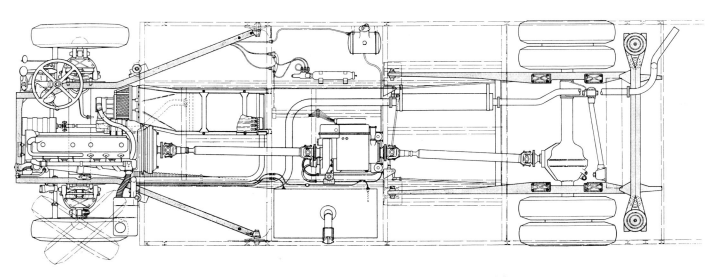

garage staff to replace. The destination displays were reduced to a single box at the front and rear, and above the platform, the latter being only of sufficient size to accommodate the destination wording and nothing else. A route number box was provided under the canopy as on the majority of RTs and, on the offside, a route number plate holder was provided, mounted midway between the end of the rearmost window and the back of the bus as on the Saunders-built RTs.

The rear registration number plate was square and was positioned centrally. Above this was a stop light, the main rear lights being positioned at the same level near the outer edge of the body, the nearside one being incorporated into the base of the rear grabrail. Horizontal direction arms for winking trafficators, then a new feature for London buses, were fitted just below the rear window, their equivalents at the front being in the form of cream painted ears projecting from the cantrail right on the corner of the body. These were much criticised for their lack of aesthetic appeal but this criticism did not stop a fairly large-scale trial of similar units being implemented on RTs in 1956.

Externally, RM 1 was painted in standard London Transport red and cream livery with black mudguards, the red oxide coloured wheels carrying the same embellishments as the RTs. Just above the front mudguard on both sides of the bus were neat little cast metal plates carrying the name ROUTEMASTER.

Above Left **Standing outside the Chiswick experimental shop where it was built, and accompanied by Arthur Sainsbury who built much of it, RM 1 is now complete with its front trafficators and ready for its first public showing at Earl's Court. The untidiness of the projecting trafficator ears, which looked as though they were an afterthought imposed upon the harmony of the overall design, caused adverse comment, but stronger still was the furore over the very restricted destination displays which, through an obsession to save weight, were reduced to a very basic level.** J.C. Gillham

Left and Below **RM 1 meets the world for the first time on AEC's stand at Earl's Court. Finishing touches have now been added including traditional enamelled AEC front hub caps and embossed metal ROUTEMASTER badges, as shown in the close-up photograph.** J. Wyndham/D.W.K. Jones

After the close of the Earl's Court exhibition on 2nd October 1954 RM 1 appeared only once more in public in its original form. This was at the Aluminium Centenary Exhibition at London's South Bank from 1st to 10th June 1955 where it was accompanied by a Commer/Harrington chassisless airport coach for BOAC and a Jensen chassis. Most of its time was spent on extensive testing and experimentation, some 7500 test miles being clocked up before the bus finally entered passenger service. This included fuel consumption tests at Northolt airport and hill climbing tests on Titsey Hill from which it was concluded that the engine needed uprating from its original setting. The Northolt tests showed that more comprehensive fuel consumption figures were needed, and these were obtained at the Motor Industry Research Association's famous proving ground at Nuneaton between 18th April and 6th May 1955 where tests with various

For the Aluminium exhibition on London's South Bank, RM 1 has lost its front posters and dummy registration numbers but the current year, 1955, now appears in the canopy route number box. The Harrington chassisless coach and Jensen aluminium passenger or goods chassis can be seen accompanying the Routemaster. An offside view (above), taken at the same location, shows the RT-style route number holder. This was positioned, as on the Saunders batch of RTs, midway along the staircase panel, but was destined never to be used.
J. Wyndham/
Lens of Sutton

On 29th June 1955 RM 1 refuels at Staines garage with the second Routemaster prototype behind it. The LONDON TRANSPORT posters have been removed and the vehicle is in the second week of its exhaustive trials at the fighting vehicle proving ground in Chobham. Alan B. Cross

weights, stops per mile and acceleration rates were undertaken. On all of these trials RM 1 was accompanied by the second Routemaster, which had now been constructed and was also being subjected to rigorous testing. Both vehicles undertook further test trials over a six-week period between 21st June and 29th July at the Ministry of Supply's Fighting Vehicle Proving Ground at Chobham, Surrey where endurance tests were carried out, accelerating body, suspension and transmission stresses in order to prove the structure as a whole. Here RM 1 clocked up some 4,500 miles under the severest conditions to test its suitability and road safety, including the effects of full-lock skidding at 30mph.

Apart from the modifications arising as a result of the MIRA and Chobham trials, such as the fitment of a heavier gauge A frame, RM 1 underwent several visible changes prior to entering service, mostly intended to improve passenger amenity. Gone was the much criticised spartan destination display in favour of London Transport's normal layout of three boxes at the front and two at the rear, whilst the box above the platform was enlarged to accommodate a route number and 'via' display identical to that at the back. Although the intermediate point boxes were shallower than those on the RT, the use of smaller lettering prevented any loss of infor-

mation, the side and rear displays being revised to incorporate the route number to the left of the route information instead of above it. A new feature was the fitting of a roller blind on the offside instead of a plate to show the route number; the winding handle was behind the fare chart door.

A further major improvement was the installation of a saloon heating and ventilation system, the presence of which was immediately apparent because of the fitting of an ungainly air intake grille at the front of the vehicle below the destination box, which also projected into the cantrail level cream band. Behind the grille lay a radiator linked to the engine water cooling system, the air entering the system through the forward movement of the vehicle and being warmed before passing through ducts into the saloon without the need for fans. In summer months, the system could be switched off, allowing cool air to enter. Before installing the system into RM 1 preliminary work had been carried out on STL 2477, the vehicle carrying the experimental 'Sainsbury' body, from which it was deduced that a satisfactory amount of heat to warm a double deck bus could be obtained from a ram air radiator mounted under the destination box on the front canopy. Credit for designing this system of fresh air heating and ventilation, which was undoubtedly more healthy than conventional methods of recirculating stale air, was claimed by London Transport although it bore more than a passing similarity to the Cave-Brown-Cave method which preceded it in the provinces, the difference being that the London Transport system retained the normal engine cooling radiator instead of doing away with it, a second heat

exchanger interconnected with it being installed behind the cant rail grille. There were two heat-cum-fresh air outlets in the lower saloon, both of them on the front bulkhead, one being just below the ceiling and the other at the foot of a duct which descended from this to an outlet at about knee level. The conductor could control the air flow on the lower deck but not upstairs. Here, there were no fewer than five outlets at the front of the saloon, two above the destination box (one on each outer edge of the ledge above it) and three at floor level (one at each side and the third in the middle). Concurrently with fitting the new heating system, the opening front windows were removed from both decks and so were the ventilators in the lower saloon front bulkhead although their counterparts upstairs were allowed to remain. The additional weight of all the new equipment imposed an additional 12cwt to bring the vehicle to 6tons 17cwt.

RM 1 was licensed for the first time on 11th January 1956. Allocated to Cricklewood for driver training on 1st February, its long awaited entry into public service occurred on Wednesday the 8th. This red letter event was well publicised and, despite cold and sometimes snowy conditions, many enthusiasts turned out during the first few days to sample London's newest bus and to hear for the first time the pronounced whirr of the Routemaster transmission, subtly different from the classical sound of the RT and destined, in years to come, to dominate the streets of the capital. Representatives of the radio and press were on hand to witness the inaugural run and a reporter travelled on the bus recording interviews. Inside were notices stating "This bus is the forerunner of the future London bus and is

on trial to test its general performance and suitability. It is of lightweight construction; embodying special features contributing to your riding comfort". Comments were invited, to be sent to the Public Relations Officer at 55 Broadway. A few months later, a higher profile was achieved by removing all commercial exterior advertising and replacing it with posters reading, in large letters, "This is the Routemaster – London's Bus of the Future". Route 2 (Golders Green to Crystal Palace) was chosen for RM 1's debut.

RM 1 bore the registration number SLT56, setting the future trend for production Routemasters in carrying registrations incorporating the letters LT. The number 56 was, of course, a reference to the year. SLT56 was not, however, the first registration number allocated to RM 1. The first, which it never carried, was OLD862 (following on from the RTs), which was considered particularly inappropriate for a totally new type of bus. This was changed nominally to SLT42 before becoming SLT56 on 5th December 1955. Likewise, RM 2 was originally OLD863 and SLT43 before becoming SLT57. Registrations SLT58/59 were reserved for the third and fourth Routemaster prototypes. RMs 1 and 2 were first allocated body numbers 9228/9 before establishing a new series from B1 upwards to coincide with the RM stock number, and an original and rather strange notional chassis/body code of 12RT12 was given to both prior to the adoption of a proper RM series under which RM 1 became coded, naturally enough, 1RM1.

As was only to be expected for so revolutionary a design, RM 1's first spell in service was far from a total success. Passengers were not keen on the foam-filled seats which felt considerably less comfortable than the RT, and the hard, thin cushions were replaced with improved ones after a short time. The slightly spongy nature of the ride did not endear itself to everybody and sometimes caused travel sickness, though others considered it very satisfactory, likening it to that of a good quality family car, and praised the lack of roll on corners. The vehicle's performance was fairly lively although gear changes were sometimes slow, possibly partly due to driver unfamiliarity, although an oil leak was diagnosed which had caused slipping to take place. To overcome complaints of noisiness in the lower saloon, revised transmission couplings

Top Left A minor transformation finds RM 1 somewhat heavier than before but now with a comprehensive set of destination displays and an internal heating-cum-ventilation system. It is seen passing its tilt test at Aldenham. LT Museum

Centre Left 31st January 1956 saw RM 1 on parade in the snow for its official press demonstration. Fully kitted out for route 2, it went to Cricklewood garage on the next day to enable staff familiarisation to commence. It is seen at Victoria. P.J. Marshall

Left RM 1 at Swiss Cottage in February 1956, its first month of service. In order to achieve the maximum service mileage, specific running numbers were adhered to, ensuring that the bus ran over 1000 miles per week except on occasions when it was due for its normal rota maintenance which was then on a three week cycle. The four line 'via' display, though comprehensive in its coverage and neatly executed, is really too cramped to read comfortably on a fast-approaching vehicle. This was ironic since the equivalent RT display had been reduced for greater clarity only two years earlier.
LT Museum 6693

were tried out in May and the drive gears for the Lockheed pump on the gearbox were changed from straight-cut to helical, but the main improvement was achieved by placing sound-deadening material under the gearbox floor trap. A creaking noise was apparent in the front bulkhead right from the start but a permanent cure was never sought as a modified design was in hand for the production run. Cracks which soon appeared on the nearside front frame were dealt with by welding in a flitch plate and replacing the bulkhead bracket bolts with new parts. Early problems also occurred with the front shock absorbers, which were replaced by an improved type. A feature universally unpopular with drivers was the steering which was very heavy. Excessive front tyre wear was also apparent, and it was quickly obvious that the whole front end design was creating major problems. The chain driven fan to the underfloor radiator was unreliable and serious overheating was encountered on the front brakes, resulting in unacceptably short lining life. The design staff at Chiswick quickly addressed all the major shortcomings and tried out modifications on RM 2, which had still not entered service, aimed at overcoming them. On 8th August 1956, RM 1's first service stint came to an end when it returned to Chiswick for major front end surgery to be carried out. Many lessons had been learned during its six months on route 2.

Variations on a design theme. RM 1's initial operating problems and the subsequent adoption as standard of a front mounted radiator led the design team to search for an improved front end styling. Several possibilities were submitted on paper by Douglas Scott on behalf of his consultancy, Scott-Ashford Associates, one of which was subsequently applied to the third and fourth prototypes, having a narrower bonnet giving improved nearside visibility compared with RM 1. In May 1956 two proposals were submitted for the forthcoming production run, one of which was basically similar to the styling subsequently adopted although the underswept front mudguards were not used and the profile was a little less flat than suggested by the drawing. The avant garde alternative with its deep, backward sloping windscreen was a notable attempt to break away from tradition which, perhaps fortunately, was not adopted. It is hard to tell whether, had it become standard, it would have stood the test of time as well as the traditionally based styling has done. No front end design was ever achieved for the Routemaster which Douglas Scott considered completely satisfactory, the production vehicles being marred in his view by the sharp curve introduced half way along the bonnet to further improve visibility for the driver.

The next public outing, which lasted for less than a day, was at the Lord Mayor's show in November, where RM 1 displayed a transformed front end. Gone was the neat front panel with its large central bullseye, and in its place projected untidily, like the afterthought that it was, a removable panel with a rather ugly rectangular grille containing, on its top edge, a small bullseye motif and, at the bottom, a built-in registration plate. A series of vertical bars occupied the front of the grille and behind them was hidden a front-mounted radiator in a somewhat vulnerable position across the open end of the A frame. The projecting panel increased the overall vehicle length to 27ft 4ins, a move made possible by a recent upward revision in permitted vehicle length to 30ft on two axles. The grille also permitted a better airflow through to the brakes, whilst further remodelling at the front end allowed a revised steering layout to permit the provision of power assistance. During this front end rebuild, the opportunity had also been taken to fit the latest type of AEC 9.6 litre engine which had been under development for some time and was still in its prototype form. Originally known within AEC as the AV600, it went into production about two years later as the AV590 and eventually became the standard Routemaster fitment. This was a direct injection unit of the same capacity as the RT engine, developing 125bhp at 1800 rpm derated to 115 bhp, but it differed in being of monobloc construction with cylinder block and crankcase in one unit and having wet liners (ie in direct contact with the cooling water) instead of dry. RM 1's original AV600, fitted early in November, presumably proved troublesome as another was fitted in February 1957 some four weeks before the vehicle re-entered service. Rebuilding had resulted in yet another increase in unladen weight which now stood at 7tons 5cwt.

When RM 1 recommenced work at Cricklewood on 6th March 1957 after a three week spell of staff familiarisation, its new frontal grille had been modified with the replacement of the vertical bars by a more conventional mesh arrangement embellished by one prominent central vertical strip. Earlier official publicity had predicted that, after a tour of duty on route 2, RM 1 would next work on route 1 and then route 60. In fact, it ran on route 260 which was an amalgam of parts of both, although Sundays were spent back on route 2. Once again, long, high mileage duties were found for it, the Monday to Friday working on W11, for example, spreading from 6.50am right through to 11.38pm and giving nine departures from Cricklewood during the day, two right through to Surrey Docks, four to Waterloo, and three to Aldwych.

During this second spell of trial running, RM 1 continued to act as a useful testbed for highlighting design faults and omissions. The need for larger shock absorbers became apparent, as did the requirement for wider brake shoes at the rear. Doubt was cast on the fitment of manual brake adjusters as against the automatic ones used on the RTs, giving an early but unheeded warning of a problem which was later to beset production models. The dynamo drive belt proved troublesome, and another then unrealised problem of the future to manifest itself early on was a slight

RM 1's first and only public appearance with its original front radiator grille was on Lord Mayor's Show day in November 1956. In its revised location the radiator was now prone to damage even in a fairly minor front end collision, but this slight disadvantage was more than offset by the much improved cooling now achieved. On the day of the Show the engine was running under reduced power as temporary cylinder heads were fitted, but with the parade being at walking pace this did not matter. LT Museum

Above **In March 1957, RM 1 re-entered service with its new front end. Route 260 was now the normal weekday abode for the bus but weekends found it back on route 2. The only externally visible sign of the major mechanical modifications which had taken place was the new protruding front grille which in no way harmonised with the general lines of the vehicle. RM 1 ran in service for over two years in this form.** LT Museum

tendency to front end vibration which became more intense later on vehicles used on Green Line operation.

RM 1 operated more or less continuously from Cricklewood until 31st July 1959, except for a spell unlicensed at Chiswick from 1st October to 19th November 1957 and the seven-week period from 5th May to 20th June 1958 inclusive when all London buses were off the road for the duration of the disastrous busmen's strike, the aftermath of which was a rapid decline in public confidence and staff morale, and a hastening of the already apparent downward spiral from which the industry has never fully recovered. After delicensing, RM 1 returned to Chiswick to undergo an overhaul. It was destined never to return to passenger service, standard Routemasters now being available for in-service test running, rendering RM 1 redundant for this purpose. Although its aggregate length of service had been less than three years, RM 1 was, nevertheless, the second most extensively used of the four Routemaster prototypes.

On 10th December 1959, RM 1 was re-licensed after its overhaul, but this time for permanent driver training duties for which purpose it was allocated initially to Upton Park and, subsequently, to a whole succession of mainly east London garages. It was often to be seen out and about fulfilling this mundane role. The body was repainted for a second time in February 1964 and, on this occasion, opportunity was taken to fit a standard Routemaster bonnet and front end assembly to bring the vehicle into conformity with the main fleet. However, its other unique external features remained and RM 1 was always identifiable, though perhaps not quite so readily as before. After the 1964 repaint, the general external appearance was allowed to deteriorate, as so often happened with permanent trainer vehicles. When finally withdrawn from trainer use in 1972, RM 1 was looking very shabby indeed.

Left **Almost thirteen years of RM 1's life were spent in the driver training fleet during which it exchanged the original bonnet and wing assembly for a standard one and the offside route number indicator was removed. The vehicle was photographed in its earlier form during trolleybus days whilst laying over in Stamford Hill depot. It was allocated to West Ham.** John Gascoine

CHAPTER TWO

RM 2

Construction of the shell for the second Routemaster began at Chiswick soon after RM 1, the same plans being used for the body structure which was identical in all main respects. However, there was no rush to display the new vehicle to the public, or to get it quickly into service; instead it was wisely used as a proving bed for many of the new components around which the Routemaster design was based, as well as for a few trial items which remained unique to RM 2 itself. As in the case of RM 1, the building of the vehicle was carried out in close co-operation with AEC and Park Royal, even though it took place at Chiswick. The construction work was sufficiently advanced for the vehicle to be officially taken into stock on 10th March 1955.

Only five days after being taken into ownership, London Transport sent RM 2 for ten days of exhaustive fuel consumption tests at Northolt airport where its performance was tested against RM 1, which had a larger capacity engine. As soon as these trials were complete,

on 25th March, RM 2 went to MIRA at Nuneaton for strain gauge tests. Still in grey primer, the new bus was tested minus its lower deck outer panels in order to assess the effects on the body framework of being submitted to various trials, which included being driven hard over very uneven surfaces including a series of planks, sharp turning sequences, and heavy braking. Strain gauges were attached to the body and to many of the running units and a good deal of valuable information was obtained as a result of the tests. Most important was the knowledge that the body structure was capable of withstanding extreme stresses, whilst information that certain units such as the A frame side members needed strengthening enabled this to be put in hand for future production. After MIRA, RM 2 rejoined RM 1 for hill climbing and re-starting tests on Titsey Hill on 13th April and the two vehicles remained together for the remaining programme of trials comprising fuel consumption and acceleration tests at MIRA from 18th April to 6th May and endurance tests at Chobham from 21st June to 29th July. If things had gone to plan, RM 2 would have been the first Routemaster in public service from as early as 20th December 1955. Under the impression that it would be available by then, the operating department decided to operate it from Chalk Farm garage on route 3 and obtained

approval from Scotland Yard (a necessity as the vehicle was 8ft wide) subject to satisfactory route testing. However, the bus was by no means ready in time and almost two more years of trial and error remained before it was to enter public service.

Apart from a flush-fitting grille hiding a front-mounted radiator, RM 2 exactly resembled its predecessor in external appearance and, like RM 1, it never entered service in its original state. Beneath the surface, there were major variations, notably a complete redesign of the steering system to enable hydraulically operated power assistance to be provided. This gave a steering wheel effort approximately equal to that of an unladen RT, thereby overcoming one of the major criticisms of RM 1; that it was too tiring to steer safely for prolonged periods. RM 2 was also fitted with fully automatic transmission on second to fourth gears with manual override, plus a kick-down facility for downward changes when required. Fully automatic control, which gave gear changes without any break in power transmission, promised improved acceleration, an easing of the driver's task, and a more comfortable ride for passengers. This fitment represented a milestone in London bus design in being the first fully automatic transmission to be tried successfully. In prewar days, STL 760 had operated for a short while in this mode

but only now had a gearbox incorporating the feature of sustained torque been developed to an acceptable standard of efficiency. Similarly to the box on RM 1, this was fitted with a hydraulic changing mechanism and though, after a bad start, it proved generally satisfactory it was not be put into volume production and the service experience gained with it was therefore of academic rather than practical value.

RM 2's first engine was the AEC AV470, the modern equivalent of the famous 7.7 as once used extensively in London on the huge STL class and others. Actually rated at 7.68 litres and producing 112 bhp, this engine was fitted at the suggestion of AEC in response to the school of thought, which was very strong at the time, that a low powered engine working hard but achieving maximum operating economy through a high mpg thanks to its lightness of weight, was preferable to a large, heavy engine. It was an attractive proposition because of the resultant reduction in the vehicle weight of some 6cwt, whilst the smaller space which the engine occupied permitted a front-mounted radiator with consequent simplification of the pipe assembly. The AV470 bore many similarities to the larger and later AV590 which became standard for the Routemaster, including one-piece 'Monobloc' construction for the cylinder block and crankcase and 'wet' liners. Originally introduced for the Mercury goods range, its horizontal equivalent on the Reliance, the AH470, was already earning a reputation for cylinder head gasket failures. In order to obtain satisfactory performance with the reduced torque output of the smaller engine a rear axle ratio of 5.87:1 was adopted compared with 5.22:1 with the larger engine; an increase in engine speed from 1800 to 2000rpm produced the same maximum speed capability as that of the 9.6 litre unit. Preliminary fuel consumption trials at Northolt showed consumption to be improved with the smaller engine at six stops per mile but worse at four stops or lower, but

RM 2's interior, while generally similar to RM 1, was brighter due to the use of light grey, shiny window surrounds. This upper deck view, looking forward, was taken after removal of the opening front windows and installation of the heating system, one of whose outlets can be seen at floor level in the middle of the photograph.
LT Museum 1506/11

the subsequent and more extensive trials at Nuneaton showed a consumption up to 4% worse than RM 1 over all running conditions. This confirmed London Transport's already held belief that a large engine, derated if necessary, was preferable to give the most economic running with total responsiveness irrespective of road and loading conditions and to achieve a long working life through never being over-stretched. Early in June 1955 London Transport notified AEC that the decision had been made not to proceed with the AV470 and requested the material necessary to enable a 9.6 litre engine to be installed.

In order to accommodate the large engine, RM 2 was given the same fussy looking projecting radiator grille as acquired by RM 1 and received the same bodywork modifications to the indicators and windows plus the same heating/ventilation system. However, it never acquired the embossed metal ROUTEMASTER

Lower saloon looking rearwards. The aluminium framed, maroon decorative panels at the end of the fourth bay stand out much more prominently than was the case on RM 1 because of the light colouring of the surrounding areas. it was still practice in those days to paint the overhaul date on the platform below the fleet number; in this case 57.4 relates to the month RM 2 was finally made ready for its first spell of passenger service.
LT Museum 1506/10

motifs, which remained unique to RM 1. It shared the same unladen weight of 7tons 5cwt. The main visual difference externally between the two vehicles was in livery, RM 2 being painted in the Country Bus & Coach Department's Lincoln green and cream which suited it very well indeed. Internally, however, RM 2 differed in various respects from its predecessor. The decor was improved by the use of grey plastic window surrounds in place of dark red rexine, which lightened the overall effect, the plastic insert in the strip above now being red in colour rather than white. The one-piece ceiling panels reaching from one cantrail to the other were replaced on RM 2 by the more conventional style with separate cove panels carrying the saloon lighting.

RM 2 could be seen out and about on test runs in full green livery for at least eight months before it finally entered service. The target date for live running was now the end of April 1957 but this could not be achieved and the first revenue earning trips actually took place on 20th May. Allocated to Reigate garage, the vehicle ran alongside RTs between Redhill and Kingston on route 406/A. Far less ballyhoo attended the arrival of RM 2 compared with its predecessor which was probably just as well since its operation from Reigate was, at best, spasmodic. Rumours of gearbox and brake problems abounded and were well founded; indeed, a complete change of gearbox was needed within four days of entering service. On 8th August 1957, RM 2 returned to Chiswick after further problems with the transmission, when the decision was made to withdraw the vehicle from country operation and to repaint it red for central area work. This came as no surprise and merely confirmed a fairly widely held view (which was believed also to be that of the country area management themselves) that out-of-town operation, even on a relatively busy route like the 406, was a strange choice of testing ground for such a sophisticated urban type vehicle. RM 2's service to the travelling public of Surrey had lasted little more than two months and a further eight years were to elapse before the commencement of regular country bus operation by Routemasters.

RM 2 received red livery during its sojourn at Chiswick and was allocated to Turnham Green from 30th August for driver training prior to taking up service on route 91 (27 on Sundays) on 18th September. The 91, like the 406, was one of a number of routes used over many years by the experimental department for testing purposes. It was very much busier in those days than now and was a useful choice of route in that it was operated by the garage closest to the experimental shop at Chiswick. Turnham Green had been the obvious base for many experimental vehicles and most of the pre-RM testing of new type gearboxes and brakes had been carried out from there. After just under a fortnight on route 91, RM 2 returned to Chiswick on 1st October, along with RM 1, for adjustments to be made to both. Service on route 91 was resumed on 1st December and remained more or less constant until 12th February 1958 when a further return to Chiswick took place. This time, the break from routine was much longer to enable major technical alterations to be carried out. It had been decided that the time was right for the experimental fitment of air suspension in

Although, except in their earliest days, RTs in country area service did not carry offside route numbers, an exception was made for RM 2. This was probably because a blind was considered more feasible to change during the course of a day's operation than plates. The word ROUTE was painted above the number aperture, a feature not found on RM 1. B.A. Jenkins

place of coils at the rear. This necessitated the provision of a compressor, so the opportunity was taken at the same time to remove the hydraulically operated gearbox and to replace it with the electro-pneumatic D182 unit. The original Self Changing Gears hydraulic box, designated the RV35, had proved impractical to put into production and an alternative needed testing urgently with the commencement of full scale Routemaster production only months away. The air suspension unit, designed and produced by Dunlop, was one of two alternatives being tried out; the other, by Firestone, was scheduled for fitment to the fourth Routemaster prototype (CRL 4) shortly afterwards.

RM 2 returned to service on 1st July 1958 and led a further sixteen months' active life until 1st November 1959 when, having reached the end of its passenger carrying life, it was demoted to a training vehicle, initially

attached to Clay Hall garage. As with RM 1, a standard bonnet and radiator assembly was later fitted, a change which took place in January 1964 at the same time as a second repaint was carried out. The vehicle spent its time in fairly continuous use on learner duties right up to 1st April 1972 and was noteworthy in that at no time during its almost 17 years' use did it receive an official overhaul.

An August 1958 view of RM 2 in Chiswick High Road, now in red livery and about to swallow a long queue of passengers on route 91 as it heads for Wandsworth Bridge. The word ROUTE was not retained above the offside number when the vehicle was repainted. J.C. Gillham

The final development of Routemaster body design is evident in RML 3 except for the untidy, pinched-looking front bonnet and wing layout which was acknowledged as being only a temporary arrangement. It is seen at the Pound Lane terminus in Willesden, opposite its home garage. C. Carter

CHAPTER THREE

RML 3

Without doubt, RML 3 was the Cinderella of the four prototypes. Its entry into service and, indeed, its whole existence, was largely ignored by the media, and its passenger carrying life of only one year and eight months rendered it the least heavily worked of all Routemasters.

Despite being numbered third out of four, RML 3 was the last of the prototypes to be completed. The contract for its manufacture was placed with the MCW organisation who arranged for the actual construction to take place in the Addlestone factory of Weymann's Ltd which, until only a relatively short time beforehand, had been heavily involved in building RT bodies on a large scale. At the time that the framework for the third Routemaster was laid down, the Addlestone works was mainly occupied in building the ungainly but highly successful MCW Orion lightweight double deck body on a variety of chassis, mainly for customers in the municipal and BET sectors of the industry. The order for the third Routemaster went to MCW in pursuance of London Transport's policy of multi-sourcing on large contracts as far as its contractual obligation with AEC allowed, though no evidence exists of any serious intent to order Routemasters from other than Park Royal in the placing of the main production contract.

With 15 months still to go before delivery to London Transport, March 1956 finds RML 3 structurally complete and under test at Weymann's Addlestone works. All the external metalwork is in grey primer, highlighting the glass fibre material used for the bonnet lid. Internally the vehicle is still a shell at this stage. G.A. Rixon

A rare colour view of RML 3 in its original form shows it at Marble Arch in March 1958, two months after entering service. The narrow bonnet lid provided much better nearside visibility than on the first two prototypes but was less attractive in appearance.
Bruce Jenkins

A chance encounter sees RM 1 and RML 3 heading nose to tail towards Marble Arch during 1958. The various differences between the two, notably in the bonnet design and in the treatment of the heater inlet, can be clearly seen.
R.H.G. Simpson

The standard Routemaster lightweight seat frames made their debut on RML 3 as did the additional ticket box on the rear platform wall. The interior decor was also in its finalised form with burgundy lining panels, Chinese green window surrounds and sung yellow ceilings. *LT Museum 1622/1*

Leyland Motors Ltd has shown a keen interest in collaborating in the Routemaster project and were the suppliers of the mechanical units for RML 3 (hence the letter L originally in the fleet number). Powered by the well tried and highly respected Leyland 0600 9.8 litre engine developing 125bhp at 1800rpm but derated to 115bhp, the vehicle was externally discernible as a Leyland only by its front wheel hubs. The same SCG Wilson-type electro-hydraulic gearbox was fitted as on the earlier prototypes and although, according to official sources, its operation was to be semi-automatic, it was actually in fully automatic mode right from the start. Power assistance was provided to the steering but of a different type from that adopted for RMs 1 and 2, being provided directly to the steering column itself rather than through an actuator inserted between the drop arm and the relay lever, a design originated by Lockheed which worked well after initial problems were ironed out. How-

ever, it was by no means universally popular with the drivers, many of whom regarded it as requiring too light an effort and lacking a positive feel. The braking system was, once again, hydraulic but, this time, the supplier was Clayton Dewandre of Lincoln instead of Lockheed although the specification was similar. Once again, coil suspension was fitted all round and the rear axle continued in the earlier vein by being of the spiral bevel type, the ratio being 5.143:1. At 16ft 10ins, the wheelbase was one inch longer than on RMs 1 and 2, and was the same as subsequently adopted for production models.

The body carried a number of refinements compared with RMs 1 and 2, the most welcome being the elimination of the fussy 'eyebrow' effect of the front dome giving sufficient curvature to avoid the former top-heavy look, though the front end was still very upright. A plainer but much neater air intake grille was provided at cant rail level whilst the flashing trafficators at the rear were now mounted vertically on either side of the advertisement space below the platform window. Conventional aluminium mouldings covered the joints between the main panels on both decks but the original arrangement was retained at window level. The body had, in effect, now reached the stage of design which was to become standard for the production batch. The

only non-standard feature was the bonnet and wing assembly which was acknowledged to be an interim measure and due to change again for the production run. The very wide bonnet top of the earlier prototypes, which had been criticised for impingeing on the nearside kerb visibility, was replaced by a narrower one surmounting a very fussy wing and lamp combination which was vaguely reminiscent of the equally untidy design used on the 9T9 coaches built for the Green Line fleet in the mid-thirties. The bonnet lid was side opening and not of the alligator type used on RMs 1 and 2, but the design of detachable radiator grille panel was inherited from these and projected from the front of the vehicle in the same untidy way.

Internally, the bodywork closely resembled the style established on RM 2, the *Vybac* plastic finishers for the window surrounds now being in the same shade of mid grey used on the seat backs, officially called Chinese green. Lining panels, though apparently the same shade as on the first two RMs, were now described as being dark burgundy in colour. The seat frames, though similar in general appearance to those used before, including a separate upper grab rail, were of slimmer profile and no longer in polished alloy. Instead *Beaton* chromium plated lightweight tubular steel frames were used. On the platform a large additional

Damage to the front end of RML 3 in its accident of January 1959 appeared to be severe but the vehicle was only off the road for a little over a month. Fortuitously this view of the vehicle in damaged condition permits a view of the radiator installation and of its Leyland engine; it also shows the side-lifting bonnet lid which was unique to this vehicle. In the background is RM 8, the only standard Routemaster in stock at the time.

From the rear, RML 3 was almost indistinguishable from the production batch of RMs which was soon to follow, though the emergency exit window and the more pronounced beading which surrounded it gave a means of identification to the keen-eyed.
LT Museum H/17226

used ticket box was provided on the rear wall. The unladen weight of RML 3 at 7 tons 5 cwt was the same as RMs 1 and 2 in their rebuilt condition. Carrying the reserved registration number SLT58, RML 3 was allocated the body number B3 and classified as the one and only 3RM3.

RML 3 was officially taken into stock from Weymann's on 1st July 1957, seventeen days after its sister vehicle was delivered from ECW. Painted in standard central area red bus livery, it went almost immediately to the Leyland works in Lancashire for adjustments and evaluation trials. The vehicle returned to Chiswick on 6th November and it was officially stated that it would be allocated to Putney Bridge garage for route 85. In the event, it was from Willesden garage that operation was to commence early in 1958 on route 8 (8B on Sundays). First licensed for driver familiarisation on 1st January, RML 3's entry into service came on 22nd of the same month. Once again, specific running numbers were adhered to, covering the longest possible working day. After just over a year in service, RML 3 was involved in a major collision with a lorry in the Edgware Road in January 1959 and suffered extensive frontal damage, by far the most serious to befall any of the prototype Routemasters up to that time. Repairs were carried out in the Chiswick experimental shop and the vehicle was relicensed for service on 1st March. However, its service career was already approaching its end. The experimental running had unearthed fan and dynamo belt problems, common also to the other prototypes, and brake lining troubles were also evident. On 1st November 1959, RML 3 was transferred, along with RM 2, into Clay Hall as a permanent learner bus, although Clay Hall closed ten days later resulting in a transfer to Upton Park.

Even in its new but lowly guise as a training vehicle, RML 3 led a somewhat chequered existence. It endured a particularly lengthy period of idleness between September 1963 and August 1965 although there were various shorter spells before and after this. On one of these, its inability to operate was compounded by the removal of its differential to keep the only other Leyland Routemaster, RMC 4, on the road. This was a 'special' derived from a Worldmaster unit and a new one had to be made. The only occasion when the bodywork was repainted under London Transport auspices occurred at Aldenham in 1965 when the vehicle underwent a thorough, if leisurely, overhaul to make it roadworthy after a long period of disuse. At this overhaul, a standard Routemaster front end was fitted, this being the last of the four prototypes to retain its original bonnet, radiator grille and wing assembly, a matter of only academic interest as the vehicle had been off the road since 1963 whereas the other three had continued working in their old form into 1964.

Earlier, on 7th September 1961, the letter L had been dropped from the fleet number, leaving the vehicle to run henceforth as plain RM 3. This change coincided with the arrival of the first 30ft Routemasters. The end of the road for RM 3 came on 1st April 1972 when its service as a trainer, latterly at Clapton, came to an end. Interestingly, RM 2, which had started its training career on the same day as RM 3, also ceased work on the same day.

CHAPTER FOUR
CRL 4

Above **Seen just after delivery from Lowestoft, CRL 4 displays the handsome livery achieved through the use of light green window surrounds, a welcome embellishment which suited the Routemaster body shape admirably. The neat rear end of CRL 4 did not feature the high-topped platform window of the open platform vehicles, giving better symmetry with the emergency window above. This was the only rear entrance Routemaster with its back registration plate sited by the offside corner.** LT Museum

In terms of timespan of passenger operation, the fourth Routemaster prototype was by far the most successful of the quartet and yet, when it was new, such a long working life would never have been predicted. CRL 4, as it was first known, (CRL standing for Coach Routemaster Leyland) was an experimental double deck Green Line Coach, and since its two well remembered predecessors in this role, LT 1137 and RTC 1, had both been conspicuous failures as coaches, there was little reason to suppose that this latest venture would enjoy any better fate.

CRL 4 was the only Routemaster on which the offside route number was sited adjacent to the rearmost side window; the word ROUTE above it was a feature which only the two green prototypes displayed. The front grille was modified with a polished central strip and registration number surround prior to entering service.

June. This had been far from completed by 11th July when the vehicle returned to Chiswick for modifications to be carried out and, although back on the road by 1st August, entry into service did not take place until 9th October 1957. In contrast to the stealthy, almost unnoticed, entry into service of RM 2 and RML 3, the new coach Routemaster was highly publicised in the extensive trade press which still existed at that time, their interest having been stimulated by a very full press release prepared and issued by London Transport's publicity department.

In basic external outline, CRL 4 closely resembled RML 3 although embellishments to suit its higher status included pale green mouldings surrounding the windows to enhance appearance, a raised bullseye motif between decks on each side, and polished lamp surrounds and front wheel trims. The below-canopy route number box was omitted and the offside one was moved forward to a position just behind the rearmost window. A major addition was that of platform doors, necessitating a redesign of the lower deck rear end to incorporate an emergency door and the repositioning, to a higher level, of the nearside blind box. A similar looking front end to RML 3 was fitted, although in this case the bonnet opened from the front rather than sideways, and there was initially no central bar to the radiator grille although one was added soon after delivery. Despite the fussiness of the bonnet design, CRL 4 was an attractive vehicle in its handsome two-tone green livery.

Running units were supplied by Leyland, the 0600 9.8 litre engine being fitted with a Glacier centrifugal filter which ultimately proved extremely effective, as was also the case on RML 3. Though the two Leyland vehicles had much in common mechanically, the CRL differed in that its full independent front suspension was effected by means of long torsion bars anchored to the bodywork behind the bulkhead, dampening being controlled by tubular shock absorbers mounted between the wishbones. This design was included at Leyland's request and was developed to provide a minimum of roll and avoid the possibility of travel sickness on long, fast runs. Coil spring-ing, as fitted to the previous Routemasters, was applied to the rear axle although, even at this stage, air bellows were being considered. AEC had carried out experiments with air suspension and its recently announced Bridgemaster double decker, which was to have many design features corresponding with the Routemaster, was intended to be air-sprung. At this stage, however, CRL 4 carried no compressor for an air system, its gearbox again being of the Self Changing Gears RV35 electro-hydraulic type, although it was now accepted that plans to incorporate this in the production run would have to be abandoned in favour of an electro-pneumatic box. The gearbox was of the fully automatic type though second and third gears could be selected manually if desired through the appropriate positions on the column-mounted gate. First was isolated from the automatic system, being needed only when starting on steep hills or when heavily loaded. Steering was of the simple manual type and, though power assistance was regarded as desirable right from the start, it could not be fitted as the linkage was the same as on RM 1 at the time.

The decision to equip one of the trial Routemasters as a coach served a dual purpose. The Green Line network had been the only part of the London Transport system on which ridership had consistently risen since the early fifties and there was a real need to test public reaction to the use of a larger type of vehicle than the single deckers traditionally employed. Also, the ability to achieve high daily mileages on fast, limited stop running would test characteristics of the RM which were out of reach on normal in-town work.

CRL 4 was built by Eastern Coach Works at their Lowestoft factory. ECW, like London Transport itself, was a state-owned enterprise under the control of the British Transport Commission, so there was little surprise in the fact that the contract for supplying one of the Routemaster prototypes should be placed within the group even though ECW's past links with London Transport had been fairly tenuous and on a minuscule basis compared with the strong trading ties, both before the war and afterwards, with Park Royal and

MCW. At the time, however, ECW was heavily involved with Bristol in supplying most of the requirements of the Tilling Group of nationalised operating companies, its star vehicle being the superb Lodekka which notched up its first thousand in January 1957, and it is hard to believe that the company could ever seriously have considered setting up a Routemaster production line in addition to all its other commitments. Viewed in this light, it is difficult to see what value ECW would have derived from being involved in the construction of CRL 4.

CRL 4 was delivered ahead of RML 3, its official handover date being 14th June 1957. In common with the other prototypes, and the production batch which followed, delivery was considerably later than originally expected, thwarting the initial hopes of putting the vehicles into service by the end of May. A programme of work for it was devised on a number of the busiest Green Line routes, starting with Romford based route 721 for which driver training commenced on 19th

The interior of CRL 4 differed quite considerably from the other three as befitted its coach status. Most noticeable was the use of high-backed, deeper cushioned seats upholstered in the same attractive, mainly green, patterned moquette as used on Green Line RFs. The basic colour scheme for the side lining panels was olive green and the ceilings were cream. Lightweight luggage racks were provided above the main side windows and consisted of an aluminium alloy frame with a nylon cord base, the lining above being of matt cream plastic matching the colour of the ceiling panels. Longitudinal slats were omitted from the floor gangways, further enhancing the semi-luxury appearance, whilst a particularly novel feature was the provision, at the rear of the lower saloon above the wheel arches, of single-width seats set at an angle of approximately 45 degrees to give a near forward view; there were two on the nearside and one on the offside. These were not the original fitment but were installed in place of conventional longitudinal seats while the coach was back at Chiswick in late June/early July and reduced the seating capacity from 57 to 55 (32 on the upper deck and 23 on the lower deck). A space left behind the offside bucket seat was used to accommodate small bags and parcels, whilst greater luggage accommodation than normal under the stairs for bulky items such as suitcases was achieved by moving the conductor's locker forward, reducing by one the seating space over the offside rear wheelarch.

Electrically operated double jack-knife platform doors were the first of their type ever fitted by London Transport to a double deck bus and were supplied by Deans. It was anticipated that they would normally be worked by the conductor from controls fitted alongside the doorway, but duplicate controls were provided in the driver's cab. An emergency release button was fitted externally just forward of the doors, and the enclosing of the platform required the fitment of a full height emergency exit door in the rear wall.

Although at an unladen weight of 7tons 10cwt, CRL 4 was the heaviest Routemaster so far, it was still lighter than the much smaller vehicles which its successors, if any, would replace. The successful and much loved RF single decker, then the backbone of the Green Line fleet, tipped the scales at just over 7tons 17cwt and seated only 39.

Top Left **Passengers entering CRL 4 were faced by the two-level luggage compartment above the battery box. The repositioned conductor's locker and farechart can be seen to the left**. LT Museum 1541/5

Top Right **Looking rearwards in the lower saloon, the original inward-facing bench seats can be seen; these were replaced soon after delivery. The well padded seats, though low-backed by coaching standards, were very comfortable. They lacked the leather edging of the buses.** LT Museum 1485/6

Centre **A frontward view across the bucket seats which reduced the seating capacity by two, shows the flat floor covering and the tungsten light bulbs situated beneath the luggage racks. The front bulkhead, including the style of top heater outlet and the control lever lower down on the trunking, was the same as on RML 3.** LT Museum 1541/7

Right **A close-up view of the bucket seats in CRL 4 at Chiswick, with a training bus STL in the background.** LT Museum

Registered SLT59, the vehicle carried body number B4 and was, predictably, classified 4RM4. CRL 4's first spell in public service was on the busy and frequent 721 Aldgate—Brentwood run. Quite different in character from the great majority of Green Line routes, the 721 was really not much more than a glorified bus service but with limited stops, having little in common with the more prestigious work for which the new double deck coach was really intended. However, it sufficed that CRL 4 should do its initial running-in trials alongside a batch of RTs which comprised the normal 721 rolling stock and were considered adequate for this particular type of work without any coach embellishments apart from livery. The new Routemaster could retain a lower profile here than would be possible elsewhere as a lone double decker amongst a fleet of RFs, and any serious mechanical misdemeanours would be less noticeable.

Heavy pounding on the well used roads of London's East End quickly produced rear suspension problems, though these had been partly induced by the vehicle specification having called for less substantial shock absorbers than had been used hitherto. This was put right and a reasonably satisfactory run was recorded at Romford, so much so that by the end of 1957 the time was considered right for CRL 4 to assume its true role in life on a 'real' Green Line route where public reaction to a double deck coach in place of the customary single deckers could be studied.

It was intended that the vehicle should operate on a number of major routes, the first one selected being the 711 (Reigate to High Wycombe). The majority of traditional Green Line routes involved lengthy runs from country towns in the inner Home Counties, across London and out to a similar destination on the other side. To maximise use of resources, it was commonplace for crews from either end to work on the other's coaches as well as their own and for vehicles to 'sleep out' at the wrong end on some nights. This meant

that drivers and engineers at both garages had to be fully trained on the Routemaster and a practice was adopted of sending the vehicle first of all to the garage to which it was not going to be allocated and, following the completion of training there, it would pass to its owning garage. Thus, on 29th December 1957, CRL 4 ceased work at Romford after about 7000 miles of public service and was received at High Wycombe next day for training, passing to Reigate a few days later. Its stint on route 711 commenced on 8th January 1958.

Public reaction to the new Routemaster appears to have been sufficiently favourable on the 711 to encourage continuation of the trial programme on other routes. Crew reaction was less positive. The loss of intimate contact between driver and conductor who could not now converse with each other during their long runs was obviously a drawback, but the vehicle proved less than popular with a good many drivers for a more tangible reason; the steering was heavy and, worse still, it showed a tendency to vibrate at speed. The latter problem, though subsequently tackled with the insertion of an additional crossmember at the front of the bus, was never totally eliminated and was still present on the production run of Routemaster coaches which resulted from these trials.

After a few months on route 711, it was decided to make some major changes to the vehicle, which was delicensed on 1st May 1958 and despatched on one of its periodic visits to the experimental shops at Chiswick. Here, the rear coil springs were removed and an air suspension system was fitted instead. This necessitated the provision of a compressor, so the opportunity was taken at the same time to remove the oil operated gearbox and to replace it with the electro-pneumatic AEC D182 unit which was now clearly going to be the one with which the forthcoming fleet of Routemasters would have to be fitted. Subsequent experimentation with the frequency of the air suspension produced varying degrees of softness

of ride (from which the lesson was that the majority of passengers preferred a firm ride to a spongy one) but, overall, the air suspension performed well enough to encourage wider scale experimentation just over a year later on a hundred units of the main production batch. Even so, problems with levelling valves and bellows, which became apparent at a fairly early stage, were never totally eliminated and air suspension never proved as successful on Routemasters as coil springs.

CRL 4's next spell of service was on route 704, for which purpose it was sent to Tunbridge Wells on 22nd July and afterwards to Windsor, where it was officially based, in readiness for entry into service on 2nd August. The long, fast, 704 gave a good opportunity to study the performance of the vehicle in its revamped condition. After the 704, it was the turn of route 715 to play host. This was the busiest of all the traditional Green Line routes, maintaining a 20-minute headway throughout the day and, as its northern base at Hertford was to be the official allocation for CRL 4, it went first to Guildford for training purposes on 1st December 1958. A spell of just over five months on route 715 commenced on 24th January 1959, terminated by its transfer to route 718 in July of the same year. Training commenced at Epping on 8th July and the vehicle returned to Windsor as its main base, where it stayed for its longest continuous spell to date, operation on route 718 lasting right through to August 1960.

Air suspension and a new-type gearbox are now installed on CRL 4, seen at Victoria in September 1958 whilst working to Tunbridge Wells on route 704. The word ROUTE is now omitted from the offside, but otherwise the vehicle still looks the same as when it first entered service. The small bill above the downstairs rear window hails the Routemaster as 'the Green Line double-deck coach of the future'. G.H.F. Atkins

24th August 1960 was the date scheduled for CRL 4 to commence operation from Stevenage garage on route 716 (Hitchin to Chertsey). The southern area garage was Addlestone whose WY plates it was also to carry on frequent occasions. Before appearing on route 716, the vehicle was repainted externally into a new light green livery similar to that being applied experimentally at the same time to sixteen RFs on route 711 as part of a series of tests carried out by London Transport's research laboratory to evaluate various types of paint. Whether or not a livery is considered attractive is, of course, a matter of taste but the general consensus of opinion appears to have been that the light green did not suit the Routemaster particularly well,

somehow managing to cheapen rather than enhance its appearance. The early days on route 716 were not a success, the vehicle now proving more prone than before to problems with the rear suspension and, more particularly, with the rear B-frame. On 1st November, it was delicensed for the B-frame to be strengthened, a process which was also necessary on the main Routemaster fleet now in production and displaying similar symptoms. CRL 4 returned to service at Stevenage on 7th December 1960 and stayed there throughout 1961. In August 1961 it was reclassified RMC 4 and in late April 1962 it reverted to its original condition, in which it never previously saw service, as a 57-seater with normal longitudinal seats at the rear of

the lower deck in place of the bucket type seats which had proved neither popular nor necessary. June 1962 saw commencement of delivery of the main batch of new RMC coaches and from November of the same year, when it was transferred back to Hertford for route 715, RMC 4 was treated as a member of the main batch despite its many differences. We shall pick up its story in chapter 14, and all that is left to record here is the loss of its light green livery and restoration of Lincoln green in November 1962. At its first, rather protracted, overhaul which lasted between April and December 1964, a standard RMC front end was fitted though, somewhat surprisingly, the three piece front destination display remained in place.

CHAPTER FIVE
THE SLAVE RIGS

By mid-summer of 1958, it had become clear that the hoped-for starting date for delivery of new Routemasters would not be met. Though the running units were all set to roll off the production lines, this was not the case with the bodies, on which there was a considerable delay. The engineering department was anxious to obtain as much operating experience as possible in advance of the start of the trolleybus conversion progamme and, in the absence of proper Routemaster bodies, it was decided to fit some early production running units to purpose built slave bodies to enable evaluation running to take place. As a result, two strange, grey painted contraptions took to the road in August 1958 and soon became familiar features of the London scene.

The first three complete sets of running units (R2RH001-003) were put aside on delivery and it is thought that there may have been plans for three slave rigs (as the mobile test beds were officially known) though only 002 and 003 actually received bodies and 001 remained as a set of units. In their bodied form, the rigs looked more like lorries than buses although half-width cabs provided a clue to their real family lineage. Generally speaking, they were so unlike anything else on the road that the casual observer would have been very hard pressed to guess their true purpose. As there was no conventional chassis frame, it was essential to provide a very rigid body and this was achieved by using a welded steel structure of rolled sections, running the whole length of the test vehicle, to which were attached the A and B frames. The

driver's cab was timber framed and steel panelled, and incorporated a standard RT windscreen, cab side and cab door in order to keep construction costs as low as possible. Behind the cab door was a full width observation saloon complete with four seats, a writing desk and provision for the attachment of various test instruments to its walls. To the rear of the saloon was a platform to carry ballast in the form of sand bags, more of which were placed on top of the cab roof to give a correct distribution of weight, the entire load being equivalent to that of a half payload of passengers. The sandbags were covered with tarpaulins to keep them dry, without which the 'passenger payload' would have increased in weight every time it rained. Space was also provided behind the cabin for access to the gearbox and compressor drive.

It was planned that the two rigs would simulate service running as closely as possible by following a normal scheduled bus (with the agreement of its driver), stopping at all the same stops and generally adhering to exactly the same pattern of work. By this means, all the novel Routemaster features such as independent front suspension, power steering, fully automatic gears and hydraulic breaking could be studied in action and monitored for shortcomings. One of the rigs was allocated to Riverside garage to run behind RTWs on route 11; the other followed similar vehicles on route 46 and was based at Willesden. After a while, the desperate staff shortage then prevailing at west London garages made it hard to provide drivers for the slave rigs and they were trans-

ferred to Battersea and Tottenham for routes 22 and 76 respectively. The use of service drivers was probably a mistake anyway, as some proved unable to accurately follow the bus in front, thereby failing to repeat the true service operation.

In due course, proper Routemasters became available as production of complete vehicles got under way and some of the earliest were quickly put to work on a number of major routes, rendering the slave rigs redundant. Although the rigs had a number of shortcomings, especially as their load factor remained constant which was seldom the case in real life, they nevertheless produced a great deal of useful information and proved very worthwhile. Eventually, the bodies were removed and the running units were put to work under new Routemaster bodies. It was originally intended that the three sets of units would form the basis for RMs 5-7 but this idea was later abandoned and unit 002, which was a 1/5RM5/1 type, started passenger service on 20th July 1960 as RM 341 and unit 003, a 5RM5, followed three months later on 26th October 1960 as RM 298. Unit 001 which had not formed a test rig was the last to be used, on 9th October 1960 as RM 459, and was also a 5RM5.

Above **With their strange combination of squared-off roof, tapered cab incorporating an RT front window, three quarters exposed radiator, and angular non-symmetrical front wings, the two test rigs must have been amongst the ugliest road vehicles ever conceived. One of them is seen at Ludgate Circus.** M. Dryhurst

CHAPTER SIX
THE RM IN PRODUCTION

In August 1956, the British Transport Commission authorised the purchase of 1520 Routemasters, which was actually twenty vehicles fewer than the current estimate of the number needed to replace trolleybuses at all depots except Fulwell and Isleworth. An initial order for 850 was immediately placed. By any standard, this was an enormous contract with a high degree of risk attached in the sense that it committed vast sums of expenditure to an almost unproven project. Whilst such total commitment in favour of the Routemaster represented a show of tremendous faith in the new bus, the fact was that the only operational experience to date had been a few months' trial running of RM 1 on route 2 which had been far from trouble-free. There was, however, no option but to go ahead. London Transport remained convinced that specially designed vehicles were essential to meet the particularly harsh operating conditions in

London. The RT was now obsolete and a new generaton of bus was essential; this had to be the Routemaster. First deliveries were required in 1958 and, in view of the long lead time necessary to set up special production lines with their associated supply chains, the placing of the initial order could not be delayed. The huge size of the order was necessary to make the task of establishing a special production facility a viable proposition, it being essential to achieve a large, regular output over which to spread the enormous development charges and the costs of all the special tools and jigs peculiar to the Routemaster which the manufacturers could not use elsewhere in their business.

It came as no surprise to anyone that the main contract was placed with Park Royal and that AEC was to supply the principal running units, even though other manufacturers were at that time still busy building prototypes.

The existence of London Transport's long standing obligation to take at least 75% of its purchases in any one year from AEC, and Park Royal's close connection with AEC as a fellow member of the Associated Commercial Vehicles group, virtually guaranteed them the work. Besides, splitting the order between manufacturers would have dissipated the benefits of economy of scale and pushed up the price for each individual vehicle.

Above **The first Routemaster to be built to the design of the production models was RM 8, completed ahead of the others so that it could be displayed at the 1958 Commercial Motor Exhibition. It followed closely the styling of RML 3 except where the new bonnet and front wing arrangement gave the design its distinctive snout.**
LT Museum H/17377

Numerically the first standard Routemaster, RM 5 is seen opposite Willesden garage from where it operated in pre-trolleybus conversion service trials. The word ROUTEMASTER above the fleet number revived a practice last used in the 1920s with the LS type LONDON SIX. For the standard RMs a three-line 'via' blind was used in place of the cramped four-line layout of the prototypes.
Lens of Sutton

If the production schedules accompanying the placing of the contract had been adhered to, the delivery of Routemasters would have been well under way by the autumn of 1958, in good time to commence the trolleybus replacement programme at the start of 1959. However various delays were encountered and the original target date proved impossible to achieve. This was no surprise; it was a malaise of the British bus manufacturing industry at the time that, despite the long lead time demanded for placing orders, they were seldom fulfilled promptly. As it happened, only one Routemaster was completed in 1958, and this was a rushed job, assembled several months before flow-line production commenced, in order to get it onto the Park Royal stand at the Commercial Motor Exhibition at Earl's Court between 26th September and 4th October. Numbered RM 8 (the missing numbers RM 5 to RM 7 having been reserved

for three sets of units temporarily set aside for test purposes, a numbering policy later changed), this vehicle was received by Show visitors with polite interest but little of the excitement which had surrounded RM 1's debut four years earlier. Bus technology was now moving in a different direction. The high capacity rear engined Leyland Atlantean had been unveiled at the 1956 Show (at which there was no Routemaster presence) and had been hailed by such superlatives as "the most revolutionary bus that has appeared for many a year", and two years later it had gone into full production and was very much in evidence at the Show. Overshadowed, the Routemaster was already viewed in many quarters as being of only passing interest to the industry in general, an expensive toy which London Transport in its privileged position could afford but others could not. Its relevance at the Show in demonstrating the principles of advanced technology was undeniable, but this was largely of academic interest as there was no intention at this time of making it available for sale to other operators. Accompanying RM 8 on the Park Royal stand was a full-fronted 30ft long front entrance AEC Regent V for East Kent, which looked by far the more modern of the two.

Despite spending much of its time in and

around Chiswick, RM 8 had not been officially taken into London Transport stock at this time (this did not happen until March 1961) and the honour of being the first production Routemaster owned fell to RM 6. This was received from Park Royal on 11th May 1959, many months behind schedule, the specially set up production lines at Park Royal having belatedly come on stream in March. Two more Routemasters were also delivered in this historic month (RM 9 and RM 11 on 21st May) and from 3rd June onwards the regular influx began in earnest, building up by the year's end to about nine per week. An uphill struggle to achieve a good reputation for mechanical reliability lay ahead but there was to grow, from these small beginnings, one of the most famous and long-lasting urban motor buses ever to be conceived.

In respect of its general external appearance, the production Routemaster differed little from RML 3, the only notable variation being in the bonnet, radiator grille and front nearside wing structure. The styles used on the four prototypes had been acknowledged as interim ones pending introduction of the definitive design which was given a seal of approval by no less an authority than the Council of Industrial Design. The result was functional but uninspired, though undoubtedly neater

43

The typical Routemaster rear end is demonstrated by RM 66 in Poplar depot prior to entering service. This aspect remained little changed over the nine year production run of the Routemaster family except for a repositioning of the offside trafficator and the use of black instead of red for the used ticket box. LT Museum 9143

Good engine accessibility was a feature of the Routemaster as demonstrated by RM 158. The small rectangular plates denoting the vehicle classification (in this case 5/5RM5/5) can be seen below the driver's nearside window above the radiator filler cap. P.J. Relf

than the prototypes with a narrowish snout projecting about six inches forward of the cab front. The bonnet top, which like the rest of the front assembly was constructed from glass fibre for lightness of weight, was of the quick release alligator-jaw type opened from the front of the vehicle. The nearside wing structure was constructed as a unit and could be removed within a matter of minutes to give complete accessibility to the engine. Small ventilating grilles for the front brakes were incorporated in the front wings and the removable front panel carried a polished surround with a red vertical central strip, the registration plate being built into the bottom of it. Above the radiator grille, mounted on the front of the bonnet top, was a raised bullseye device.

The exterior was painted in standard London Transport red with a central cream band and black mudguards and lifeguards, and the brand name ROUTEMASTER was carried in small gold letters above the fleet number on both sides as a subtle way of indoctrinating the public into learning and accepting this as the title for London's 'Bus of the Future'. The external appearance was marred by London Transport's studious avoidance of polished embellishments for lamp surrounds and wheel trims, etc which could have done so much to enhance the vehicle, elimination of polished trim (except on trolleybuses) having been adopted as a cost-cutting measure early in 1956.

Internally, the decor was the same as on RML 3. Retention of tungsten-style lighting was a little surprising as the general trend countrywide was towards the use of fluorescent tubes because of their better lighting qualities; it was done to reduce manufacturing and maintenance costs.

Saloon heating, similar to that on the prototypes, was specified as standard for the first time on a London bus, and the ergonomic principles applied to the cab design of the experimental vehicles were also perpetuated. In its mechanical specification, the production Routemaster embodied improvements to coil springs, shock absorbers, engine mountings, brake shoes and rear axle pinion race assembly which had been found necessary as a result of the service trials with the prototypes. The engine was the AV590 production version of the AEC 9.6 litre unit as tried out on RMs 1 and 2. It was derated to 115bhp to ensure, as far as possible, complete combustion with smoke-free exhaust. The gearbox was the electro-pneumatic AEC D182 with automatic operation on second to fourth gears plus manual override. Mounted at the forward end of the gearbox was a belt-driven reciprocating air compressor. Braking was activated by a continuous flow hydraulic system and had no automatic adjusters; hydraulic power assisted steering was fitted, as was coil suspension front and rear. The back axle was of the spiral bevel type, the ratio being 5.22:1. Unlike the four prototypes, and the complete RT family, the production RM was fitted with an offside fuel tank which gave better balance but caused complications over refuelling arrangements in years to come where Routemasters and RTs shared common fuel islands. 900x20 tyres were fitted all round, with 14 ply rating on the single fronts and 10 ply on the double rears.

RM 101 featured in a widely used advertisement in the trade press during the autumn of 1960 on behalf of Lockheed. Despite this, hydraulic braking systems never really became popular outside London.

An instruction card was given to all Routemaster drivers, being deemed necessary because of its many differences from the fleet's other standard class, the RT. This one dates from the period when the original water system was being replaced by a pressurised one, necessitating two sets of instructions for filling the radiator.

Such is the fine reputation justifiably built up by the Routemaster over its many years of intensive operation that it is now hard to believe that it was not universally well received when new. However, it is a matter of historical record that, in the early days, numerous problems were encountered and mechanical failures were common. Naturally, this did not endear it to many of those whose task it was to run the Routemaster in its original role as a replacement for London's huge trolleybus fleet which, though by and large now elderly and overdue for replacement, was still in the main operating extremely reliably and producing few mechanical problems which could not be easily handled. In comparison with the trolleybuses, the RM was a very complex machine, in fact the most complex bus of its day. From the public viewpoint too, the Routemaster was by no means the ideal in its early days. The much-vaunted heating system frequently produced seemingly uncontrollable blasts of ice-cold air on winter days, and the ride was such as to produce names like 'Jerkmaster' and other derogatory epithets.

None of this should have been too surprising. In a totally new design embodying so many novel features, it was inevitable that problems would surface which had not shown up in the small scale running of the four

ROUTEMASTER BUSES
INSTRUCTIONS FOR DRIVERS AND CONDUCTORS

The Routemaster is basically different in design from the RT bus. It is of chassisless construction manufactured in light alloy with coil spring independent suspension at the front, and a coil spring suspension at the rear specially designed to ensure stability. The vehicle incorporates fully automatic transmission with over-riding control; power assisted steering; high efficiency power hydraulic braking; with fresh air heating and ventilation on both decks.

FOR THE DRIVER

Starting the Engine

First check that the handbrake is hard " on ", that the gear selector lever is in neutral, and that the engine stop control is pushed fully home. Press the accelerator pedal right down and operate the starter switch until the engine fires. Release switch as soon as engine fires, release pedal and engine will idle.

Driving the Vehicle

The transmission changes gear automatically according to conditions of road speed and accelerator pedal position.

To move off, place the gear selector lever in the normal top gear position. Release hand-brake against the pull-away of the vehicle. The vehicle may then be driven solely by use of the accelerator and brake pedals.

It is particularly important that the handbrake should be applied each time the vehicle is stopped to prevent it running backward or forward. Such movement is likely on a slight slope.

When descending hills which are scheduled for descent in low gear, or in any other abnormal circumstances, the required gear should be engaged manually. While the selector gate is similar to that on the RT bus, third and top gears cannot be engaged unless the vehicle is in motion; first and second gears can be engaged manually when the vehicle is stationary and at relevant road speeds.

Reverse gear must only be engaged when the engine is at idling speed and the vehicle is stationary with the handbrake on.

When manoeuvring in garages or confined spaces, drivers should use the second speed manual gear, and not the automatic.

In the event of the rear wheels skidding, a relay trips in the automatic mechanism causing neutral to be engaged. The drive can be restored by stopping the vehicle and depressing the selector lever down through the gate with the reverse catch pulled and held there for 10 seconds. **In no circumstances must the accelerator be pressed whilst so doing.** If this action is not successful, then the garage must be telephoned for instructions. For emergency operation, first, second and third gears will still be obtainable manually. The power assisted steering must not be turned while the vehicle is stationary.

The power hydraulic braking is very responsive to pedal movement and is lighter in application than the RT air brake. It is best operated by keeping the heel in contact with the floor plate.

Pressure Indicators

Low brake pressure is indicated, as in the case of the RT bus, by means of a white light and a warning flag. A separate indicator in the form of a red light gives warning of low gearbox pressure. When either warning is given the vehicle should be stopped and the engine revved up in neutral for 30 seconds. If either the brake or gearbox indicators fail to respond, then contact should be made with the garage.

When leaving the Vehicle

Apply the handbrake, select neutral gear on the gear change lever and pull the engine stop control, leaving it in the " out " position.

Filling the Radiator

STANDARD RUBBER CAP

The water level in the radiator should be checked by means of a separate push button level cock, which can be reached after first lifting the bonnet. If no water comes out when the button is depressed, the main filler cap should be opened with caution and the radiator topped up to the level of the filler hole. It is dangerous to stand directly in front of the filler cap. After use it is essential that the filler cap is screwed down **hard.**

METAL TYPE PRESSURE CAP

Where a metal type pressure cap is fitted no attempt should be made to remove it to check the water level. With this sealed system there should be no loss of water under normal operating conditions, but, if due to a defect there is an obvious water shortage, the garage should be contacted.

Emergency Fuel Shut Off

To turn off fuel supply in an emergency, lift bonnet and turn hand wheel in fuel line clockwise. See sketch overleaf.

Saloon Heating

A blind is provided in the front of the saloon heater and this blind can be drawn to prevent air passing over the radiator. The blind is drawn to cover the radiator by pulling a cord with a white knob located in the corner of the driver's cab roof and locking the knob into the retaining slot in the adjacent bracket.

During cold weather the blind should be drawn to cover the saloon heater radiator for at least 20 minutes after the bus has left the garage in the morning, and for 10 minutes after leaving a stand, if the bus has been standing for more than 30 minutes. To introduce heat into the interior of the vehicle after the intervals stated above, the knob should be released from the slot so that the blind rolls up.

Cab Heating

The cab heater is operated by moving a white painted handle which simultaneously switches on the fan and opens the vent to admit fresh air to the heater.

prototypes and a couple of mobile test beds described in the previous chapter. One by one the defects were tackled. Many came to light during the production years and consequent improvements were incorporated on the assembly line with retrospective action taken where necessary on vehicles already built. The more important modifications are described later in this chapter. Others occurred only in later life, often as a result of the ageing of structures which were new in concept at the time of manufacture and for which no historical knowledge as to fatigue potential could be called upon.

Viewed superficially, the production Routemaster as operated by London Transport appeared to be a highly standardised vehicle with just four variations on the basic theme, each with its own specific class designation. By far the most numerous variant was the basic 27ft 6ins long RM although the 30ft RML also achieved a creditable production run; each had their coach derivatives in the RMC and RCL classes respectively. The production run of 2756 vehicles attracted no fewer than 24 combinations of mechanical and body codes signifying that, despite external appearances, all was far from standard. These codes, as will be seen later, related almost solely to varying combinations of proprietory items of electrical and braking equipment, but in addition some forty of more major modifications were introduced on the body or mechanical fitments during the production run. Further to this, numerous experiments were carried out, most of which were not perpetuated but nevertheless added still more to the variety within the Routemaster fleet for so long as they remained current. Even after production had ceased, modifications continued to be made, some significant but many of a very minor nature, with the result that, by the start of the nineteen-eighties, London Transport was able to claim that the Routemaster had undergone over two thousand modifications, major and minor, during its career.

Although standardisation had been the keynote of London Transport's vehicle design policy for many years, the Routemaster was in fact a less standardised product than its predecessor, the famous RT. However, in one major concept, the Routemaster never changed: namely in the basic construction and layout of its main body shell and associated components, and therein lay one of its major strengths. The complete interchangeability of units, notably pillars, panels and glass, and of many mechanical fitments enabled factory-type production line methods of overhaul to be developed to the highest degree ever achieved in a bus fleet, and greatly reduced the call on diagnostic skills in garages because the majority of items could be replaced speedily rather than repaired in situ. The drive, already implemented with the RT, to reduce the number of skilled craftsmen in garages was maintained and non-revenue earning time could, theoretically, be cut to a minimum. Quick replacement of parts enabled London Transport to aim for a phenomenally low 2.5% spare bus float in garages and 5% in the fleet overall.

The first year's run of Routemasters produced an incredibly mixed bag of vehicles, reflecting the willingness of London Transport's designers and engineers to adopt an

By today's standards the Routemaster cab was almost primitive, yet for its time it represented the latest in comfort and technology. From left to right are the handbrake, the gear control lever attached to the left of the steering column with the knob releasing the control for reverse engagement facing the driver, the horn button on an extension arm on the right of the column, and the flashing indicator switch on the console adjacent to the speedometer and above the headlamp and wiper switches. The headlamp dip switch is on the floor to the left of the steering column. Originally an AEC motif was fitted at the top of the column to hide the steering wheel nut, but as on this vehicle, they were continually found to be missing and their use was dispensed with from January 1964 onwards. LT Museum 21001

Apart from the speedometer, the only instrumentation consisted of a red light at eye level to indicate low gearbox pressure and a white one for low brake pressure, the latter supplemented by an RT-type 'STOP' flag. In typical London Transport fashion the starter switch was above the driver's head on the nearside and was adjacent to the main light switches. The button controlling the blind for the heating-cum-ventilating system is clearly marked. LT Museum 1773/12

open-minded approach, almost a trial and error method, for ascertaining which proprietory equipment would be best for any given purpose. The production Routemaster was novel for its time in having been developed around an AC electrical system theoretically better suited to the vehicle. Claimed advantages were lighter weight, less maintenance and maximum power output at a lower engine speed enabling smaller batteries to be fitted, with improved life through discharging less frequently. However, the first twenty units received a conventional DC system with heavy duty batteries. Of these, RMs 5-11, 341, 398 and 459 had CAV built control panels and transmission equipment (the latter comprising the accelerator switch and gearbox auto control panel), and Lockheed brakes. RMs 5-7, 398 and 459 were coded 5RM5 whilst RMs 8-11 and 341 were 1/5RM5/1, denoting that a different make of dynamo was fitted. The three higher numbered buses were constructed using the electrical equipment and running gear set aside for the mobile test beds (see chapter 5). The remaining DC RMs had SCG instead of CAV transmission and were divided into 2/5RM5/2 (RM 12-16) and 3/5RM5/3 (RM 17-21), again according to the type of dynamo fitted. By equipping twenty

buses in the old manner, it seemed almost as though London Transport was keeping its options open in case its preferred system employing alternators failed. It did not, however, and within two years all twenty had been converted to AC although their heavy duty batteries remained in place until June 1963. With removal of the dynamos, the differences between the various categories vanished and codes 1/5RM5/1 and 3/5RM5/3 were officially discontinued on 1st June 1961, being merged into 5RM5 and 2/5RM5/2 respectively. After removal of the DC equipment, the buses were used for experiments with a revised type of CAV alternator, being just a few of the very many early RMs to feature in alternator, control panel, rectifier or starter experiments. Indeed, no fewer than 91 buses numbered between RM 5 and 543 were involved in one experiment or another in these particular fields.

Alternator equipped buses started from RM 22, the generators being mounted on the right hand side of the crank case bottom half, and driven by three vee belts from a pulley on the front of the crankshaft. RM 22-121 formed a sub-type of one hundred technically identical vehicles coded 4/5RM5/4. Like RM 5-11, they were equipped throughout with CAV electrics.

CAV control panels and alternators were to be found on RM 122-209 of type 5/RM5/5, although these had SCG built transmissions. Further 4/5RM5/4s were RM 210-252 and 333-339 whilst RM 340 and 464 were two more 5/5RM5/5s. Code 6/5RM5/6 brought Simms built control panels and alternators into service for the first time, introducing a policy of dual sourcing of these components which was to continue through to the end of Routemaster production. The Simms products differed in design from those of CAV and the two were not interchangeable. The first Simms Routemaster to enter service (RM 253 at West Ham) did so some eight weeks in advance of others in the batch which comprised 240 buses in all, being RMs 253-332, 342-397, 399-458, 460-463, 465-504. Further Simms equipped vehicles were the large 7/5RM5/7 sub-type, of

Above **Looking forward in the lower saloon of RM 9, the standard ceiling mounted heater outlet can be seen. Below it on the heater ducting is the vertical advertisement frame, which remained unused, above the circular heater control which required a budget key to operate in place of the fixed handle provided on the prototypes.** LT Museum 1773/14

The mesh of the front grille barely hides the radiator of RM 101 at Aldgate, one of the vehicles with experimental alkaline batteries and rear air suspension. The front trafficator mounting brackets of the production RMs were improved in design compared with those on the prototypes.
Lens of Sutton

which 325 were purchased during the initial Routemaster production run of 850 vehicles; these were RMs 505-781, 802-849. They differed from the 6/5RM5/6 in having SCG transmission rather than CAV. Further 7/5RM5/7s were built during later production runs, the last new sub-type to be created within the first order being the 8/5RM5/8, RMs 782-801 and 850 onwards. These reverted to CAV electrical equipment but of an improved type, though transmission was by SCG.

One of many lines of experimentation saw the fitment from new of alkaline batteries, of two different types, on RM 22-121 instead of the usual lead-acid type. London Transport already had extensive experience of alkaline batteries on its trolleybuses and the hundred Routemasters retained them for a number of years, being always allocated to Poplar or West Ham Garages even though their identity changed on overhaul.

The Routemaster was designed to incorporate air suspension at the rear if required in place of the standard coil springs, the locating holes and fixtures on the sub-frames and bodies being identical for coil or air. RM 8 was equipped at the 1958 Show with Firestone-built rear suspension and it was decided that fifty of the early production run (RM 75/87-135) should be air sprung. Four types of suspension were tried out; RM 75 and 87-105 with

Firestone rolling diaphragm type 1 'Airide', RM 106-110 with Firestone type 2 'Airide', RM 111-130 with Dunlop triple convolution 'Pneuride' and RM 131-135 with Dunlop combined convolution and rolling diaphragm type 'Dillow'. Ancillary equipment common to all versions comprised an air storage reservoir, charge valve and two levelling control valves, one nearside and one offside. Air supply was taken from the compressor via the existing reservoir for the gearbox to the air suspension charge valve and storage reservoir. The charge valve acted as a non-return valve to prevent air escaping from the gearbox system in the event of a leak in the air suspension. Acknowledged as giving a softer ride and thus advantageous on prestige work such as Green Line, air suspension was also thought to be worth trying on urban work for the theoretical benefit it offered in keeping the platform at the same height above the road whether the bus was full or empty. A further 184 bodies, those on RM 76-86/136-308, were fitted with conduits below the floor in the third and fourth body bays in case air suspension was required, but it never was. The generally held view was that the air suspension was never sufficiently beneficial in urban use to justify the higher maintenance costs of the equipment which often proved troublesome. Replacement of the air bags with coil springs on the hundred vehicles began at a fairly early date but only on an 'as and when' basis, and some of the air sprung vehicles continued in their original state well into the 1980s. By this time, however, their original fleet numbers had been long lost upon successive overhauls. Each Routemaster body, irrespective of the fleet

number allotted to it on overhaul, retained its own original coding and, usually, any experimental or other non-standard features which went with it.

The first visual manifestation of changed design came with RM 254 onwards, on which the plain front windows on the upper deck were replaced by quarter drop opening ones similar to those fitted at the sides. The change came in response to complaints that the fresh air flow through the heating/ventilation system was inadequate in hot weather. In order to accommodate the upper contour of the quarter drop windows, the separate air scoop in front of each window had to be omitted although a less prominent but continuous outer scoop was retained. These served the small ventilators, one above each window, which erroneously had been thought would provide adequate additional hot weather ventilation, but which effectively became redundant and were omitted from RM 355 onwards. This modification was visible from the outside of the vehicle, the remaining air scoop above the windows within the dome being eliminated as it no longer served any purpose. Within a few years, many of the bodies of the RM 254-354 batch, which started life with both opening front windows and ventilators, had the latter plated over. As we shall see later, many of the body modifications which were adopted during production were later fitted retrospectively to existing vehicles but, generally speaking, this was not the case with the plain front window bodies, most of which remained distinctive throughout their career. At an early date, six bodies (those on RMs 34, 106, 168, 199, 215, 227) were given opening front windows and it was

Left **Dual sourcing of electrical equipment commenced with the delivery in February 1960 of RM 253, the last vehicle with non-opening front windows. Simms Motor Units were the supplier, but equipment from the original manufacturer, CAV, proved longer lasting within the fleet as Simms spares became increasingly hard to get.** Fred Ivey

Centre **Opening front upper deck windows were soon found to be desirable and were fitted as standard from RM 254 onwards. They were capable of being locked in the winter months. The upper deck of RM 319 shows the combination of dome-mounted ventilators plus opening front windows found only on the batch of 101 vehicles RM 254-354. On later deliveries, which omitted the ventilators, the advertisement panel was dropped to a lower level.** Alan Nightingale

Bottom **The lip projecting slightly below the moulding in front of the windows of RM 345 indicates that it is one of the batch equipped with old style interior ventilators in addition to the quarter-drops.** Alan B. Cross

generally anticipated that a full-scale modification programme would follow, but it did not. However over the ensuing years bodies B5, B9, B16, B38, B40, B68, B74, B91, B110, B149, B151, B169 and B247 also received opening front windows, usually when repairs were carried out following accidents.

The much vaunted heating-cum-ventilation system soon became the subject of modification. In the lower saloon, there was a neat outlet grille mounted just below the ceiling in the centre of the front bulkhead and at the foot of the heater duct below it was another much smaller outlet, the whole system being controlled by the conductor by a key-operated switch in the trunking. The main, upper, outlet proved to be too high to be effective and the switching arrangement proved troublesome. As an experiment, RM 104 was re-equipped with a revised design through which all the air was diverted to a low-placed ventilator pointing directly into the saloon rather than downwards at the foot of the duct as was the case previously. The decorative upper ventilator was removed and replaced by an upwards continuation to ceiling level of the trunking case to the detraction of the general appearance of the bulkhead but resulting in much more effective distribution of the heat output than before. The control switch was now placed at the top and no longer required a key, and a novel feature was that, by sliding a lever, the conductor could now select the level of heat instead of it being preset. Soon after the conversion of RM 104, a batch of fifty new vehicles (RMs 525-574) was built similarly equipped. On these 51 vehicles, the Chinese green duct was slightly narrower than usual and thus could not accommodate the burgundy-coloured advertisement panel, which mattered little as it was never used anyway. The equipment was a success and, with the start of production of the second batch of Routemasters, from RM 855 onwards, the new layout was adopted as standard. However, with a view to converting the existing fleet retrospectively, the production models now incorporated a neater duct of standard dimensions (complete with advertisement panel) and a more robust air outlet grille. The original aluminium grille on the 51 prototypes had been prone to damage and was replaced by the new standard type from June 1963 onwards, although slightly modified to suit

The longest run of externally identical vehicles in the RM class comprised 570 numbered between RM 355 and 948. The 500th Routemaster, delivered in October 1960, is seen at Moorgate shortly after entering passenger service. Lens of Sutton

the narrower heater duct. A programme of converting all the RMs before RM 855 to the new design was undertaken quickly, the converted vehicles being distinguishable from those built new because a small strip of the yellow ceiling colour, forming part of the new upper duct housing, projected below the horizontal decorative aluminium moulding. However, with the later fitting of illuminated interior advertisement boxes on all Routemasters, this feature was covered up and the pre-RM 855 bodies were then indistinguishable from the rest.

From RM 855 onwards, various contracts for the supply of new Routemasters flowed one after another, the size of the individual orders tending to become blurred in the continuous production schedules. A run of 598 took the class up to RM 1452 (although within this was included the trial batch of RMLs, 880-903, and the experimental RMF 1254, both described in later chapters). Fleet numbers 1453-1520 were set aside for RMC coaches, and subsequent orders for 195, 91, 350 and 61 vehicles took the conventional RM production up to the

end of its run at RM 2217. The 7/5RM5/7 sub-type continued to be specified, RMs 1052-1054, 1174-1253, 1521-1719 bringing the total to 607 units, the largest single sub-type of any within the RM family. Added to the 607 were two float bodies built in February 1963 and given body numbers (without a B) in the pre-Routemaster series. It was an old established practice of London Transport, and the LGOC before it, to purchase float bodies for all large batches of vehicles as an aid to the overhaul programme where bodies invariably took longer to handle than chassis. The two Routemaster bodies marked the end of this tradition. They were finally used in September 1963 (body 9986) and October 1963 (9985) on RM 90 and RM 162 respectively.

Another large sub-class, 8/5RM5/8, also continued in production. It was current at the time of the commencement of construction of the second Routemaster order and continued up to RM 879, and then on RM 904-1051, 1155-1173, 1255-1452, rendering it the second largest sub-type at 415 vehicles. New sub-types came with the comparatively small 84 strong

9/5RM5/9 (RM 1071-1154) and the even smaller batch of sixteen 10/5RM5/10 (RM 1055-1070). These brought into use for the first time, in January 1962, a Clayton Dewandre design of hydraulic braking system which differed significantly from the Lockheed built one fitted so far. The 9/5RM group had CAV electrical equipment whereas the 10/5RM had Simms; all had CAV transmission.

After RM 1719, almost all remaining deliveries reverted to the 2/5RM chassis classification, RM 1720-1799, 1801-1809 being of the 2/5RM5/2 type last delivered with RM 12-16 in June 1959. Meanwhile, RM 1577 had been fitted experimentally with illuminated advertisement panels, one measuring 17ft 6ins by 1ft 9ins on the offside between decks and the other (2ft 5ins by 11ins) inside the lower saloon above the front bulkhead windows. It was recoded 2/5RM9 and was used as a demonstration vehicle to test the reaction of potential advertisers. Encouraged by the response, London Transport arranged for RMs 1923-1985, 2036-2121 to be built as 2/5RM9s. On these vehicles, the generator for the offside

The lower deck of a Routemaster equipped from new with an illuminated bulkhead panel. Vehicles converted from the earlier style can be recognised by the existence of an advertisement panel on the heater duct upon which the control switch will have been superimposed. This photograph also shows the plain moulding above the windows which from November 1962 replaced the polished strip with plastic insert.
LT Museum A70/1085

panel was located under the upstairs nearside rearmost seat. The switch, which conductors were instructed should always be in the ON position except in emergency, was situated next to the saloon lighting switches. When switched on, it ensured that the interior advertisement was illuminated whenever the engine was running and that the external advert was lit when the engine was running and the side lights were on. The presence of the interior advertisement required the re-siting of the heater control switch from its horizontal location above window level to a vertical slot on the heater duct itself, from which the advertisement panel was omitted. All remaining vehicles in the RM production run had interior illuminated advertisements, including those which did not carry the outside one, vehicles in this category (RM 1800, 1810-1922, 2122-2217) being coded 2/5RM9/1. Not yet mentioned are RM 1986-2035, which had both exterior and interior illuminated panels but Simms rather than CAV electrical equipment, earning them the separate coding 11/5RM9/2. With the subsequent fitment of interior illuminated panels to all RMs, the 9/1 classification later became obsolete, all 2/5-RM9/1s being officially recoded 2/5RM5/2 in January 1966. This was the month in which the fitment commenced of illuminated advertisement boxes to the interiors of all Routemaster family vehicles except Green Line coaches, a massive programme involving over 1800 buses which was carried out at Aldenham on overhaul and also on a 'run-in' programme from garages requiring each bus to be in works for two days. The programme took until September 1968 to complete, except for RM 830 at Camberwell which somehow managed to escape the net and was not caught up with until January 1969.

Illuminated advertisement panels, with their promise of enhanced revenue generation, were embraced as heartily by London Transport as by many provincial operators, though few outside London went as far as to fit them inside the vehicles as well as on the offside. Victoria garage's RM 2020 displays the panel at work.
LT Museum 3966/R/1

The full, complex list of codings allocated to production RMs when new can be summarised as follows:

		Transmission	Alternator & Control Panel	Brakes
5RM5	RM 5-7, 398, 459	CAV	–	Lockheed
1/5RM5/1	RM 8-11, 341	CAV	–	Lockheed
2/5RM5/2 (first series)	RM 12-16	SCG	–	Lockheed
2/5RM5/2 (second series)	RM 1720-1799, 1801-1809	SCG	CAV	Lockheed
2/5RM9	RM 1923-1985, 2036-2121	SCG	CAV	Lockheed
2/5RM9/1	RM 1800, 1810-1922, 2122-2217	SCG	CAV	Lockheed
3/5RM5/3	RM 17-21	SCG	–	Lockheed
4/5RM5/4	RM 22-121, 210-252, 333-339	CAV	CAV	Lockheed
5/5RM5/5	RM 122-209, 340, 464	SCG	CAV	Lockheed
6/5RM5/6	RM 253-332, 342-397, 399-458, 460-463, 465-504	CAV	Simms	Lockheed
7/5RM5/7	RM 505-781, 802-849, 1052-1054, 1174-1253, 1521-1719	SCG	Simms	Lockheed
8/5RM5/8	RM 782-801, 850-879, 904-1051, 1155-1173, 1255-1452	SCG	CAV	Lockheed
9/5RM5/9	RM 1071-1154	CAV	CAV	Clayton
10/5RM5/10	RM 1055-1070	CAV	Simms	Clayton
11/5RM9/2	RM 1986-2035	SCG	Simms	Lockheed

Above Left **The ongoing search for improvement in front end appearance resulted in the introduction of a central polished strip on the radiator grille in September 1961 in place of the red-painted strip used previously. RM 1125, which demonstrates this feature, is one of the first batch of Routemasters to be fitted with Clayton hydraulic brakes rather than the Lockheed variety which always remained far more numerous.** Alan B. Cross

Above and Left **Evidence that a search was under way for a revised frontal style surfaced when a quantity of Shepherds Bush RMs were fitted with new panels consisting of the current type of stainless steel surround superimposed on a new base whose V configuration at the top centre was clearly intended to take a traditional rectangular AEC-style badge. RM 351 was one of the vehicles involved in the experiment. The V-style grille was duly adopted as standard as shown on a pair of Edmonton RMs, 693 and 1806. However the former Shepherds Bush fronts remained distinguishable, even after conversion, due to the prominent ridge of red inside the polished surround (as on RM 693) which the neater, standard ones did not have.** A.J. Wild/Alan B. Cross

On the motive power front, no fewer than 745 of the 2120 production RMs were equipped with other than AV590 engines, though without invoking any change to the type coding. Of these, 575 (RMs 632, 870, 1009, 1255-1452, 1521-1719, 1811-1985) had Leyland's renowned type 0600 9.8 litre engine and are described more fully in chapter 9. The remaining 170, RMs 1991-2160, were fitted with AEC engines, but of the more powerful 11.3 litre AV690 variety derated to give the same power output as the AV590. Specified for comparative purposes, the AV690 proved significantly more thirsty despite being set to produce the same power, and comparative tests were carried out, some at Chobham and some in the form of bench tests, to ascertain the reason. These tests were inconclusive but it was assumed that greater friction caused by the larger piston ring contact was the most likely cause. In fact, the standard AV590 was more than adequate and no further 690s were purchased for use in conventional RMs, and existing ones were gradually phased out as they became time expired. The use of wet liners resulted, in the early days, in corrosion on the

water jacket side, which was cured by ceramic spraying of the liners but by and large the AV590 was a splendid engine being well designed, well built, smooth running and, above all, economical; factors which combined to contribute in no small way to the fact that the RM could claim an approximate 5% better fuel consumption than the 8ft wide RTW which had 13% fewer seats.

Whereas there had been no apparent external body modifications during the first production contract for Routemasters up to RM 854, apart from the obvious one involving the front upper deck windows, in later batches several changes were made in fairly quick succession. Most were subsequently extended to all other vehicles as a retrospective fitment, either in a phased way or piecemeal, so that within a decade of production starting only the last hundred or so to be built (those which had incorporated all the latest design features from new) were likely to be seen in completely original condition. The first external modification, and a fairly innocuous one at that, was the replacement of the polished aluminium radiator grille surround with stainless steel

on which the central vertical strip was also bright to match the grille instead of being painted red. As with several of the modifications which followed, it was introduced as part of a continuing quest to improve the frontal appearance of the RM and was to be found on RM 949 upwards. Starting with RM 1064, all external glass fibre items such as front wings and bonnet top were overpainted in red, the unpainted red-impregnated glass fibre used previously having been prone to fade with the passage of time, turning firstly pale red then an unsightly pink. The same vehicle saw the introduction of black used ticket boxes instead of red. From RM 1067 upwards, the horizontal wearing strip on the driver's cab door was in stainless steel, the original red painted ones quickly becoming badly marked through use. A much more obvious design change occurred in July 1963 when RM 1662 was delivered with a completely redesigned style of front grille, followed two months later by RMs 1665/1680/1682 onwards. The new styling incorporated a V shaped top to the centre strip to accommodate an AEC style LONDON TRANSPORT badge of the type familiar on

the RT and earlier Southall built classes. The separate raised bullseye at the front of the bonnet lid was rendered redundant and was omitted, although the motif fixing screwholes lasted up to RM 1697, suitably plugged. This new style, which was introduced on purely aesthetic grounds, had first been tried in October 1962 on RMF 1254 (see chapter 13) and its full scale introduction was presaged by a trial on 25 Shepherds Bush based RMs in the spring of 1963, using front valance panels incorporating provision for the triangular motif but still retaining the old style full height stainless central strip and exposing the new type V shaped glass fibre moulding below it. Once it became the standard fitting, the new grille quickly spread to older vehicles on overhaul or after accident damage and, though an instruction was given that the new grille should not be fitted with the old bonnet top unless the bullseye was removed, this inevitably was ignored. Before long, it was by no means difficult to find RMs with two motifs at the front, or even with none at all where an old style grille was matched up with a new type bonnet top.

The next exterior modification came in November 1963 on RM 1743 onwards from which the offside route number was omitted. A change of policy had decreed that route numbers should no longer be shown on the offside of any vehicles and, towards the end of the month, an instruction went out to all garages to remove the offside blinds and bulbs from all Routemasters. This was quickly complied with; in most cases the glass was

painted red at the same time. As vehicles went into Aldenham for overhaul, the wiring, terminal block, bulb holders, and the glass and its rubber surround were removed. On some vehicles, a new plain panel replaced the old one but, more often, a panel which just fitted within the existing vertical and horizontal mouldings was pop-riveted over the top of the old one.

From RM 1902 of April 1964 onwards, the air ventilator apertures in the front headlamp panels were omitted. Earlier trials on RMF 1254 and RMC 1469 had shown that ventilators were unnecessary, and design of a new type of front wing was put in hand, omitting the ventilator apertures and giving a lower sweep at its bottom edge to align with the foot of the radiator grille. As the new type was not then in production, RM 1902 merely carried the old style wing with solid plates where the ventilators would have previously been. A November 1964 instruction to garages outlined the procedure for converting existing vehicles by sandwiching a plate between the panel and the grille, but no co-ordinated programme of conversion took place and, for a while, it was common to see RMs with grilles on one side but not on the other. From June 1964 onwards, plastic wing valances using a material called 'Royalite' were used instead of metal.

From October 1964, the ROUTEMASTER name was omitted from above the fleet number on both sides of the vehicle, it presumably no longer being considered necessary to proclaim its title now that the Routemaster fleet was so large. RM 2046 was the first to appear without ROUTEMASTER transfers. In the same month, RM 2063 onwards appeared with the cream band carried continuously around the front of the vehicle, obscuring the bottom half of the upper front grille. This modification, for which RMF 1254 and RMC 1469 had again been guinea pigs, was another of a series aimed at improving external appearance and it in no way hampered the effectiveness of operation of the heating and ventilation system despite the fifty per cent reduction in air flow. Modifications of existing RMs did not commence immediately, although the RMC coaches were dealt with en bloc from May 1964 onwards, but from January 1965 a programme commenced of modifying vehicles as they went through Aldenham for overhaul. This took some years and an occasional vehicle slipped through the net with the result that total modification was probably not completed before 1980 when the 'Showbus' craze commenced whereby garage staff voluntarily beautified vehicles for rallying and often, in doing so, restored the heater aperture to its original state by removing the masking plate.

No further external modifications were made to the RMs during the course of their production run, although the new style front grilles with the registration number plate mounted below (introduced with RCL 2218) and front headlamp panels downswept to meet the bottom of the grille (from RML 2261), were modifications which quickly began to find their way on to RMs. The introduction of the new style headlamp panels to RMs was accompanied in February 1966 by the instruction that they must always be fitted in pairs to

The standard illuminated advertisement vehicle is illustrated by Hendon's RM 2006 mounting a City pavement. For several years a conscious effort was made to allocate these to garages from where they could operate through central London for maximum effect, but this was abandoned in due course as was the interest of advertisers in sponsoring illuminated panels. This view also shows the omission of the offside route number box on RMs 1743 onwards.

Facing Page The ultimate RM styling, with a continuous band and moulding across the lower half of the heating and ventilator grille, is represented by Hackney's RM 2199. The use of a cream relief band was on the verge of ceasing when this vehicle was built in favour of an insipid pale grey. Ken Blacker

avoid an unbalanced effect but this instruction was never adhered to and it became increasingly commonplace thereafter to find RMs with one headlamp panel deeper than the other.

Very late in the RM production programme, from RM 2210 delivered in April 1965, a livery change saw replacement of the cream cantrail relief by pastel grey, a prototype for this having been RM 2128 which entered service at Bow three months earlier. Grey was used as the relief colour for all of the red RMLs which followed on after the cessation of RM production at 2217, though the pastel shade which was an insipid colour closer to off-white than grey, was superseded in November of the same year by mist grey which was a noticeably darker shade.

In addition to the obvious external variations, the RM class underwent a number of internal changes to bodywork during the course of the production run. The earliest modification was not immediately visible though it could certainly be felt. One of the major criticisms of many earlier RMs was the uncomfortable seats compared with the RT, an impression caused mainly by the cushions which felt thin and insubstantial to the extent that, if sat upon too hard, the sitter would feel the cushion ground on the base below. The

problem lay in the seat filling of polyether foam which, though much vaunted at the time of introduction, soon showed itself prone to premature collapse which, in addition to causing discomfort to the passenger, resulted in premature wear of the moquette coverings. From RM 407 onwards, a harder wearing *Vitafoam* filling was used. In September 1963, another novel seat feature introduced with the RM was abandoned as a failure when the seat back boards, which had been made of moulded fibreglass, were replaced with conventional plywood ones with metal sides and bottom plates. The new seat backs came into use from approximately RM 1400 onwards and were later fitted to all existing vehicles, a mammoth task taking into account the number of seats on each bus.

Minor visible alterations included the fitment of a polished finisher strip at the top edge of the rear destination box lid on which the rexine tended to become badly frayed through continual handling by conductors (fitted to RM 1815 onwards and retrospectively to the remainder), and the provision of a cleaning outlet slot at the top of the staircase on the foot of the panel adjacent to the nearside rear seat (RM 1385 onwards and, again, fitted retrospectively not only to RMs but also to all remaining members of the RT family). More

immediately visible was the November 1962 change in internal decor, introduced with RM 1356, which substituted the polished aluminium moulding with maroon plastic insert above the windows on both decks with a plain band stove-enamelled in sung yellow to match the ceiling panels. This, like several other modifications subsequently adopted as standard, had originally been tried out on RMF 1254. Slightly earlier in the production programme, commencing with RM 1335, the conductor's bell push on the platform bulkhead adjacent to the staircase was repositioned from approximately thigh height to head height, a modification which remained a slight source of irritation to conductors ever afterwards because earlier vehicles were not altered to bring them into line and the conductor could not be sure, on taking over a bus, which position the bell push was in. It was claimed at the time that the modification was made to put the bell push out of reach of small children allegedly making a nuisance of themselves by ringing the bell for fun, though it would hardly have been effective against even more troublesome older children!

Larger staircase panels and a new design of panel at the bottom of the stair riser were minor new features introduced on RM 1285 whilst, in a similar vein, a revised finish with

larger kicking panel on the rear wheel arch assembly, below the longitudinal seats, was to be found on RM 1255/1257 onwards. A further small addition, like the foregoing aimed at reducing wear, was the provision of a chequer plate kicking pad on the upper saloon rear nearside seat riser commencing with RM 1385. Few, if any, of these small detail changes would have been noticed by the casual observer, but the use of a four piece Treadmaster mat on the platform in lieu of slatting tread, on RM 1705 onwards, was rather more apparent. Even more noticeable was the replacement of the offside armrest to the upper deck rear nearside seat by a plain, sloping, rexine covered panel starting with RM 1703. The moquette covered armrests had been extremely prone to wear and were subsequently removed from all RMs previously fitted with them. One final modification, applied only to RM 2188-2217 but not perpetuated on the ensuing RMLs was the fitting of plain, quarter inch thick Treadmaster gangway mats in both saloons instead of the normal individual slats. Though only a comparatively minor modification, the completely flat floor effect which this produced gave a totally different visual impact when entering either saloon. Most, if not all, of these bodies later received normal slatted gangway floors.

Being chassisless, Routemasters were not allocated chassis numbers in the normal sense, the RM number usually being designated as the 'chassis' number if one was required to be given. All buses were, however, allotted unit numbers starting from 001 which, in later years, tended to be more commonly quoted as the 'chassis' number. These followed a prefix denoting the type of Routemaster which, in the case of a standard 27ft 6ins long, rear entrance, AEC engined vehicle was R2RH. The unit numbers actually applied to the separate front and rear assemblies more than to the complete vehicle, so that whilst, for example, RM 5 would be quoted as R2RH004, its front and rear units were A004 and B004 respectively. The situation is confusing because, for licensing purposes, the original unit number has always remained constant with the bonnet number. In real life, not only have Routemaster bodies frequently changed identity – receiving after each overhaul the unit number originally allocated to the fleet number concerned – but the actual units have also moved around very considerably. Although a large number of front and rear units have remained as a pair throughout their lives, they have seldom stayed with the same body. Routemaster unit numbers are given in appendix 2.

CHAPTER SEVEN
BUILDING THE RM

A vast amount of complex planning and organising was needed to get the manufacturing programme for Routemasters on stream. Supply chains had to be negotiated and established in addition to the setting up of the large number of special tools and jigs essential in a design whose central theme demanded construction to unusually close tolerances for interchangeability purposes. It was a series of delays in the tooling-up process, particularly at Park Royal, which caused several months' slippage in getting production under way. So extensive was the amount of special tooling required that AEC alone incurred expenditure of some £75,000 on items relating solely to Routemasters and requiring to be borne within their purchase price plus a further £36,000 which had partial commonality with AEC's other manufacturing work and could therefore be partly offset against other customers' orders.

Above **A general view of the erection shop at Park Royal shows the relationship to each other of the upper and lower saloon assembly lines, with a number of RMLs being built simultaneously. In the stores area on the left can be seen several partially completed roof and other sections.** AEC

The components which go to make up the front unit of a Routemaster, including A frame, boat, engine and auxiliaries, have arrived at Park Royal from a number of sources. After assembly, a steel frame representing a bus cab is used to test clearances and wheel alignment.

Above Left **In the body shop at Park Royal an upper deck, already fully panelled and glazed, is seen being swung gently into position onto the lower saloon which at this stage is in a much less advanced state and totally without its cab and platform structures.**

Above **A workman fixes a window pan into an upper saloon section using a blind rivet gun operated by air pressure. Even at this early stage the upper deck pans are already in their red top coat.**

Left **With the basic lower deck structure now complete, the mechanical components and the main floor structure are checked before the floor is laid.**

Because the Routemaster was chassisless, it was not possible to drive it to the bodybuilders in the normal way. Instead, the completed front and rear assemblies were delivered to Park Royal by lorry. Originally the front units were to be built in the AEC plant at Southall and the rear units in the Maudslay plant at Coventry which, under AEC ownership, specialised in rear axle production, but later these too were produced at Southall.

The Routemaster production line at Park Royal was probably the most streamlined and automated ever dedicated to bus building up to that time and certainly used systems of building and prefabrication which most other British manufacturers of the time could not emulate. It is interesting to recall that, at the same time, bus bodies were being built elsewhere in the works by conventional means for numerous other operators, often in small job lots, whilst other labour teams were constructing high quality bodywork for Bristol GT motor cars and glass fibre cabs for AEC lorries. Park Royal was at its zenith, and the catastrophic slide into low output, productivity and quality, leading to its eventual demise, was still some years ahead. No-one would have thought that Park Royal's future was anything but totally secure back in 1959 when the Routemasters began to roll.

Construction of a Routemaster commenced with the underframe and the three rigid transverse cross members essential for distributing the body load to the mechanical subframe units. Next, the lower saloon side frames and bulkheads would be assembled on jigs (as was everything else to ensure complete interchangeability) with the side pillars extending from the lower saloon floor to the upper saloon floor. These would be attached to the underframe and then the lower deck ceiling would be added before the completed upper deck, which was built on a separate line and came fully panelled and glazed, was lifted into position. The lower saloon was then completed and fitted out, an unusual feature being the special mushroom headed stainless steel screws used for fixing the outer panels which required hardened steel bushes to be pressed into the exterior flanges of the pillars and rails to accept them. Elsewhere on the bus, rivets were used for attaching panels.

The main structure now being complete, the rear end framing and platform which were supported from the upper deck, and the drivers' cab, which was cantilevered from the front bulkhead, would be put in place. The vehicle was then ready for the mechanical units to be fitted prior to finishing the flooring and interior trimming, and the installation of

seating and lighting. With construction completed, the vehicle went to the paint shop for hand painting which Park Royal considered longer lasting than spray painting. The original intention was that most external fittings including panels, mouldings, window pans and even screw heads, would be painted (officially stove enamelled) in top coat prior to erection so that an almost fully painted vehicle emerged with just a minimum of finishing off paintwork to be done. This may have occurred early in the production run but, generally, most of the larger items, notably panels, were in primer and required further coats after assembly.

Park Royal paid much more attention than was usually the case at the time to anti-corrosive treatment, all body parts being treated with a process and then painted, hardened and sealed by heat. All parts and prefabricated sections which were hidden for life after the vehicle was assembled were stove enamelled prior to assembly. Such was the high quality and effectiveness of this treatment that, even thirty years later, a Routemaster body, stripped of its panels, looks as good as new under the surface. With the Routemaster, Park Royal achieved a level of quality in bus body building which has seldom, if ever, been surpassed.

CHAPTER EIGHT

TRIALS AND TRIBULATIONS

Many of the coachwork modifications mentioned in chapter 6 as having taken place during the RM production run were purely cosmetic, trivial when compared with the plethora of design changes which had to be made to correct mechanical and electrical problems, some very serious. In its early days, the Routemaster was, without doubt, an engineer's nightmare. The shortcomings seemed endless, ranging from comparatively minor irritants such as bursting hydraulic pipes or throttle spring failures, through a whole host of electrical problems to structural and design defects in major units. Brakes, gearbox, steering column, suspension, rear axle, and main A and B frames were all units which demanded close examination and much expenditure of time and money to get them right. Several of the worst problems became evident more or less concurrently and, as a result, an extensive review of all aspects of Routemaster performance was undertaken during the twelve months commencing April 1963. Every perceived problem was tackled, placing a demand on the design and development teams to find cures within the shortest possible timespan. In fairness it must be recorded that by no means all were design defects, some were due to contractor error such as hydraulic pipe failures which arose through the use of an incorrect flaring technique, or A-frame failure through the manufacturer adopting cost-cutting techniques.

The defect most obvious to the travelling public was the jerk, sometimes quite violent, associated with almost every gearchange. Not only was this an irritant to passengers, it was also frustrating for drivers who were advised, in training, to ease off the throttle just as each new gear was about to be engaged. However this was a tedious process and the correct moment for the release of the throttle was not always easy to judge, particularly as each bus tended to change gear at differing road speeds despite a supposedly common setting for them all. The trouble lay in the largely unproven

Above **Problems with the earlier production RMs came to a head in November 1961 when some 25 were delicensed and up to six months were to elapse before they were all back at work. Here RM 27, RM 25 and an unidentified radiatorless compatriot stand in Poplar garage awaiting attention.** John Gascoine

Below **Severe jerking on the automatic transmission required urgent research to be carried out to overcome the problem. A large scale experiment on this theme was the conversion of Hanwell's entire fleet to semi-automatic control. RM 501 was one of the vehicles participating in this experiment.** Alan B. Cross

performance of the D128 gearbox which had been forced on London Transport late in the day as an air operated substitute for the hydraulic unit around which the Routemaster transmission had been designed. To make matters worse, in addition to causing jerks between gears beyond the control of the driver, the gearbox also caused a jerk when starting up from rest, perpetuating one of the few defects of the trolleybus which the Routemaster was designed to replace. The jerk start was caused by the automatic transmission being set to idle in neutral, no gear being engaged until the accelerator pedal was depressed, at which point the gear would often come in with a thump. The jerkiness of the RMs on the road was acknowledged by A.A.M. Durrant himself who admitted in September 1963 that tests had proved that 25% of all Routemasters jerked, though the casual observer would almost certainly have put the percentage figure very much higher. After intensive research into the problem, a programme was initiated for the fitment of improved automatic brake hand adjusters, (which AEC had earlier refused to fit despite LT's forebodings), and gradually thereafter the Routemaster lost its reputation for giving a bad ride. Even before this, the problem of the jerk start had been tackled in a programme instituted in the latter part of 1962 under which automatic selection of neutral when stationary was abandoned, the normal gear for starting from rest, which was second, being engaged instead. Drivers were then instructed to select neutral manually if they expected to be stationary for any undue length of time. Strangely, despite the earlier experience, this decision was reversed in 1966 on fuel economy grounds when all Routemasters were to be converted back to neutral idling, but this caused an outcry and vehicles which had been so converted were once again converted to idle in gear. These conversions excluded all the RMs at Hanwell Garage which had been engaged since new in an experiment under which the automatic transmission facility had been sealed off, the vehicles being driven in the semi-automatic mode with driver selection of all gears.

Hanwell Garage apart, there was a strict instruction to drivers in the early days that, in normal circumstances, they should not drive using manual gear selection except when manoeuvring in garages and tight spaces. Dictated by a wish to optimise fuel economy, this instruction was justified on the rather dubious assertion that the automatic setting through the vehicle's control panel was better placed than the driver to judge the correct point at which to change gear. Many drivers, finding performance sluggish due to delayed changes in automatic, resorted to manual selection; officials were instructed to report those who did so. The position changed after April 1964 when a modification within the accelerator switch terminal box removed the kickdown facility for hastening lower gear selection when overtaking or hill climbing which henceforth had to be achieved manually. At the same time, the previous two-pressure throttle range, which had proved unnecessary and added further to the driver's difficulty in giving a smooth ride, was also eliminated. These two modifications were excluded

Thick smoke billows black from RM 1768 whose life has come to an untimely end at Marble Arch, bringing traffic to a standstill. It was travelling out of service because of mechanical problems when the fire occurred. Associated Newspapers

initially from vehicles at Edmonton Garage which remained for a while in their original form as a control batch for evaluation purposes.

Both the A and B frames proved a source of trouble with fractures forming through stresses which were higher than foreseen at the time of design, although in the case of the A frame the adoption by the manufacturer, Thompson Pressings, of cold bending proved unwise and hot pressings were later insisted upon. A major problem with the 'A' frame lay in the 'boat' where the welding of the two halves began to crack, a problem which the operation of the four prototypes would not necessarily have revealed as the design had been changed for the production run. Reinforcement had to be provided in the form of a diaphragm plate within the boat, whilst the thickness of the materials themselves was increased for future production to give greater strength. On the B frame, the fracture occurred on the stiffening web ahead of the axle which, again, was overcome by the addition of a strengthening plate, in this case along the upper edge of the offending unit whilst, once again, new production incorporated a design revision to overcome the problem. At the time that all this was going on, London Transport was fortunate that Vauxhall Motors was experimenting with a brittle lacquer stress coat technique for determining structural areas on road vehicles which might need further investigation into stress patterns

resulting from the application of varying degrees of load, and it was arranged for RM 1278 to go to Vauxhall's proving ground at Chaul End to undergo tests.

Engine problems were comparatively minor and, if anything, the AV590 proved longer lasting than the RT engine, achieving an average inter-overhaul life of over 250,000 miles without any problem. However, flywheels proved troublesome through overheating despite their greater robustness and comparatively exposed position. This was a problem which came to prominence only after the changeover from idling in neutral to idling in gear, the final straw being in July 1966 when RM 1768 was completely gutted by a flywheel fire while running light to Middle Row Garage from route 7, its body being a total write—off. Prevention of similar fires was achieved by fitting each unit with a fusible plug containing a central core through which oil was expelled with force when overheating reached a level short of the oil catching fire.

Overheating was also a fairly frequent problem in the water system which was much more complex on the RM than on other buses because of the lengthy trunking and the dual tank system associated with the heater design. Conversely, the emission of cold air through the heater ducts was a common problem, particularly noticeable in winter and a constant source of irritation to passengers and conductors alike. The heating system was probably the Routemaster's greatest deficiency in the early days and it was comparatively rare to find a bus whose heaters were blowing truly warm air. The many troubles included air ingress into the heat exchanger, caused by even the slightest gasket leak, rendering it inoperative. Often there was water loss through the numerous hose linkages. Very many cylinder head gaskets or *Ranko* thermostatic control valves in the heating system were changed unnecessarily before the problem was solved under a crash programme instituted late in 1964 for replacing the original water system with a pressurised one requiring considerable re-piping. Freezing up of the system was another problem which occasionally kept whole fleets off the road; sometimes buses froze whilst in service. This was solved from 1964 onwards by the winter use on all Routemasters of antifreeze, the first time that its use had been found necessary on a regular basis by London Transport. Even the blind which should have been drawn by the driver over the matrix of the saloon heater radiator during the engine's warm up period, to prevent icy blasts in the saloon, embodied a design fault which resulted in the centre portion of the blind blowing backwards, allowing cold air to enter the ducting past the edges, but a November 1963 modification allowing the blind to be backed by a frame prevented this from happening. On the 800 early RMs on which the conductor was required to switch the heater on or off by budget key, the nylon ball valve operated by the key absorbed water

causing it to swell up and jam, which meant that it would not work. This problem was eliminated when the revised type of sliding switch was fitted. Despite all the effort put into it, the Routemaster heating and ventilation system is probably the aspect of the vehicle which has remained the least satisfactory over the years.

A major defect was uncovered when fractures were found in the steering columns of three RMs late in 1961; one column totally collapsed when a driver used it to steady himself when climbing into the cab of an RM at the East Ham stand. Ultrasonic testing at AEC showed that a better material was needed for the column tube and a campaign change was quickly instituted. This required the whole fleet to return to Southall one by one for new columns to be fitted and started with a mass delicensing of RMs at Poplar on 1st November 1961. In October 1964, following a number of failures of the steering track rod, centre rods of a strengthened design were introduced by AEC for all new vehicles. A steering feature which caused little trouble was the power assistance which was incorporated into the steering linkage and normally worked well, although at times of failure (generally when the fluid level fell too low) manual operation of the steering could prove very heavy.

Early days saw the loss of large amounts of scheduled mileage through allegedly weak brakes. The hydraulic braking system itself

worked well except, of course, in the event of a fluid leak where pressure could not be replaced automatically as it would with air brakes through the atmosphere. The real problem lay in the decision to abandon the fitment of automatic brake adjustors which, on the RT, had maintained shoe clearances within acceptable limits. The revised design of brakes as used on the Routemaster, far from being so efficient that it did not need the expense of automatic adjustors as originally predicted, quickly proved unable to last between scheduled rota checks without frequent manual adjustment. This placed an undue burden on garage engineering staff but, when not carried out, caused drivers to reject buses as unroadworthy. Eventually, London Transport bowed to the inevitable and, in January 1964 from about RM 1898 onwards, introduced automatic brake adjustors on all new vehicles together with a campaign change to bring existing buses up to the same standard.

Freezing of the entire water system was not unknown in the early days, resulting in the expensive use of antifreeze which had never been necessary on earlier types of vehicle. Wood Green's RM 634 has the remnants of a destination blind stuffed in front of the radiator in an attempt by garage staff to make the engine run warmer.
Alan B. Cross

Another problem area was in the shock absorbers and their mainstays. Most trouble was experienced at the front end, but those who have experienced a ride above the rear axle with the shock absorbers adrift are unlikely to forget it, and this was not an uncommon feature in earlier years. Extensive tests were carried out along roads in the Morden area, resulting from which it became clear that shock absorber velocities had been badly underestimated at the design stage. Earlier trials with alternative materials had proved unsuccessful and it was realised that a redesign would be needed for the front absorbers. The original spigot mounting top and bottom in a conical bush was modified at the bottom to accept a Metalastik bush which considerably improved unit reliability. These modifications also speeded up unit replacement time, the front absorbers having previously been difficult to change. Shock absorbers are required to do a lot more work when associated with coil rather than leaf springs, but even so the anticipated life was never really achieved. On the other hand, the coil springs themselves proved very reliable and though occasional breakages occurred at the front, they were comparatively rare at the rear.

The rear axle was an interesting feature in that, in abandoning the efficient and proven worm-type final drive in favour of the spiral bevel axle, the designers were consciously trading proven reliability for the promise of reduced friction loss and the associated cost savings which they hoped would be achieved in the event of the product working well. These hopes were not immediately realised and various design changes had to be made, including an increase in the number of crown wheel fixing bolts from sixteen to twenty to overcome the persistent failure of these items. It is doubtful if any real economy ever was achieved, particularly as the crown wheel and pinion had to be discarded after the expiry of their original life span whereas the worm and wheel of the more conventional design could be reground for further use.

Electrical failures were commonplace in the early days and were sometimes caused by manufacturing faults such as the diodes not being correctly burnt in. However this was one field where the problem lay not so much with the vehicle and its design as with the quantum leap which the maintenance staff were required to make but sometimes could not. The advent of electronics was something totally new as was A.C. generation, added to which the automatic gears with their transistors simply compounded problems. As knowledge broadened and skills developed, competence in handling the Routemaster's complex electrics gradually grew.

In contrast to the numerous mechanical and electrical troubles, the excellent design and construction of the vehicle body structure was such that it needed little basic modification during the construction run, the only real defect, which was serious, being a tendency for the lower saloon floor to distort. Flexing between footstalls caused longitudinal angles supporting the floor to twist, the combined movement in some cases breaking the bond between the slats and floor plate and loosening the floor fixing rivets. This problem was tackled from July 1965 onwards by fitting

RM 8 found a full time occupation as experimental hack for no less than 15 years and was the guinea pig for numerous modifications including many later adopted as standard. The revised front end carried when these photographs were taken indicates experimentation in engine and brake cooling. M. Dryhurst

reinforcing angles connecting together the nearside and offside floor supports. Various other underfloor modifications were carried out later around the floor traps, rendering this area of the Routemaster body the most rebuilt of all and probably leaving few original fittings once all the changes had taken place. Close by, at the very front of the lower saloon by the flywheel cowl, problems occurred from an early date when the Treadmaster strips around the aperture began lifting. Oil contamination was a major cause, coupled to which the floor fixing plate at the offside of the aperture tended to give much trouble with rivets actually pulling through the floor plate. These problems were overcome, again from about July 1965 onwards, by replacing the tread plate with a steel plate and by fitting a new type of floor fixing plate by the aperture whenever signs of 'working loose' appeared.

There can be no denying the fact that the Routemaster gave more than its fair share of cause for concern in the early days but so, also, have many other advanced designs such as the Leyland National and even the hallowed RT. In most cases, these problems have tended to be forgotten once a satisfactory standard of reliability has finally evolved. This has certainly been the case with the Routemaster whose technical problems were, ultimately, resolved allowing it to settle down to a degree of reliability almost comparable to that of the RT. Only in the realm of electrical problems has the Routemaster remained the inferior of the two, always being responsible for more road calls and lost mileage because of this than would be expected from a normal front-engined bus. This fact is however hardly surprising when one takes into account its technical complexity.

CHAPTER NINE

LEYLAND ENGINES

The throaty roar of the Leyland engined Routemaster was once a commonplace sound on the London street. Almost a quarter of the standard RM class at one time ran with Leyland engines and some garages had large fleets of vehicles thus equipped. In the fullness of time, the experience of the RT family was to occur all over again in that the Leyland content would disappear to leave only the AEC design prevailing during the final years of operation but, for more than two decades, AEC and Leyland engined Routemasters ran side by side.

Two strong commercial pressures combined to bring about the equipping of 575 RMs with Leyland engines. Leyland Motors Ltd had hoped all along to play a significant participating role in the Routemaster construction programme while London Transport, for its part, had been keen to encourage this as a means of avoiding the placing of all its orders with one manufacturer. Discussions between the two parties had taken place on a preliminary basis as far back as 25th June 1956 when A.A.M.Durrant travelled to Lancashire to explore with Sir Henry Spurrier, Leyland's Managing Director, and Donald Stokes, their Sales Director, the possibility of the company supplying twenty-five per cent of RM mechanical units. Durrant had in mind that Leyland should supply not just engines but a far more

comprehensive kit as they had done for the third and fourth Routemaster prototypes. For their part, Leyland were very anxious to supply the units because of the prestige attached to London Transport's orders, but examination of the proposition led them to conclude that they would be unable to quote economically for supplying at the rate of two buses' worth of units per week which is approximately what their quarter share of the total Routemaster output would have amounted to. Leyland proposed that, instead of building in uneconomically low numbers on a continuous supply basis, they should manufacture larger quantities periodically in carefully timed batches which would be financially viable to construct and could be programmed in with their other commitments. London Transport, in turn, had to put this proposition to AEC whose co-operation was essential in agreeing to spread the 75% of new vehicles which London Transport was required to purchase from them over a number of years rather than requiring each year to stand on its own, the operator having acknowledged Leyland's view that this was the only way in which orders placed with them could be of sufficiently large size to permit economic production. The suggestion to amend their longstanding trading agreement in this way was put to AEC in November 1956 but came to nothing. In the

end, the only mechanical units which Leyland was to supply for the production run of Routemasters were engines.

The first move towards fitting a Leyland engine came in January 1961 when newly built RM 632 was earmarked for an initial trial fitment. It was despatched to Leyland, stopping off on the way at Self Changing Gears in Coventry for a prolonged, four month stay. A further month at Leyland's works saw the removal of the AEC engine and the installation of its replacement unit, upon completion of which the vehicle entered passenger service on 21st June 1961. This prototype installation saw the fitting of Leyland's well renowned 0.600 9.8 litre power unit which, like the AV590, was derated for London use through its fuel pump and governor settings to produce 115bhp at 1800rpm. The specification incorporated the design features of Leyland's Power Plus range of engines but, as always with London Transport, modifications could

Above **December 12th 1962 was the first day of large scale Leyland Routemaster operation. RM 1277 takes the foreground in this scene at Stoke Newington whilst RM 1297, another Tottenham based vehicle, passes RTL 890, itself a Leyland and making what may well have been its final appearance on route 73.** John Gascoine

not be resisted, notably with the omission of the air filter. London Transport had never favoured the use of air intake cleaners or silencers, regarding their benefits as minimal in London conditions especially as they could become clogged; fires on the RTLs and RTWs had been a further factor influencing this view. In any case the Leyland filter could not be accommodated within the standard Routemaster bonnet shape. The Leyland engine was designed in the expectation that the filter would always be used, and its omission led to the induction roar associated with Leyland powered Routemasters. Tests showed that these could be up to two decibels louder than the AEC engine, although the effect of this would differ according to many factors including the proximity of buildings, whether a vehicle was accelerating or cruising, and even the volume of noise from other traffic in the vicinity.

The engine in RM 632 was the first of a batch of 406 which had been ordered in a contract valued at over £320,000; a quantity of spare parts was also ordered to go with them. The first standard Routemaster to carry a Leyland engine as its original fitment was RM 870 in September 1961 and it was followed by RM 1009 two months later. Initially, all three Leyland Routemasters ran from Hanwell Garage where their performance was monitored against the normal AEC-engined contingent but, once their initial trial period was over in April 1963, they were transferred to Cricklewood. Leyland engines were commonplace by this time and Cricklewood was one of the garages in which they were concentrated whereas Hanwell was not. It was intended that, of the remaining 403 engines covered by

the contract, 197 would be installed in vehicles being built under the then-current programme, these being RMs 1255–1452. A further 199 would be fitted to further vehicles on order for 1963, RMs 1521–1719 which actually followed on directly from RM 1452 in production terms, leaving six engines as spares. Leyland engines really came into their own in November 1962 when large batches took to the road from Tottenham, Mortlake, Stockwell and Cricklewood garages. For a few years afterwards, efforts were made to concentrate Leyland engined vehicles at these and certain other garages such as Rye Lane, Peckham, Croydon, Holloway, Upton Park and Barking although few remained exclusively Leyland for very long and, conversely, garages which were predominantly AEC often received the odd Leyland or two.

A second Leyland engine contract covered the 175 vehicles numbered RM 1811–1985 delivered between January and July 1964. Completion of the contract marked the end of Leyland's connection with the Routemaster for no further orders were forthcoming and, in late 1965, it was officially announced that no more new vehicles would be fitted with Leyland engines. By that time, there was no point in buying from Leyland anyway. The whole reason for breaking with the cherished concept of total standardisation by splitting the engine order had been the avoidance of total commitment to one manufacturer; the shock announcement of August 1962 that the Leyland and Associated Commerical Vehicles groups were to 'merge' (in effect Leyland was to take over ACV) meant that, henceforth, both manufacturers were in the same group.

As with many other major derivations on

the basic Routemaster theme, the fitment of a Leyland engine was not distinguished by any variation in their type code. The Leyland RMs thus spanned four code variants: 2/5RM9 (RM 1923–1985), 2/5RM9/1 (RM 1811–1922), 7/5RM5/7 (RM 632, 1521–1719) and 8/5RM5/8 (RM 870, 1009, 1255–1452). However, the difference in engine was marked by a revised classification for the running units to which a prefix 2 was added, making them type 2R2RH. In performance terms, there was little to choose between an RM fitted with an 0.600 and one fitted with an AV590; some drivers preferred one and some the other but many remained unaware of the difference. Apart from an early problem of excessive oil leakage from the engine backplate joints which was cured at Leyland's expense in 1964, the 0.600 was no more and no less satisfactory than would have been expected. The fact that, in the 1980s these engines were phased out in preference to AECs was due more to a desire to reduce a proliferation of spares holdings in a reducing fleet than for any other reason.

As we shall see in later chapters, the fleet numbers of vehicles carrying Leyland engines became widely dispersed on overhaul and finally spanned a range between RM 9, which was the lowest numbered Leyland, to RM 2134 the highest, although one RML (initially numbered RML 2368 and subsequently RML 2397 and RML 2295) was also Leyland engined for many years. Generally, each body which had started life Leyland powered continued to be so even though the actual units to which it was attached may have been exchanged on overhaul, though in later years this rule was broken and instances occurred of Leyland engines being replaced directly by AECs.

A Leyland 0.600 as fitted into a Routemaster. Prominent in the foreground are the radiator header tank and lubricating oil filler cap. The air intake is visible at the rear; following London Transport practice this does not incorporate a filter but a breather connection from one of the rocker covers is fitted. Commercial Motor

CHAPTER TEN

RM 664 – THE SILVER LADY

With public transport of all types, except of course the booming aircraft industry, under severe economic pressure from the early nineteen fifties onwards through falling trade, the search for economies became ever more important. One cost saving idea, which was often promulgated though seldom implemented, was to leave rolling stock unpainted to reduce running costs through lighter weight and to save the fairly high expenditure necessary on repainting on overhaul or after accident repair. London Transport was at the forefront in 1952 when its first experimental unpainted Underground rolling stock was built. Its success ultimately led to the replacement of the entire Underground fleet with unpainted cars. Inevitably the extension of this principle to buses was also examined and judged to be potentially worthwhile, offering a saving in weight of possibly 3cwt per bus.

As it happened, the concept of unpainted buses was destined never to catch on in Great Britain. The main proponent of the unpainted bus was Liverpool Corporation but few other operators evinced much interest. London Transport's effort in this sphere never got beyond a single vehicle and its earlier intention of mounting a wide scale experiment never materialised.

Above and Left **With its panels shining in the summer sunshine, RM 664 speeds towards the West End en route for Streatham early in its career. The opportunity to study the rear of the vehicle in stationary mode whilst laying over at the Nags Head, Holloway, shows the many differences in coloration which were apparent even in its earliest days.**
Michael Dryhurst/
Ken Blacker

The vehicle selected for this experiment was RM 664, which was totally unpainted externally, except that the moulded plastic parts (bonnet top etc) were painted silver to match the natural colour of the aluminium cladding. When new, it looked quite shiny and smart but numerous prophets of doom predicted, with total accuracy, that it would quickly tarnish. Allocated initially to Highgate garage, RM 664 was scheduled to operate on route 276 from Mondays to Saturdays and route 127 on Sundays. Licensed for service from 13th July 1961, it seldom if ever strayed from its allocated routes in its first fifteen months or so although it was later to be found on route 17.

Much attention was focused on RM 664 both by the public and by London Transport's own staff. Opinion was divided but, in the main, the unpainted vehicle was much less popular than the red bus which many regarded as being a traditional feature of the London scene. Drivers tended to dislike it because the silver bonnet top reflected the sun's rays into the cab and also onto the nearside mirror, reducing its effectiveness. In rainy weather when general visibility was less than good, the silver Routemaster tended to merge into the greyness of its surroundings and was not as easily seen as a normal bus, whilst in a combination of tungsten lighting and fog it almost disappeared from sight altogether. It also looked more cold and uninviting than its red-painted counterparts especially in snowy or icy conditions. The vehicle attracted press comment because of its novelty and was even the subject of a letter to the *Times* asking why

THIS BUS is one of London Transport's latest Routemasters. Its aluminium body has been left unpainted so that it can be compared, in terms of wear and maintenance, with those painted in the standard red livery.

Londoners and visitors are invited to write to the Public Relations Officer, 55 Broadway, S.W.I, saying what they think of it.

Poster inside unpainted RM 664 inviting comments from passengers. Capital Transport

anyone should want to change the colour of London's buses and citing the red London bus as an institution like the policeman's blue uniform. Inevitably, perhaps, the nickname 'Silver Lady' soon came into vogue for RM 664 although it was also referred to, probably just as frequently, as the 'White Lady', reflecting the colour which it often appeared to be, especially in dull light and more particularly after its initial sheen had worn off.

Views of RM 664 at two of its varied locations show it at Shepherds Bush as a Hanwell vehicle on the 207A, and at Kingston when Fulwell-based for route 285. Whilst at Fulwell, after this photograph was taken, the disused offside route number glass was removed, presumably as the result of an accident.
LT Museum/Alan B. Cross

After almost eighteen months at Highgate, RM 664 set out on a round of reallocations for evaluation purposes, the intention being to test public and staff reaction in a variety of operating environments. Ten garages were visited in just over two years:—

1st December 1962	Poplar	23
28th January 1963	Rye Lane	36B
6th September 1963	Mortlake	73
1st December 1963	Stonebridge	18
24th January 1964	Finchley	260
9th March 1964	Cricklewood	16
6th May 1964	Hanwell	207A*
13th July 1964	Fulwell	285
19th October 1964	Shepherds Bush	220
1st February 1965	Walthamstow	123
		*207 Sundays

By the time RM 664 reached Walthamstow in the early months of 1965, its novelty value had greatly diminished. Furthermore, it was looking decidedly dowdy, the uneven wearing of the panels and the necessity to replace certain of them after accident damage having combined to produce a patchwork effect which was most unappealing. The experiment was deemed to have been unsuccessful and steps were taken to bring it to a close. On 18th July 1965, RM 664 ran for the last time in unpainted condition; next day it was de-licensed and transferred to Dorking garage whose staff had agreed to etch and prime it ready for conventional coats of paint to be applied. The completion work was carried out at Hounslow garage from 26th July onwards

and, on 4th August, RM 664 appeared in service at New Cross looking no different from any other member of the Routemaster fleet. Though unpainted aluminium surfaces had proved acceptable for Underground rolling stock, they were clearly not suited to the very different constructional methods and operating environments of the urban bus, and have not been tried again. In view of the mindless but prolific graffiti daubings of a later age, this is probably just as well.

By the time of its final stint in unpainted form, at Walthamstow, RM 664 was looking very grubby, especially around the mouldings where accumulation of dirt was apparent around screw and rivet heads. The Daily Express posters, which it had carried from the start, were now reduced to the side panels only, in-house material having replaced them at front and rear. Alan B. Cross

After being painted red, RM 664 arrived at New Cross where it ran for seventeen months up to the time of its first overhaul, indistinguishable now from any other member of the fleet. Alan B. Cross

CHAPTER ELEVEN

THE TROLLEYBUS CONVERSION YEARS

Although RM 8 had been given its public preview at Earls Court in September 1958, time ticked by and 1959 arrived with no immediate sign of any further Routemasters being completed, still less of any entering public service. London Transport was anxious to get on with the task of ridding itself of most of its huge trolleybus fleet (all of it, in fact, except the south-western network based at Fulwell and Isleworth depots) and had long since decided that the first stage of the programme, under which the Bexleyheath and Carshalton trolleybus services would be eliminated, must take place in March 1959 using RTs. It had, later, reluctantly concluded that, in view of the huge surplus of RT-family vehicles following the post-1958 strike service reductions, these would also be used for stage 2 (Clapton and Lea Bridge depots) in April 1959. As late as September 1958, the newest version of the 'firm' Routemaster delivery programme had promised that sufficient would be

available for stage 2 but continued slippage in the production programme made it obvious by December that this was not to be the case. Sights were then set on introducing Routemasters for stage 3 (Bow and Ilford) scheduled for August and, even as late as March 1959, there was every intention of doing so but, yet again, this proved impossible to achieve and it was not until stage 4, on 11th November 1959, that the RM finally came into its own.

Meanwhile, Routemasters had, at last, started to arrive from the production lines, the slow trickle of May and June 1959 turning, in due course, into the fully blown output destined to last right through to February 1968. The Executive's engineers were anxious to get some trial running completed as quickly as possible to identify any problems in operating the new vehicles in advance of their first large scale introduction, and it was decided that fifteen of them would be put into service alongside RTs on a number of central London bus

routes. Additionally, a further twelve were to be commissioned for the training of trolleybus drivers at Poplar and West Ham depots in preparation for stage 4. Earlier, before the progressive slippages in the manufacturing programme had become evident, the engineers had proposed much larger scale running, preferably by the advance conversion of a selected trolleybus service, for which several alternatives including routes 611, 654 and 698 were proposed, but each of these presented snags to make them unsuitable and, in any case, the ensuing delivery delays left no scope for any such scheme to be implemented.

Above A scene which was to be repeated many times over during the course of the trolleybus abandonment programme was the accumulation of Routemasters in readiness for the appointed day. Many are to be seen in this view inside Poplar depot along with some time-expired trolleybuses, on the right, and still active members of the fleet on the left. LT Museum

The first licensing of new RMs took place in June 1959. Several garages had been nominated as recipients of the new vehicles with a view to operating them on a variety of routes and fate decreed that Willesden was to have the honour of being the first garage to put production Routemasters into revenue earning service. RMs 7 and 24 were licensed on 4th June and RM 5 on the 5th; all three entered service on route 8 on 6th June. Next into service was RM 14 at Riverside which was licensed for route 11 on 5th June and commenced operation on the 12th. Also licensed in June were RM 19 at Cricklewood for route 2 and RM 18 at Battersea for route 22, but the latter may not have operated and it was transferred later in the same month to Hackney (the first standard RM to be involved in an inter-garage transfer) when Battersea was found unsuitable to house RMs at that time and route 22's other garage was substituted.

In addition to Routemasters for public service, the first of the training buses were also brought into use during June; in fact, RMs 6, 9 and 11 which were licensed on the first of the month were the very first standard Routemasters to take to the road, being a few days ahead of Willesden's initial trio. Over the next ten days, they were joined by RMs 12, 13, 15, 16 and 17, all being allocated to Clay Hall garage which was chosen because it happened to be the garage nearest to Poplar trolleybus depot at which housing and maintenance facilities were available for this influx of new buses. This new contingent, although intended only

for training duties, marked the swansong for Clay Hall garage which, though fairly modern and well equipped, was scheduled to close with the implementation of stage 4 of the trolleybus conversion programme in order to make more effective use of the large amount of spare space in the former trolleybus depot at Bow. The training of Poplar trolleybus staff commenced on 17th June, the vehicles having been employed prior to this on miscellaneous

instruction work at other locations. This was a few weeks ahead of the training for West Ham drivers required for stage 4 who were fewer in number and were catered for by RMs 20, 23, 26 and 27 licensed at Upton Park from 1st July. Eleven of the proposed twelve trainers were now in use; the twelfth was RM 46 which was commissioned at Clay Hall in September whilst a thirteenth, RM 58, was based at Hackney from 1st October.

With stage 4 of the trolleybus abandonment programme now imminent, RM 92 bounces across the cobble streets on delivery to Poplar depot under trade plates. This was one of the previously unused vehicles which comprised part of Poplar's first allocation, supplemented by some formerly used as trainers. Fred Ivey

Returning to the vehicles in passenger service, every month which passed saw further Routemasters being licensed, the final one being on 1st November, only ten days prior to the date earmarked for conversion stage 4, when the class would finally come into its own in replacing trolleybuses. As early as the third week in July, the original intention of placing fifteen buses in trial service was exceeded and, by the time that RM 111 was licensed at Turnham Green on 1st November, the number which were, or had been, operational exceeded the originally intended figure three-fold. In addition to the original trial routes (2, 8, 11 and 22), Turnham Green's route 91 (27 on Sundays) was added in August and Tottenham's route 76 (with its subsidiary peak-hour route 34B) in September. The full list of vehicles licensed month by month from July onwards was as follows:–

July
Willesden – RM 22, 25, 28
Cricklewood – RM 30, 31, 35, 39, 42
Riverside – RM 29, 32, 33, 34, 37

August
Cricklewood – RM 10, 41
Hackney – RM 43
Turnham Green RM 36

September
Cricklewood – RM 38
(later transferred to Hackney)
Hackney – RM 40, 47, 54, 55
Riverside – RM 52
Turnham Green RM 57, 75
Tottenham – RM 44, 45, 48, 49, 51, 56

October
Willesden – RM 86
Hackney – RM 99
Turnham Green RM 89, 94, 95, 96, 101

November – Turnham Green RM 111

Turnham Green's RM 75 was the first with air suspension to enter service, being licensed on 16th September, but problems occurred and it was withdrawn on 14th October. Troubles were also experienced with RM 18 (at Hackney), RM 25 (Willesden) and RM 34 (Riverside) which were all delicensed on 1st October. It is worth pointing out that the utilisation of early production Routemasters was very intensive and, of those numbered between RM 5 and RM 58 excluding the still undelivered RM 8, the only ones not used either for service or training purposes prior to the stage 4 trolleybus programme implementation were RMs 21, 50 and 53.

On 5th November 1959, six days prior to the 'big day', Turnham Green's RM 94 was transferred across to Poplar for reasons now unknown, this being the first Routemaster to be licensed to any trolleybus depot. On the night of 10th/11th November, four more of Turnham Green's RMs moved eastwards for trolleybus replacement: RM 57 to West Ham and RMs 95, 101 and 111 to Poplar. Of the remaining 36 RMs still in service up to that date, nine were transferred to training duties and the remaining 27 were withdrawn into store. Conversely, most of the existing trainers, ten out of the thirteen, were put into passenger service for the first time: RMs 6, 9, 11, 12, 13, 15, 20, 23 and 27 at West Ham, and RM 26 at Poplar.

Commercial Road, the busy artery leading eastwards from Aldgate towards London's dockland, was the first setting in which the Routemaster was to come into its own. On 11th November 1959, stage 4 embraced the elimination of all trolleybuses along its length, these being the 567, 569 and 665 which, between them, served the main central core of the route with various offshoots at each end. Poplar depot's entire trolleybus fleet was swept aside in one fell swoop with a minor

Routemaster allocation also based at West Ham, a large depot which was to require two more conversions to eliminate all of its trolleybuses. Poplar required an allocation of 59 RMs (including two spares which was all that was thought necessary at that time) whilst West Ham received 15 including one spare. These totals, by and large, permitted Routemasters to replace trolleybuses on a one-for-one basis, the lower seating capacity of the new vehicles not being regarded as critical in view of the continuing fall in passenger demand. Poplar's RMs were scheduled to work on new bus routes 5, 5A, 48 and 238 plus night service 284, with West Ham helping out on routes 5 and 238. In addition, Poplar operated RMs alongside Barking based RTs on old-established bus route 23 which was augmented as part of the overall conversion scheme, and they also appeared on routes 9 and 56 on Sundays.

In the days leading up to the conversion, much activity occurred, particularly at Poplar, in assembling the new fleet of Routemasters, a picture that was to be repeated time and time again across the trolleybus network as the conversion programme rolled on. With the exception of the four vehicles from Turnham Green and one former trainer, Poplar's initial Routemaster fleet consisted of brand new and virtually unused vehicles. West Ham, on the other hand, received a motley collection of former training buses with only four of its buses being new. Unfortunately, the opportunity of placing pristine buses into service was lost because the policy was to post all vehicles fully with advertisements prior to sending them to their garages and, throughout the whole of the time that Routemasters were being built, it was very rare indeed to see a new one in service without advertisements except, of course, for the Green Line coaches. Shortly before midnight on the evening on

The honour of being the first Routemaster to operate a trolleybus replacement journey fell to Poplar's RM 82, seen in the Commercial Road at about midnight on 10th/11th November 1959 passing L3 class trolleybus 1495 just completing its last inward run.
M. Dryhurst

10th November 1959, RM 82 left Poplar garage for its first service run on night route 284; a new era had begun.

As was, perhaps, only to be expected, this first large scale and intensive period of Routemaster operation produced its full share of problems. Engineers at the two garages concerned, accustomed to the comparatively trouble-free operation of trolleybuses, quickly became exasperated by a whole host of problems which came to light and, inevitably, service reliability suffered. Drastic measures were called for and, in December and January, many buses were temporarily withdrawn and replaced by others, and the stock of spare buses held for maintenance purposes was also increased.

The first trolleybus conversion of the nineteen-sixties was stage 5, under which routes 557, 669, 685, 689 and 690 were due for Routemaster replacement on 3rd February 1960. Most of the ground to be covered lay in the eastern suburbs, although the 557 penetrated into the City of London at Liverpool Street. A second and much larger RM contingent went into West Ham on this occasion, to which was added Walthamstow's first allocation in a two-fold conversion programme, the second stage of which was due to be completed along with West Ham at stage 6. New routes for RM operation were 58, 69, 162 and 272 at West Ham, the 58 being shared with Walthamstow who also operated new routes 256 and 257. The 256 was of interest in breaking completely new ground through Chatsworth and Powerscroft Roads in Lower Clapton, and the 162 was interesting in another way through being the first mainly RM route to have a minority RT allocation in the form of a four-bus contingent provided by Barking garage. With one exception, all of Walthamstow's RMs were completely new vehicles. However, a different situation prevailed at West Ham where

One of the first cases of weekend RMs being used on routes worked by RT types during the week was the 56. Poplar's RM 22 is seen at Millwall.
Gerald Mead

West Ham remained predominantly a trolleybus depot after stage 4, albeit not for very much longer. One of its small initial allocation of motor buses was RM 70, seen by the unusual wooden shelter at Fair Cross.
Lens of Sutton

22 of the RMs temporarily withdrawn at Poplar were reinstated to join eight which had been delicensed since the end of the pre-trolleybus conversion trials (mostly ex Willesden and Riverside buses) plus 24 brand new ones.

West Ham was more fortunate at stage 6 on 27th April 1960 when the great majority of the 61 RMs it received were brand new, most being of the revised design with opening front windows which made their public debut at this conversion. Walthamstow's 44 buses included only four of this new type and they also included the final five buses from the preconversion trials of the previous year but these stayed only a week before being transferred to training duties with further new buses arriving as replacements. This conversion witnessed the end of electric traction in the eastern suburbs with the passing of trolleybus routes 623, 625, 687, 697 and 699. The replacement programme was particularly complex, none of the routes being replaced exactly as they had been in trolleybus days. Walthamstow and West Ham both found themselves running RMs alongside Tottenham-based RTWs; for Walthamstow this was on new route 123 which covered a long section of bus route 41 between Walthamstow and Ilford, the 41 being diverted via former trolleybus territory to Stratford, becoming the route which West Ham shared henceforth with Tottenham. Walthamstow also found itself on new route 275, which was particularly noteworthy in opening up new bus territory between the old Woodford trolleybus terminus and Woodford Bridge, and on route 249 which was shared with West Ham. West Ham also had new routes 249A and 278 as well as night service 299 replacing the former

One of the routes introduced with West Ham's second intake of diesel buses in February 1960 was the 58. RM 18 was amongst many of the class revived at this conversion after having been stored since the end of the previous year's trial running on central bus routes. It was one of the small batch of 20 production RMs fitted with traditional DC generating equipment instead of the technologically advanced AC system employing alternators which was adopted as standard.

Walthamstow's trolleybus fleet was disposed of in two batches, with RM 168 and route 257 having been introduced at the first conversion in February 1960. The 257 was one of several major projections beyond the traditional trolleybus termini; in this case London Bridge marks an extension right across the City to link up with former tram operating territory south of the river. *Lens of Sutton*

staff journeys on route 699 which, in normal trolleybus fashion, had been available for use. On the day of conversion, the bus garage at Forest Gate was closed and its fleet of RTs transferred into West Ham. To achieve the most economical use of resources, a number of RT workings were scheduled on route 69 (which had commenced at stage 5 and was now extended from Stratford to Chingford Mount) and also on route 249A. RMs were no longer looking strange on RT routes or vice versa and, later on as other garages joined West Ham in having allocations of both types, such workings became even more common, either through official scheduling (the most frequent examples being of RMs allocated to RT routes on Sundays) or on an adhoc basis.

Stage 7, which took effect on 20th July 1960, saw an abrupt expansion of Routemaster territory. Instead of the trolleybus abandonment continuing in a progressively westerly sweep as might logically have been expected, Hammersmith depot (working routes 626, 628 and 630) was selected as the next for conversion along with a solitary route from Highgate. This was the Highgate Hill route 611 whose abandonment eliminated the need for trolleybuses with special coasting and runback brakes, no such niceties being stipulated for the RMs on replacement route 271. Concurrently with the conversion, Hammersmith depot closed to normal service operation, being required instead as a new base for the airport coaches operated by London Transport on behalf of British European Airways which, though not suspected at the time, were to be replaced by a fleet of special Routemasters a few years later. The existing bus garage at Shepherds Bush was the base for most of the replacement RMs on new routes 220 and 268, the former taking Routemasters as deep into

Top **Walthamstow's second and final phase of conversion at stage 6 saw the first entry into service of RMs with opening front windows. Outside the old ivy-clad tramway offices at Manor House, now the local bus operating headquarters, RMs 232 and 335 terminate on new bus route 123. The whole of the overhead wiring remains intact at this juncture as all other trolleybus routes past this major point still operate as witnessed by K1-type Leyland 1150 on route 679. In 1960 the general use of aluminium garage plates finished and these vehicles have the code newly stencilled on the body side in white paint.** Ken Blacker

Centre **The arrival of RMs shattered for ever the quiet, clean atmosphere of former trolleybus depots and at several of them engineers faced the task of maintaining both modes of transport during the changeover period. Here RM 440 is still in a minority against Highgate's large and mixed trolleybus allocation, but not for much longer.** Fred Ivey

Left **Shepherds Bush was the first traditional bus garage to receive a large RM allocation, which it did upon closure of Hammersmith depot. Almost opposite the old depot, RM 369 heads towards Harlesden beneath the embryo of the new Hammersmith flyover.** Tony Belton

A surprising Routemaster outpost created in south London in July 1960 was Elmers End's seven bus fleet for route 64. All were received secondhand from West Ham where RM 283 had entered service as a new vehicle only three months beforehand.
Pamlin Prints

Above Left **Calamity strikes!** Shepherds Bush's RM 380 suffers a front end collision on route 220 whilst still only two months old, and is hooked onto a venerable AEC towing lorry, itself a former bus, for an ignominious return to garage. Repair work took four months to complete. Alan B. Cross

Above **When RM 422 appeared at Earl's Court in 1960 it was noteworthy in being the only double decker in the Show to carry an open rear platform. Kitted out for route 271, it finally entered service at Highgate in February 1961.** Bus & Coach

Left **The task of training trolleybus drivers to handle Routemasters was a massive one and 'learner' vehicles such as RM 48, seen standing alongside chassisless trolleybus 1441 at Stamford Hill traffic lights, were a common sight. After running at Tottenham for two months in the 1959 trials, RM 48 saw only three weeks passenger service between November 1959 and October 1962, being virtually a full time trainer for this period.** Tony Belton

The first RT route to be taken over in its entirety by Routemasters was the 143 at stage 9 on 1st February 1961, which was much extended at the same time from its formerly purely suburban role. Highgate's RM 597 is seen at Farringdon Street.
P.J. Relf

south London as West Croydon. Part of the service on the lower end of the former 630 was covered by an extension from West Croydon to Wimbledon Stadium of bus route 64 whose Croydon RT allocation was augmented by a contingent from Elmers End which, rather surprisingly, comprised RMs, the first to be allocated to a Central Bus garage in south London. Elmers End's fleet of RMs amounted to a mere seven vehicles, all of which had formerly been used at West Ham on stage 6 and had been delicensed afterwards for various reasons.

The biennial Commercial Motor Exhibition opened on 23rd September 1960 and, as ever drew hosts of bus industry personnel and bus industry watchers to Earl's Court. Featured as one of the exhibits was RM 422 displaying blinds for route 271 but it attracted little critical attention. The Routemaster was no longer a novelty, eyes being focused instead on the revolutionary Guy Wulfrunian, of which no fewer than three were on view, and the prototype Daimler Fleetline. Outside, in the heart of west London, preparations were well advanced for the conversion of Hanwell depot to motor buses at stage 8 of the trolley-bus conversion programme, scheduled for 9th November. Uxbridge Road trunk route 607 and the meandering 655 were replaced by RMs as the 207 and 255, with an eastward projection numbered 207A taking the Route-master inwards towards town via bus route 49 to terminate at Chelsea. This conversion took RM fleet numbers above the 500 mark but, for many of these buses, their stay at Hanwell was destined to be very short. From 21st November, they began to be withdrawn from service and, in most cases, delicensed, with a particularly large withdrawal on 1st

December. By the end of the year, just over half of the original allocation had been replaced by further new vehicles, the majority languishing temporarily in spare corners at Stonebridge, Cricklewood and Holloway garages awaiting a further call to service. The reason for this changeover was that Hanwell's fleet had been selected for an experiment whereby the Routemaster's standard fully automatic transmission and the associated kickdown facility were disconnected, leaving drivers to change gears manually, the aim being to test unit life and fuel consumption under these circumstances.

As with stage 8, the ninth conversion on 1st February 1961 involved only one depot and these were the only two conversions to do so, all the remainder witnessed a wider spread of the Routemaster's net. This time, it was the turn of Highgate which already ran a few RMs

on route 271 and, even after a massive influx of 117 more, would still be left with a few trolleybuses on route 627 (plus 609 on Sundays). The routes which disappeared were 513/613, 517/617, 615, 639 and 653, the replacements being new routes 17, 214, 239, 253 and N93 plus lengthy extensions of existing bus routes including two which gained an RM allocation. The 143 was taken over in its entirety by Highgate and was the first RT route to go over completely to RMs; on the 63, a few RMs shared the road with Peckham's much larger contingent of RTs. One of the incoming vehicles was the Earl's Court show bus RM 422; many others were former Hanwell buses relicensed. Shortly afterwards, on 7th March, RM 8 was at last taken into stock but it remained in experimental use and a further 17 years were to elapse before its eventual entry into service.

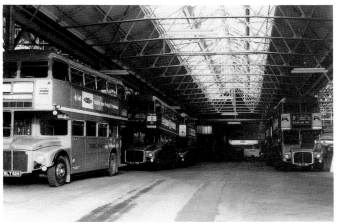

With large numbers of new vehicles to be introduced overnight at each stage of the conversion programme, storage beforehand was often a problem, especially where the depot concerned was unable for capacity reasons to hold many of the new buses itself. Brand new RM 626 was one of many RMs destined for Highgate at stage 9 which were stored principally at Poplar, where some of this garage's own complement of vehicles, including RMs 108 and 39, can be seen.
Fred Ivey

Four locations received RMs for the implementation of stage ten on 26th April 1961 and three depots (Edmonton, Highgate and Wood Green) lost trolleybuses although only at Highgate did this mark their final abandonment. Trolleybus route 627 (worked jointly by Edmonton and Highgate with peak hour workings from Wood Green) was discontinued along with routes 629 (worked by Wood Green) and Edmonton based routes 659 and 679. Motor bus routes 127, 259, 269 and 279 were direct replacements, although the 127 was projected into the heart of London at Victoria, and a new route 279A augmented much of the northern end of the old 679 but was extended beyond the traditional trolleybus terminus at Waltham Cross to take RMs to their most northerly point yet at Flamstead

End. In addition to all this, Highgate gained a completely new route 276 which was totally unrelated to trolleybus routes and provided new links over a complex routeing between Tottenham and Brixton garages. There were two particularly interesting aspects to this conversion. One was the surprise inclusion of West Green garage, whose closure was well known to be imminent but which nevertheless received a handful of RMs for a minority allocation alongside Wood Green on route 269. The five buses concerned (RM 753–757) thereby gained the doubtful honour of forming the shortest lived Routemaster allocation to any garage. West Green was due to close just over six months later but its RM allocation did not even last that long and was lost at stage 12 on 8th November. The second item of interest

West Green's small allocation was the shortest lived of all, and although the garage lives on largely unaltered to this day, its use by London Transport was rapidly drawing to a close when RM 756 was received in April 1961. Although they also carried blind displays for route 144, West Green's RMs were never known to operate on any route but the 269.
Tony Belton

A rare photograph of Edmonton's RM 724 operating southbound in Tottenham Court Road on route 127. Abandonment of trolleybuses at this terminus was hastened to permit introduction of the one-way traffic scheme which still exists, diverting the southbound traffic flow via Gower Street. RMs followed the old routeing for only four days from their first Wednesday of operation, 26th April 1961, up to the introduction of the traffic management scheme on the next Sunday. J.C. Gillham

Much photographed during its 6½ months of existence was the joint RM/trolleybus Sunday working on route 609. At the Moorgate terminus, Highgate's RM 580 passes Finchley's 1472, one of the few trolleybuses in the fleet with sliding rather than half drop side windows.
Alan Nightingale

was the manner in which Highgate's Sunday only allocation on route 609 was tackled. This route, which was primarily a Finchley depot responsibility, was not yet due for conversion but it was necessary to retain a Highgate allocation to achieve a satisfactory balance of Sunday work. The solution chosen was to substitute Routemasters for trolleybuses on the existing schedule, producing the only instance of both types of vehicle running together under a common route number and the only example of Routemasters working on a route numbered in the trolleybus six-hundred series. Some curious allocations, brought about by the need to balance work levels between garages, resulted in route 259 being shared between Highgate and Wood Green whereas, in trolleybus days, the 659 had always been worked by Edmonton, whilst part of route 253 was reallocated from Highgate to Edmonton involving a long dead run to pick up the line of route at Stamford Hill. Stage 10 was by far the most ambitious conversion to date with no fewer than 148 new buses being licensed at Edmonton (74), Wood Green (46), Highgate (23) and West Green (5) and spanning a range of fleet numbers between RM 518 and RM 775.

The impetus of the trolleybus scrapping programme continued unfalteringly and reached the eleventh stage when routes 543/643, 647 and 649/A (all worked by Stamford Hill augmented by an Edmonton allocation on route 649) were replaced by RMs on 19th July 1961, eliminating electric traction from two more depots and from any points east of the almost straight line of route 641 (Winchmore Hill to Moorgate) which was itself due for conversion next time round. With the new Routemasters now reaching into the upper eight hundreds, the class had ceased to hold any novelty value and was now very much an everyday part of the London bus scene and inroads made into the ranks of the trolleybus fleet were such that all the older and less structurally sound vehicles had been disposed of and vehicles in good condition were now going for scrap. New routes on the bus scene were 67, 149 and 243, a concurrent event being the extension of old established bus route 47 northwards from Liverpool Street to Stoke Newington but without any Routemaster involvement. At the northern end of route 67, Routemasters opened up new bus territory between Tottenham and Northumberland Park whilst the southern end of route 149 saw a lengthy and circuitous extension beyond the old Liverpool Street terminus to Victoria, crossing the River Thames twice en route. Sundays only route 243A replaced the only trolleybus route to carry a suffix letter, the 649A, and a new night route N83 covered the former 543/643 night journeys with an extension to Charing Cross. At the time of conversion, Stamford Hill was not ready to receive its full complement of motor buses, the intention being that it should accommodate the uneconomic Edmonton allocation on route 253 which had only been started as a temporary expedient. This arrangement ceased on 11th October when rebuilding work at Stamford Hill was sufficiently advanced to accept the 253, and 34 RMs moved in from Edmonton. It is interesting to record that, almost alone amongst ex-trolleybus garages, neither Edmonton nor Stamford Hill subsequently acquired an allocation of the ubiquitous RT family.

The north London conversions resulted in a few unusual allocations of garages to routes which were soon modified. One such was Wood Green's short spell on route 259 with which it had never been associated in trolleybus days when it was the 659. Malcolm E. Papes

Three types of road transport are evoked in this Lower Edmonton scene where RM 719 and K3-type trolleybus 1682, both Edmonton vehicles, meet outside the Trolleybus cafe at the end of Tramway Avenue. The building on the corner is now a thing of the past as, indeed, is the depot at the end of the avenue.
Tony Belton

Trolleybuses were very thin on the ground after stage 12 was implemented on 8th November 1961. The withdrawal of Finchley's routes 521/621 and 609, and Wood Green's route 641, all lengthy routes whose companion trolleybus services had already given way to Routemasters in most cases, saw the end of electric traction in many areas, including central London where the Moorgate and Holborn termini had been the last to survive. Wood Green's final trolleybuses were replaced by RMs and a very long southwards extension of route 141 to Grove Park in place of the 179 needed an RM allocation at New Cross.

Highgate's famous Sunday RM share of route 609 remained under the 104 number but the joint trolleybus/motorbus operation was, of course, at an end. A feature inaugurated at this conversion was the use of lower-case lettering for intermediate route displays on bus blinds. Though not introduced for legibility reasons as was later popularly supposed but on aesthetic grounds, the new style of lettering seemed very strange at first but soon gained acceptance.

1962 was only a few days old when, on 3rd January in almost arctic weather conditions, Finchley's remaining trolleybuses were withdrawn along with the entire fleets at Stonebridge and Colindale. The latter depot closed for business on the same day. Under the original scheme of things, this was to have been the final conversion with the remaining trolleybus network based at Fulwell and Isleworth remaining a few years longer until the post-war rolling stock based at these depots was worn out. However, a market had been found amongst various operators in Spain for the fine Q1-type post war trolleybuses which had now been replaced in London service by older vehicles, the result being that stage 13 had now become the penultimate in the withdrawal programme, with the final abandonment scheduled to take place four months later. This conversion saw RMs with fleet numbers above the one thousand mark entering service for the first time, a remarkable achievement in less than three years of manufacture. RM 1000 itself was completed at Park Royal on 16th October 1961 and was the subject of a small ceremony to mark the milestone in Routemaster achievement. It introduced reversed registration numbers to the RM fleet for the first time and its one-off registration number of 100BXL was also the first on a Routemaster which did not incorporate the letters LT; they were, however, re-established with RM 1001 (1CLT) onwards.

Insufficient new RMs were available to meet the whole requirement for stage 13 and it was necessary to use eighteen older vehicles, largely in the one and two hundreds and mostly ex-trainers, to make up Stonebridge's requirement. Other garages to receive RMs at the same time were Cricklewood (the original home of RM 1 and also a participant in the 1959 trials, which now resumed RM operation after a lapse of more than two years), Middle Row (which had never previously run RMs)

and, of course, Finchley. Completely new RM worked services were 245 (allocated to Cricklewood), 260 (Finchley and Stonebridge), 266 (Cricklewood and Stonebridge) and peak hour 293 (Middle Row). RMs also enjoyed a major presence on existing bus route 18 which gained a lengthy extension to London Bridge via the now-withdrawn 18B, the three garage allocation comprising RMs from Stonebridge and Middle Row and RTs from Alperton. Trolleybus services that ran for the last time were 645, 660, 662 and 666. Quite unconnected with all this was the reallocation from Wood Green to Tottenham of its share of route 259, giving Tottenham its first permanent RM allocation although, like Cricklewood, it had participated in the 1959 trials.

On 1st April, New Cross received a small additional quota of RMs to enable the Round London Sightseeing Tour to operate with the latest vehicles. Soon afterwards, on 9th May, Elmers End lost its few RMs to Thornton Heath through a reallocation of route 64 and would not receive any more for another eleven years. For a far more significant reason, this was a historic day in London's transport history, marking the last occasion on which trolleybuses were to operate on the streets of the capital (or, to be more precise, the streets of suburban south west London). The last full day of trolleybus operation was Tuesday 8th May, and when trolleybus 1521 made its historic last run into Fulwell depot amongst a large crowd of well wishers in the early hours of 9th, the event marked not only the end of an era for electric street traction but also the completion of the Routemaster's first major task. Next on the agenda lay the even more daunting prospect of replacing the RTs, RTLs and RTWs which were everywhere to be seen and represented London's transport system at its best and most efficient. The commencement of this task lay several months ahead with a spate of acrimonious debate between management and unions intervening, and meanwhile the immediate task was to inaugurate the final round of new and revised routes brought about by the scrapping of trolleybuses.

The time-expired and the still-unused meet in Fulwell depot yard on 29th April 1962. Preserved 'Diddler' trolleybus No.1, still in the same condition in which it was withdrawn from service more than a decade earlier and now being prepared for the final trolleybus ceremony, makes an interesting comparison with RM 1078. A.J. Wild

The final trolleybus services had been the 601 to 605 and 667 operated by Fulwell plus the 657 from the Isleworth depot which closed when its last trolleybus ran in. There was ample spare space in nearby Hounslow bus garage to accommodate all the former Isleworth work, the 657 being covered by an extension of existing bus route 117 which was converted from RT to RM at the same time, resulting in RMs appearing as far west as Staines and Egham. In converting Fulwell, the existing local bus garages at Norbiton and Kingston also became involved with a complicated set of route reallocations, included

amongst which were the provision of RMs at Norbiton for an extended route 131 plus new routes 282 and 283 whilst Fulwell itself received RMs for ex-trolleybus routes 267, 281 and 285. Fulwell found itself running RFs as well as its new Routemasters, having received route 206 as part of the wide-ranging reallocations which were also of interest in that they resulted in the Kingston fleet becoming entirely single deck. This last conversion of all took Routemaster fleet numbers over the twelve hundred mark with Hounslow's RM 1212 being the highest numbered member of its class used for trolleybus conversion.

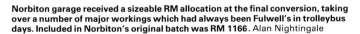

History is made in the early hours of 9th May 1962 as London's last trolleybus, No.1521, creeps into Fulwell depot and the door is half closed behind it. Ready for the first RM departure is RM 1058 on a staff bus duty. Alan Nightingale

Norbiton garage received a sizeable RM allocation at the final conversion, taking over a number of major workings which had always been Fulwell's in trolleybus days. Included in Norbiton's original batch was RM 1166. Alan Nightingale

CHAPTER TWELVE

THE FIRST THIRTY-FOOTERS

By the end of the nineteen-fifties, when the Routemaster finally went into full production, London Transport had already passed its zenith and was heading gently towards decline. In times past, it had generally been accepted that where London Transport led others followed, but this was now rarely the case. Once hailed the most gifted and far-sighted authority in urban transport, not only in the United Kingdom but arguably through the western world, it was now widely perceived to be trailing in a number of ways. The advanced design of the Routemaster certainly enabled London Transport to claim continued pre-eminence in this particular sphere but, at the same time, it dealt a self-inflicted blow to its own credibility with its insistence that the most effective vehicle for intensive urban operation was the relatively low capacity 64-seater double decker. Even within Britain, where operators were still largely committed to the double decker, few believed this decision to be correct. The worsening economics of bus operation dictated that larger vehicles should become the norm wherever possible and it had been largely as a result of strong representations from within the bus industry to prove this very point that the Construction and Use Regulations had been amended to permit 30ft long double deckers to operate on two axles instead of the three previously required. The London Transport argument in favour of low

capacity vehicles was not even consistent with its own experience of running a large fleet of 70 seat trolleybuses in a highly successful manner. By the time that RM 422 appeared at the 1960 Earl's Court Exhibition a good deal of criticism, and sadness too, was being expressed that the Routemaster had not been produced in a longer, more updated format.

Even within London Transport itself, and especially at the lower echelons, the inconsistency of its position was clear, and it was certain to be merely a matter of time before the decision makers bowed to the inevitable. The announcement duly came that a small number of 30ft long Routemasters with 72 seats was to be tried out to assess the feasibility of operating vehicles of this size. The 24 vehicles ordered under this face-saving exercise marked a tentative start to the RML class which was to prove undoubtedly the most successful Routemaster variant ever devised.

Although integral construction was criticised as being vulnerable to damage in the event of heavy front or rear end collision, a criticism which the excellent Routemaster design largely overcame anyway, its great advantage was that it lent itself to variations and particularly length extensions with a minimum of modification and tooling much more readily than a bus of conventional design. Thus it was a comparatively simple matter to convert the Routemaster into a 30ft,

72-seater merely by inserting an additional central bay of 2ft 4ins and extending the wheelbase from 16ft 10ins to 19ft 2ins (rather longer than normally favoured on front engined vehicles of this length), thereby permitting an additional row of seats on each deck to increase the capacity by eight. Whilst quoted for brevity as being 30ft in length, the RML was actually 29ft 10 9/16ins. A very high standard of interchangeability was achieved with the RM, even to the extent that the same AV590 engine was employed despite the heavier work load which would be imposed upon it. The vehicles received the classification 7RM7 and were basically a lengthened version of the 8/5RM5/8 with CAV electrical equipment, SCG transmission and Lockheed brakes. They were given unit numbers R2RH876–899 within the current RM sequence with nothing to denote the major difference in length.

Above **The ER classification was not carried in service, but fortunately it was recorded on film by AEC's official photographer. The insertion of a small, non-standard sized bay to achieve the desired 30ft length had not been a device employed in other designs up to that time and there was no mistaking that it was an afterthought superimposed upon the original design. AEC.**

The RMLs were the first 30ft long double-deck motor buses ever to run regularly in London, although the trolleybus fleet had long been standardised on vehicles of this length. RML 884 stands at Finsbury Square at the start of its career. P.J. Relf

The main distinguishing feature between the standard Routemaster and the stretched version was obviously the additional bay which looked very much the afterthought it was, but this did allow the maximum use of standard RM body parts. The commonly aired view at the time was that, being much shorter than the surrounding windows, this marred the otherwise well balanced appearance of the Routemaster but, as always happens with the passage of time, it eventually gained acceptance to pass almost unnoticed. Also new was the provision of a quick release emergency window in the second offside bay of the lower saloon to provide the secondary means of escape required by law for vehicles of this length. Otherwise, there were no special features, inside or outside, to distinguish it from the current RM apart from a cautionary notice in the driver's cab.

The new model was originally classified as ER (for Extended Routemaster) and the first four were actually delivered as ER 880–883. However, the same change of policy which saw the renumbering of RML 3 and CRL 4 to RM 3 and RMC 4 respectively, also saw the adoption of the now familiar RML designation (RM Lengthened) for the batch. RML 884–903 were delivered as such, the original four being officially rechristened as RMLs on 30th August 1961, well before their entry into passenger service. ER 883 was renumbered on the same

A posed view shows the offside and rear end of the last of the initial batch of 24 RMLs, RML 903. This vehicle was one of several in the batch employed on overseas tours in their early days although, unlike some of the others, it had actually seen a short spell of service before being despatched abroad, in this case to the USA. LT Museum

Above **The lower saloon push-out type emergency window can be seen in this RML interior view, and also the modified heater ducting and control switch introduced from RM 855 onwards.** LT Museum

Below **The release mechanism at the base of the lower-deck emergency exit.** LT Museum

day that it was delivered as a new bus from Park Royal. As originally built, the unladen weight of the class was recorded as 7tons 12cwt. In terms of weight efficiency, based on the premise that for each additional pound of dead weight the fuel consumption cost increased by 6d per annum per bus, the 1961 reckoning made the RML the most weight efficient of all London buses at 236lb per seat compared with 254lb for the RM and 330lb for the 8ft wide version of the RT class, the RTW.

The twenty-four vehicles were delivered from Park Royal, mostly in numerical sequence with only a few out of order, over a period of almost six months between 10th July 1961 and 8th January 1962. In Routemaster terms, this was a comparatively slow rate of construction with deliveries ranging between one and six buses per month, the peak month being October 1961 when RML 888–893 were received. By contrast, the new standard length RMs built during the same period ranged between RM 865 and RM 1084. In common with the contemporary RMs, the RMLs saw the switch to the modified radiator grille with polished central strip which took place with RML 886, 887, 889 onwards. The

last three vehicles, RML 901–903, arrived with red painted exterior glass fibre panels and black ticket boxes.

Having publicly committed itself to the 64-seater as being the optimum size for a double decker, London Transport was faced with the tricky task of convincing the Transport & General Worker's Union that there was a case for trying out anything larger. From the union point of view, a successful trial, even on a limited basis, could pave the way for job reductions in the future, which it strongly opposed on principle despite the acute shortage of bus crews which then prevailed. London Transport's initial desire to use the RMLs on a central London route met with blank refusal and it was finally agreed that they would operate on a former trolleybus service where the capacity of the new vehicles would not be so different from the ones they were to replace. The route selected was the 104 which was scheduled to supersede trolleybus route 609, which Highgate's RMs were already working on Sundays. The starting date for the 104 was 8th November 1961 and, as the maximum Monday to Friday peak requirement was for nineteen buses, there would be a few RMLs for

Later members of the batch, such as RML 900, carried the revised front grille with polished centre strip. This bus was one of several to spend long spells after driver training work in which capacity it is seen in July 1965 whilst attached to Hounslow garage. In fact it notched up only eight months' passenger service in its first six years of existence. Alan B. Cross

which no work would be found. Sixteen RMLs were actually in stock at the start of operation, of which fifteen (RML 880–894) were licensed to inaugurate the 104, supplemented by a few standard RMs. Three of the batch (RML 880, 882, 883) had, in fact, been licensed since 30th October for the training of drivers who, having passed their motor bus test on normal length RMs, were then given additional tuition on the longer variety.

Finchley's RML fleet was augmented on 1st December 1961 by the arrival of RML 895–897, and RML 899 brought its holding up to the correct level on the next trolleybus conversion date, 3rd January 1962. The remainder came in dribs and drabs after varying lengths of time in storage at Aldenham; RML 900 in September 1962 and RML 901/903 in March 1963. The two vehicles not mentioned so far were earmarked prior to entering service for promotional trips overseas. RML 898 went twice to the USA in 1962 and RML 902 made two forays into Europe in 1963. Both finally entered service at Finchley on 1st May 1964, by which time they were more than two years old. Meanwhile, RML 903, which had seen three months' service at Finchley, went

off for a spell in the USA during 1963; all these tours are described more fully in chapter 24.

As far as is known, Finchley's RMLs never strayed away from route 104 during their early years of service. However, as there was a surfeit of them, it was inevitable that some would be used as trainers for the much larger RML batch which came into service elsewhere in the fleet from November 1965 onwards. Five of them (RML 882, 894, 896, 900) comprised the first batch diverted to training work in May 1965, and it is interesting to note that over the years which have followed, only one vehicle from the entire batch of twenty-four has escaped doing at least one stint on trainer duties; this is RML 897.

Despite their temporary sojourns on trips abroad or as trainers, the batch became indelibly associated with Finchley Garage where the great majority could be found for almost ten years. Only a few strayed to other garages for passenger service, the first being RML 885 which turned up at Holloway in September 1967, followed by RML 891 at Willesden at the start of the following month. RML 900 found its way to Upton Park in February 1968 and RML 902 to Highgate a month later.

It is well known that none of the 24 original RML bodies have ever strayed outside their original batch of fleet numbers although there is, of course, no reason why they should not have done so. Exchange of bodies at overhaul has taken place within the batch on various occasions but there remain five vehicles which still carry their original bodies: RML 898 and 900–903. The late entry into service of these five resulted in delayed overhauls whereby it was impractical to set up the customary float to enable an exchange of bodies to be organised. During the course of their lives, all the modifications which were carried out on contemporary standard length RMs were also carried out on RML 880–903. Though nowadays there is nothing to distinguish them externally from a standard RML, apart from their fleet and registration numbers, the polished strip above the windows inside the saloons acts as an instant reminder to the knowledgeable passenger that the vehicle is one of those which marked London Transport's first tentative step into the realms of high capacity double deck motor buses over a quarter of a century ago.

CHAPTER THIRTEEN
RMF 1254

The October 1962 Commercial Motor Show at Earl's Court was chosen as the occasion for the debut of an interesting Routemaster, RMF 1254. Developed and constructed quietly and with very little publicity, this bus drew the inquisitive in large numbers to Park Royal's stand to catch their first glimpse of a front entrance Routemaster. Here, somewhat belatedly, was the Routemaster's answer to the now unstoppable quest by operators for high capacity double deckers which, in the fullness of time, might prove suitable for driver-only operation. The front entrance double decker, initially popularised by the Leyland Atlantean, had come to stay. The front entrance was favoured because it enabled the driver to have closer control over boarding and alighting, thereby freeing the conductor to concentrate on fare collection, a useful consideration on vehicles with seventy seats or more, and the rear engined Leyland Atlantean and Daimler Fleetline had been developed specifically around this concept. These two models, along with the front-engined Guy Wulfrunian, had the entrance doorway immediately to the left of the driver and ahead of the front axle. They differed considerably from the great variety of models, including new ones such as the AEC Renown, Albion Lowlander, Bristol Lodekka and Dennis Loline, and traditional ones like the AEC Regent, Daimler CVG, Guy Arab and

Above **RMF 1254 on the only service it worked in London — the BEA contract. New front wings and a continuous cream band had been applied by the time operation commenced on the airport run. An additional nearside rear view mirror has also been fitted. The destination blind was permanently set to read 'B.E.A.'** throughout the spell of operation on this service unlike the AEC Regal IV half-deckers which displayed the destination of the flight with which they connected. Ken Blacker

Left **Close-up view of the entrance and stairs taken on the Park Royal stand at Earl's Court in September 1962 showing the double step from pavement level into the saloon. The protrusion of the offside blind box into the staircase area was an unsatisfactory feature of the design. For the period of the Show, RMF 1254 carried blinds for route 104 and it was officially stated that this was where it would operate, but it did not do so.** LT Museum

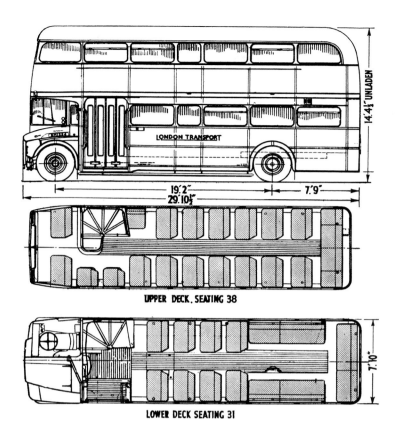

UPPER DECK. SEATING 38

LOWER DECK SEATING 31

A general arrangement drawing for RMF 1254 shows the general dimensions of this handsome vehicle and the layout of staircase and seating. The longitudinal seats over the rear wheel arches each accommodated five.

Leyland Titan, which retained the engine-above-front-axle concept thus placing the doorway behind a conventional front bulkhead. This less satisfactory arrangement was known in the vernacular of the time as forward rather than front entrance, and it was into this category that RMF 1254 fell.

The total flexibility offered by the Routemaster's modular type design meant that the new version could be built using a very high proportion of standard components. It was lengthened, as in the case of the 24 RMLs, by the insertion of an additional central bay but incorporated a repositioned entrance and staircase plus a fully enclosed rear end. The bulkhead was arranged so that the vehicle could be operated on the one-man principle, should this become permissible, with the driver turning round to deal with passengers through an angled opening. The net result was generally agreed to be a vehicle which was particularly handsome and well balanced in appearance, and modern too. It was exhibited at the Show in standard red bus livery carrying blinds for route 104 and bearing the 'London Transport at London's Service' posters which normally appeared on special occasions.

As built, RMF 1254 was a 69-seater, carrying 38 passengers upstairs and 31 downstairs. The rearward facing staircase was immediately opposite the front entrance doors which were electrically operated double jack-knife type supplied by Deans. Each leaf had one-piece glazing for maximum outward visibility. The main control was with the driver although an auxiliary control for the conductor was placed high up on the corner of the front bulkhead just below the curve of the

canopy. Towards the rear of the vehicle, the lower half of the conventional rear bulkhead structure was retained and strengthened, with an outward opening offside emergency door added behind it. The interior decor was exactly the same as on the standard Routemaster except that the polished strip above

the windows was omitted, pre-empting the design change that was to occur on the main batch from RM 1356 onwards. Another foretaste of things to come was the radiator grille which incorporated the traditional AEC triangle at its top centre, the raised bullseye motif familiar in the RM being omitted from the bonnet lid above. This, of course, was the modification adopted as standard in the summer of 1963. A full set of the usual destination boxes was provided front and rear but no nearside display was carried where one might have been expected above the entrance. Perhaps it was thought that the under-canopy route number box would suffice in view of its proximity to the doorway. On the offside, the route number aperture was situated in the staircase panel close by the bulkhead pillar.

From a mechanical point of view, RMF 1254 contained nothing new apart from stronger rear coil springs. It was powered by the conventional AEC AV590 engine and achieved much the same road performance as the RML with the standard rear axle ratio of 5.22:1 and a fairly similar unladen weight of 7tons 14cwt 2qtrs. Its London Transport code was 1/7RM8.

The rear end design of RMF 1254 was very neat with its single, wide lower deck rear window. The full depth emergency door can be seen at the rear end of the lower saloon. LT Museum

The official handover date from Park Royal was 19th October 1962, and exactly a week later the vehicle moved north to Liverpool for a month's experimental operation with the Corporation Transport Department. The Routemaster had now been offered for sale on the open market and both Park Royal and London Transport were anxious to achieve outside sales so that the development and overhead costs could be spread more widely. Park Royal quite rightly judged that, if any interest was to be stimulated at all, a front entrance model would have to be available and this was a significant factor in bringing about the construction of RMF 1254 in the first place. London Transport itself never appeared to be more than lukewarm over the idea, and though there was an initial intention to try the vehicle in experimental service in London, this never actually took place. RMF 1254 made its service debut on Liverpool's route 27 on 29th October and passengers were invited to submit their comments. It was well liked, being a cut above the average Liverpool bus for comfort and smoothness of ride. Returning to London on 26th November, it went into storage at Aldenham and did not appear again until the following spring.

Whilst those in London waited expectantly for the entry into service which never came, RMF 1254 departed for the provinces again on 1st March 1963, this time for a spell of work based at Canterbury. Its period of service on East Kent's route 4 was from 4th to 20th March and it had arrived back at Aldenham by 1st April. At the same time, East Kent was also experimenting with an AEC Renown demonstrator but neither impressed sufficiently to lead to a purchase. Similarly to Liverpool who stayed with their Atlanteans, East Kent continued to favour its Regent Vs and the provincial order book for Routemasters remained empty.

The RMF was now destined to stay out of the limelight for more than a year though it was not completely idle for the whole of this period. It was used for the experimental fitment of new-style deeper front headlamp panels without ventilator grilles, of a type later introduced as standard on the main production run of RMLs, and for a revised upper front air intake with reduced aperture and the cream band continuing unbroken across the front of the vehicle. This latter modification was adopted as a standard Routemaster fitment in October 1964.

At the time, the Minister of Transport was taking steps to permit buses to pull trailers, a move which was of particular interest to British European Airways, on whose behalf London Transport ran a coach service between Heathrow Airport and the West London Air Terminal in Gloucester Road. A surprise appearance towards the end of 1963 of the normally elusive RM 8 with a trailer in tow signalled that BEA was studying the feasibility of running a fleet of double deck coaches with trailers for the carriage of suitcases and other bulky luggage, and this scheme moved

Interior views of RMF 1254 in August 1965 while at work on the airport service. Capital Transport

to a more positive stage with the decision to employ RMF 1254 as a guinea pig for service trials. As early as August 1963, the lower saloon seating capacity had been reduced by five with the removal of the rear seat to increase space for hand luggage, and it was subsequently fitted up with towing gear including connections for an overrun brake. On Monday 21st January 1964, RMF 1254 was demonstrated at Chiswick with trailer attached. A few more months were to elapse before operation commenced; on 1st June the vehicle was relicensed for training purposes and its entry into service finally came on 4th August. It ran alongside the BEA fleet of Regal IV half-deckers and an experimental Regent V from the old Hammersmith trolley-bus depot and soon became a familiar sight on the main roads of west London.

Its stint on the Heathrow airport service was destined to be the only revenue earning work which the RMF would ever undertake within the capital under London Transport ownership, and it spent just under two years and two months gainfully employed in this way. During this time, between 15th and 30th August 1964, a third trip to the provinces was undertaken, this time for a fortnight's trial running in the hilly terrain of Halifax Corporation. It was reported to have given a good account of itself but, as in the two previous cases, no firm order resulted. On 20th July 1966, the BEA fleet left Hammersmith depot, which was scheduled for redevelopment, and was relocated in the old Chiswick tram depot (nowadays better known as Stamford Brook garage) and RMF 1254 went with them. However, its days in London were now numbered. The bus and its trailer had proved so successful that BEA had purchased its own fleet of Routemaster coaches and no longer had any need for the RMF. On 24th October 1966, it was delicensed and parked up in Hounslow garage, moving just three weeks later to Chiswick. With only four years of its originally assumed life of eighteen years used up, and its original cost of £8938 written down to £6954, this Routemaster was sold to Northern General on 25th November 1966 with Leyland (who now owned Park Royal and AEC) probably acting as an intermediary in the sale. Nearly fourteen years of hard work in and around Tyneside lay ahead.

Top **Disused tram tracks are silent testimony to a past era in Liverpool's transport but RMF 1254 is glistening new as it works circular route 27. At this stage its destiny as the white elephant of the London Routemaster fleet was not foreseen.** Roy Marshall

Centre **Canterbury bus station finds RMF 1254 amongst a host of East Kent's AEC Regent Vs all of which, with the exception of the one on the far left with its back to the camera, carry the final, ugly style of Park Royal body produced for this type of vehicle. Correctly-sized destination and route number blinds have been specially prepared for the RMF.**

Left **For the period of its fortnight's trial with Halifax Corporation, RMF 1254 retained its BEA advertising material but the towing eye was removed from the rear. In Halifax on a wet day, the RMF cast a drab appearance compared with the colourful orange, green and cream of the native fleet but probably surpassed any of them in performance.** Colin Routh

CHAPTER FOURTEEN
THE RMCs

As early as 1960, the rumour was beginning to circulate that London Transport was about to place an order for sixty double-decker Green Line Coaches based on a modified Routemaster and that these would enter service after the trolleybus conversion had been completed. The rumour was, in fact, well founded. The Executive had been very encouraged by the public reaction to CRL 4, which had clocked up somewhere in the region of 200,000 miles in passenger service, and had noted that it was normally the upper deck which filled up first. This, and the potential savings achievable by using larger capacity vehicles in place of the standard RF, particularly by reducing the need to operate duplicates, encouraged the decision to order a fleet of new double deckers. Contrary to most trends, the total usage of Green Line services had continued to increase up to 1960, even though the number of long distance passengers had fallen, and it was felt that larger, more attractive, vehicles would stimulate further growth. Also, it was hoped that the availability of upper deck seats with their good view over the countryside would encourage more people to travel to the quieter outer ends of routes. In the summer of 1961 came the official announcement that 68 vehicles were to be purchased. These would be 57-seaters with enclosed platforms, fluorescent lighting and auxiliary 12-gallon fuel tanks.

They were to be called the CR class (Coach Routemaster), reviving the designation which had passed out of use only a few years earlier with the demise of the well intentioned but mainly unsatisfactory rear-engined Leyland 20-seaters which had also been CRs. News of a more specific nature emerged in June 1962 when it was officially stated that the new coaches would be introduced over a five month period commencing in the autumn and would take over routes 715/A, 718, 720/A, 719 and 716/A in that order. All except the 715/A served new towns in the northern country area where traffic was expanding; the 715 had been selected in order to cut it from a 20-minute to a 30-minute headway with the loss of only three seats per hour.

Construction of the new coaches commenced at Park Royal in the spring of 1962 and the first one was handed over on 28th June. The RMC classification had now replaced the original intention to call the vehicles CRs, and the bonnet numbers RMC 1453 to 1520 had been reserved for the batch. This meant a jump upwards from the standard RM production run which had only reached RM 1282 at the time. As was to be expected, the new coaches closely resembled RMC 4 except for their front end layout which followed the general lines of current RM styling but, unlike RMC 4, they were in standard Lincoln green rather than

light green livery and it suited their handsome lines very well. Their entry into service was marked by a large scale publicity campaign featuring RMC 1453 against a leafy background in a full-colour photograph which showed the vehicle at its very best.

Double headlamps on each side marked a major frontal difference between the new RMC and the standard Routemaster. At the rear, the electrically operated double jack-knife doors enclosed the platform in the same way as on RMC 4, access to the operating mechanism being via a hinged external flap. This caused the nearside indicator box to be raised, with the result that it was operated from upstairs instead of from the platform. The emergency door layout was the same as on RMC 4 although the access handle was located towards the foot of the door rather than at waistrail level. RMC 4 had been the only Routemaster built to date with the rear registration plate mounted near the offside; on the standard RMC this was located in the centre with a bullseye transfer applied directly above it. A surprising, though not illogical, change was the abolition of the separate front route number box, a combined route number and via blind being used instead. At 2ft 9ins wide, this was narrower than the 3ft 6ins destination screen but had the advantage of using the same blind as at the side and rear.

Facing Page **A few days old, RMC 1454 pauses to set down passengers on the long cross-London run to Guildford, where its home garage is situated. Many of the features of CRL 4 are repeated in the production batch including the handsome livery. The destination blinds on the RMCs were in orange (officially amber) and black.** Colin Routh

Left **Brand new RMC 1453 pauses in a sylvan scene, ostensibly whilst working on the 715. This is, in fact, the official photograph which was widely used to publicise the entry into service of these attractive vehicles.** LT Museum

Below **Inside AEC's Southall works in July 1962, the final checks are made on RMC 1457 shortly before its delivery on the 18th. The Lincoln green paintwork, which always looked splendid when new but tended to lose its richness quickly, contrasts very effectively with the red of the central area Routemasters standing on either side.** G.A. Rixon

Underneath and inside the vehicle, the differences from the standard RM were more radical than those affecting its outside appearance. The normal coil suspension was retained at the front but, at the back, air bellows were employed, the air pressure being applied from the standard gearbox operating system and controlled by levelling valves, one on each side, mounted on the underside of the body and connected to the suspension sub-frame. The shock absorbers, which on the normal Routemaster were mounted co-axially with the coil springs, were sited inboard of the suspension units on the coach, 34 vehicles being equipped with arm-type shock absorbers and the remainder with telescopic units. Because the number of gear changes per mile was some 70% fewer than on central bus work, the automatic gear change facility was not provided and, although the standard AV590 engine was fitted, a rear axle ratio of 4.7:1 permitted significantly higher road speeds to be attained. A 41-gallon fuel capacity was specified instead of the normal 29 gallons which, being mounted on the offside in the standard RM position, left RMC 4 (now the only one of the four prototypes to remain in passenger service) very much the odd man out at the daily refuelling.

The main feature of note inside the RMC body was the seating. Although the dove grey, black and maroon moquette could perhaps have been a little more cheerful in appearance (the design was borrowed from the more recent Underground stock) the deeply upholstered cushions and squabs gave a real feeling of luxury. Spacing was more generous than on the normal RM, with 1.25 inches more knee-room in the lower saloon and 1.75 inches upstairs, the total capacity of the vehicle being only 57 (32 up and 25 down). A complete row of seats had been omitted from the upper deck in the interests of comfort, whilst downstairs the rear longitudinal seats were shortened to seat only three on the nearside and two on the offside. The seatbacks were covered with red rexine to match the side panelling and the upstairs seats had ashtrays fitted. Much brighter decor was adopted, with sung yellow window surrounds and white ceilings. Parcel racks were provided, comprising stainless steel tubing with detachable aluminium frames and red nylon netting; the coving panels above them were grey. Instead of the normal incandescent lighting, fluorescent tubes were fitted as these were felt to be necessary for the long distance traveller who might wish to read, the lighting level being improved some 2.5 times by this means. Six 2ft 20watt tubes were installed downstairs and eight upstairs, including one above the rear emergency exit, the fourteen tubes being driven by seven transistorised inverters, each driving two tubes in series, grouped together

on a panel behind the nearside rear passenger seat upstairs. Though dearer to install initially, the total lighting load was reckoned to be no higher than with conventional bulbs, the latter still being present in the destination boxes. Other deviations from normal bus fitments included the omission of internal stanchions, a standard Green Line practice, and the replacement of gangway slats by flat, cork-rubber Treadmaster tiles in the same shade of brown. The conductor's bell on the platform was the only one; elsewhere on both decks buzzers were fitted.

The RMC was, naturally, somewhat heavier than its RM counterpart and, as weighed when first built, it stood at 7tons 12cwt 1qr. Expressed in terms of weight per passenger, this was equivalent to 299lbs which represented a significant improvement over the Green Line RF which turned the scales at 443lbs per passenger. The RMCs were finally licensed at 7-15-0 which, though slightly above the original estimate, was still a remarkable achievement for such a well built and comfortably appointed vehicle. The class was coded 6RM6 in the London Transport scheme of things and no changes were ever made to cause any sub-codings to be issued. They were fitted out with Simms electrical gear, SCG transmission and Lockheed brakes. In true Green Line style they bore no advertisements. This factor, plus the additional embellishment to the livery provided by the light green window surrounds, made them appear to sparkle more than the average Routemaster and gave the air of class that their Green Line status demanded. Polished lamp fittings in place of the usual painted ones were another good feature and it was such a pity that polished wheel trims were not fitted to complete the picture.

The class was delivered almost, though not completely, in numerical sequence. RMC 1453 was taken into London Transport stock about

three weeks ahead of any other on 28th June 1962. Delivery proper commenced on 18th July and took place at the rate of between ten and thirteen vehicles a month up to 20th December when RMCs 1519 and 1520 arrived at Aldenham to complete the batch. The first licensing took place on 10th August when RMC 1455 at Hertford and RMC 1456 at Guildford commenced driver training, one at each end of route 715, ready for the big day on 29th August when the coach Routemasters would come into their own for the first time. Just enough vehicles were in stock on 29th August to provide twelve vehicles for Hertford and eight for Guildford, RMC 1453-1472 being shared between the two garages, with the larger allocation at Hertford. This garage also worked route 715A which ran between Hertford and London Marble Arch so had no Guildford involvement. Though the actual allocation was RMC 1453-55/57-59/66-71 at Hertford and RMC 1456/60-65/72 at Guildford, this distinction would not have been apparent to the casual observer. As in the case of a number of other Country Bus & Coach Department operations, but most notably on the longer Green Line routes, it was common for vehicles to sleep out at the other end of the route, appearing next day with the foreign garage's allocation plates. Although the general use of aluminium stencil plates gave way on the Country Bus fleet in the latter part of 1962 to the already established Central Bus practice of painting the garage code direct on to the bodywork, vehicles working from the wrong end still tended to carry old style plates to obscure the painted code.

Routes 718, 720 and 720A were next in line for conversion, on 24th October, the 720 being reduced in frequency from half-hourly to hourly at the same time. Before this, Hertford and Guildford had both been given an additional coach during September, the original allocation presumably having proved too tight.

Epping was the major recipient of new vehicles, being responsible for all these routes whereas Windor's involvement was limited to a half share in route 718. Just over a week later, on 1st November, RMC 4 which had been keeping a lone vigil at Stevenage, was transferred to Hertford to join the mainstream RMC operation. Still in its rather unattractive light green livery at this stage, it was very soon afterwards repainted into Lincoln Green. Although treated henceforth as a more or less normal member of the RMC fleet, RMC 4 remained non-standard in many ways and was less than popular with many staff, engineers and drivers, who tended to compare its speed, handling and ease of maintenance unfavourably with the standard RMC.

The third of the four planned stages of RMC introduction took place on 21st November 1962 with the conversion of route 719. This was the simplest of the four schemes because only one garage was involved, Garston, which received an unbroken block of vehicles, RMC 1499-1506, which were destined to stay together on route 719 for the full period of almost five years up to their first overhaul.

The fourth and final RMC conversion was on 2nd January 1963, on routes 716 and 716A. For this occasion, Stevenage received eight vehicles and Addlestone received nine although, a few days later, the position was reversed with the transfer of one of Addlestone's to Stevenage. At the October 1962 conversion of the 718 and 720/A, the vehicle allocation had been complicated by the use of certain coaches which had already seen service elsewhere to make up the numbers, and the same thing happened this time. One of the inter-garage transfers involved was that of RMC 4 which returned to Stevenage after only two months at Hertford. Its renewed operation on route 716 was destined to be of very short duration and was terminated on 8th February when it was sent to Epping in exchange for a

normal RMC, its intended use on the 720 group presumably being regarded as less demanding than route 716.

An interesting feature of the Green Line network had long been the scheduled operation by certain garages of the odd coach or two to cover journeys on local bus services. Designed to achieve maximum vehicle and staff utilisation, these workings made a fascinating break from the run of the mill coach operation for the vehicles concerned. Full provision for these operations was normally made when the coach destination blinds were produced, with the result that anyone who happened to be in the right place at the right time could expect to find RMCs blinded up for some obscure and interesting workings. These changed from time to time but initial RMC allocations made provision for operations on routes 393A, 396 and 805 from Epping, 417 at Windsor, 347 at Garston, 303 at Stevenage, and 420 and 463 at Addlestone.

The first reallocation of any consequence took place on 22nd May 1963 when the new garage in Fourth Avenue, Harlow opened for business, replacing the premises at Epping which, though still comparatively modern, were ill sited for Harlow New Town whose rapid development necessitated a great deal of dead running. Sixteen Routemaster coaches were included amongst Harlow's first complement of vehicles (RMCs 4, 1471/73/75/76/78/80-84/87/90/91/92 and 1494), representing the largest fleet of RMCs held by any garage. Though Harlow's coach working remained little changed from the previous Epping based timetables, route 393A was dropped from the bus schedules but journeys on routes 397 and 804 were added. Not long afterwards, in the autumn of 1963, RMCs began to appear with external advertising beneath the rear lower deck windows, obscuring the Green Line bullseye transfer. This marked a complete break from tradition, it having been the strictly observed policy until then not to display commercial advertising material on any vehicles used permanently on Green Line work. The temptation to earn additional revenue had prompted the change of heart but fortunately this never extended to the acceptance of adverts on the upper panels.

The RMC coaches were quite well received by passengers but probably did not prove as popular as had been hoped. It is certainly doubtful whether they did much to stimulate additional patronage, but they were unfortunate in coming on the scene when demand throughout the system was taking a definite downturn. They were not as reliable as the RFs which they replaced. Front end vibration at speed was an early problem which required modification of the shock absorber rubber mounting, whilst another early area of maintenance difficulty lay with the ingress of road dirt into the brake drums. The brake drum dust shields had been removed from all Routemasters from June 1963 onwards with the idea of facilitating ease of maintenance, but the problem that this caused on the coaches resulted in them being refitted in November 1964. Undoubtedly, the biggest area of unreliability lay with the rear suspension. Right from the start, problems arose with exhaustion of air from the suspension because of leaks in the gearbox air system and, as early as May 1963, it proved necessary to provide a redesigned and stronger Westinghouse valve

Heading north through Hatfield with its paintwork still gleaming after almost six months of service, Addlestone's RMC 1518 glistens in the sunshine of June 1963. Gerald Mead

spring following an experiment on RMC 1503. However, problems with the levelling valves and bellows continued and in January 1965 the Firestone Tyre and Rubber Co Ltd provided new 'Airide' springs to improve service life. The 34 vehicles with telescopic shock absorbers experienced recurring failure of the mounting plates and as these were of a less effective design than the alternative, being mounted in-board of the wheels, arm type absorbers were fitted in due course bringing all 68 to the same specification. Eventually, as with all early Routemaster problems, most of the troubles were ironed out and a satisfactory standard of reliability achieved, although the air suspension never became as reliable as the excellent coil springs. Though it is easy to be wise in hindsight it would have been better not to have fitted the coaches with air bags at the rear, for the trouble which the air suspension caused was out of proportion to the very scant benefit which it endowed upon the travelling public.

The RMCs had been on the road for less than two years when changes to their appearance were decided upon. Spurred on by the fact that plans for a further batch of Routemaster coaches, the RCL class, were well advanced, RMC 1469 was withdrawn from service at Hertford at the end of May 1964 to serve as a guinea pig for minor structural changes and livery modifications in readiness for the forthcoming new vehicles. All were purely cosmetic and aimed at enhancing the overall appearance; whether or not they succeeded remains purely a matter of personal preference. The main structural changes were carried out at the front end of the vehicle where the wing and grille assemblies were replaced by a revised design, the main feature of which was the use of deeper front edges for the headlamp panels and the omission of the registration plate from the grille panel, resulting in a smooth bottom line running in an unbroken sweep from one side of the vehicle to the other. This modification, which was also carried out on RMF 1254, eliminated the brake cooling grilles which were no longer considered necessary, and the grille panel itself now carried the latest type of V shaped badge at the top instead of the separate raised bullseye motif which had been removed from the bonnet lid. Higher up, the band and moulding at cantrail level were continued across the lower half of the saloon ventilator and heating grille to provide an unbroken line for the light green relief and, above this, the intermediate point blind box was enlarged to the same width as the destination screen. The value of this last change was particularly doubtful as it necessitated production of a special blind (the side and rear boxes having remained at their old width) which carried no more information than the one it replaced. A completely new set of fleetname transfers had been devised and, in order to accommodate them, the offside route number box, disused since November 1963, and the raised bullseye motifs were removed, although the motifs still left their impression when viewed from certain angles. Large new bullseyes were positioned on the main upper deck panels just below the first window on each side, but transfers were now used instead, and these incorporated the title LONDON TRANSPORT in place of GREEN LINE.

Advertisements made their appearance on Green Line vehicles for the first time in the autumn of 1963, albeit confined to the lower rear panels. RMC 1492, photographed at Aldgate on a 720A duty, was one of Epping's original batch transferred to the new Harlow garage when it opened in May 1963. The light green window surround differed from the one on RMC 4 in that it did not encompass the small corner window. Alan Nightingale

The latter name was carried, like an uncomfortable afterthought, in plain block capitals just to the rear of the bullseye below the second window. Smaller bullseyes were also carried on the lower deck, the nearside one being above the rear wheelarch with the offside location being at the rear end of the old route number panel, the words GREEN LINE being placed forward of it. No name was carried in the normal position on the main lower panels. Sadly, in the search for modernity, the traditional and handsome Green Line motif with large initial G and final E and the Lon-

don Transport title carried below the remaining seven letters in an elongated box, was discarded. Also out was the standard light green relief, replaced by a new shade of porcelain green which was reputedly lighter and more distinctive but which really seemed little different from its predecessor. RMC 1469 re-entered service in its new guise on route 715 on 9th July 1964. London Transport made much in its official press release of the revamped appearance but the changes probably remained unnoticed by all but a tiny percentage of travellers.

RMC 1469 emerged in its revamped form with new front wings and grille, continuous front band, wider front 'via' box, and revised fleetnames in July 1964. It is seen soon afterwards at the Hertford end of route 715. Frank Mussett

The May 1964 instruction to garages to blank over the lower half of the front heater and ventilator aperture was quickly complied with, although in the case of many vehicles some time was to elapse before the vertical strips on either side were repainted pale green to match. Hertford's RMC 1453 in unaltered form passes Guildford's RMC 1463 in Hertford bus station. Alan Nightingale

One of RMC 1469's modifications was adopted as standard for the whole of the RMC fleet with almost immediate effect. This was the continuous between-decks band, an instruction to implement this locally being despatched to all RMC operating garages on 29th May 1964. Within a few weeks, a start had been made and, gradually during the remaining half of 1964, all RMCs were dealt with, giving a foretaste of the wider application of this principle to the red bus fleet in 1965. A modification adopted gradually for all Routemasters from the latter part of 1964 onwards was the blanking over of the cooling grille apertures on the headlamp panels of existing vehicles, a process in which the RMCs participated.

While this was going on, RMC 4 was also being subjected to alterations to its appearance. On 14th April 1964, it was delicensed for its first, long overdue, overhaul and was transferred from Harlow into Chiswick works as the first stage in this process. The overhaul was a protracted affair which took very nearly eight months to complete, but it provided a good opportunity for the vehicle to be examined structurally to assess the effects on it of seven years fairly constant wear and tear. The final stages of overhaul, including repainting, were carried out at Aldenham in October and November bringing RMC 4 into a state of readiness to be relicensed at Harlow on 9th December. The result was not totally dissimilar to RMC 1469, RMC 4's original bonnet and wings having been swept away and replaced by the same style of front end as on the Hertford vehicle. The front cantrail band was likewise now a continuous one and, again like RMC 1469, the offside route number box and both raised bullseyes had been removed to permit the same new style bullseye transfers to be applied, although the words GREEN LINE were no longer adjacent but appeared instead on the main lower saloon panels allowing the lower offside bullseye to be positioned centrally on the staircase panel. Although RMC 4 now resembled a standard RMC much more closely than before, its non-opening front top deck windows remained an immediate giveaway as to its identity. So too did the surprise retention of the three piece front indicator layout which meant that special sets of blinds would continue to be needed.

The second half of the nineteen-sixties was a hard time for the Green Line network which was badly hit by increasing congestion on the roads resulting in worsening timekeeping, whilst modernisation schemes by British Railways and the Underground took their toll.

Badly hit by the Great Eastern electrification were Harlow's 720/A which reverted to RF operation on 4th November 1964, single deckers being more than capable of coping with the available trade. The eight displaced RMCs went, four apiece, to two new garages, Hatfield and Swanley to commence operation on route 717. Hitherto operated only between Welwyn Garden City and Victoria, this route was extended on the same date to Wrotham to cover the southern half of the 703 which was then withdrawn, a casualty of the Metropolitan main line modernisation.

When RMC 4 emerged from overhaul in December 1964 it sported a front wing and grille assembly identical to that on RMC 1469, and also a similar livery style. However retention of the three piece blind display and non-opening front windows ensured that it was still easy to recognise. Here it is seen some two years later at Hyde Park Corner when allocated to Hatfield. W T Cottrell

June 1965 saw the RMCs being joined in the Green Line fleet by new, longer, consorts in the shape of the RCL class. The original intention in ordering 43 of these new vehicles was that they would replace all existing Green Line vehicles at Romford and Grays but a problem occurred when it came to light that doubtful clearance on a bridge at South Stifford would preclude the use of RCLs on route 723B, one of the variants of the Grays based operation. To overcome this, five RMCs including the revamped RMC 1469 moved from Hertford to Grays on 1st July 1965 to be replaced, somewhat wastefully, on route 715A by new RCLs. In October 1966, RMC 4 made a surprise transfer to Hatfield where it stayed for thirteen years, the most settled spell in its life.

The years 1966 and 1967 saw further alterations to the external appearance of the RMCs. In April 1966, an instruction went out to garages to remove the external handrails from either side of the entrance doors, experience having shown that they regularly became fouled with dirt and mud thrown up by the rear wheels. Two new handrails were fitted on the inner faces of the entrance doors in their place, and this rendered redundant a handrail on the nearside partition which was also removed. In effect, this modification brought the RMCs into line with the RCLs which had never been fitted with the external handles. The 1967 modification was distinctly retrograde and resulted from the first RMC overhaul programme which got under way in April. The first two vehicles to emerge in overhauled condition, RMC 1470 at Hertford and RMC 1484 at Guildford both on 12th May, displayed the new livery which included all the revised transfers as finalised on RMC 4 and subsequently applied to the RCLs, but it also abolished all the light green window reliefs. With only the cantrail band now picked out, the overall effect was one of drabness. One by one, the whole batch of 68 was dealt with in this way, the last in the old livery being RMC 1520 which went into overhaul from Addlestone on 27th December 1967. The only RMC then still in old colours was RMC 4 which lasted for another year until repainted in December 1968. The main overhaul programme had been carried out using the customary float system with the result that all vehicles changed their identity in the process, the odd man out, RMC 1469, reappearing on 31st October as RMC 1502. In its new guise, it was allocated initially to Stevenage but, probably because this garage had no suitable front blind for it, a move was made three days later to Grays.

The Green Line story from 1966 onwards was one of continuous decline as traffics continued to dwindle and single deck, driver only operation became inevitable. On 13th June 1966, route 715A, which had not long before grown up from RMC to RCL, was reduced to RF operation. A bigger move came on 2nd December 1967 when the whole Grays RCL allocation on the 723 group was downgraded to RMC operation using vehicles no longer required at Stevenage. This garage had lost its 716A workings to Hatfield to compensate for the loss of route 717 which was truncated from that date to work Wrotham to Baker Street, route 716A being diverted between Welwyn Garden City and Potters Bar

The conversion from RT of route 723B brought RMCs to Grays on 1st July 1965. Ex-Hertford RMC 1468, seen at Aldgate, has had its brake grille apertures blanked out under the programme commenced late in the previous year. Alan B. Cross

A retrograde step was the simplified livery applied on overhaul from May 1967 onwards. RMC 1459, rounding Marble Arch in March 1968, displays the new drab look and also the loss of its external platform grab handles. Alan B. Cross

to cover for it. Very soon afterwards, on 20th December, routes 717 (worked by Swanley) and 719 (Garston) received RFs and the displaced RMCs moved to East Grinstead and Hemel Hempstead to work on route 708 at a reduced frequency, odd journeys also being worked on bus routes 318 and 334 at Hemel Hempstead, and 435 at East Grinstead. A move in the other direction, from RF to RMC, occurred in December 1967 when the spare Green Line vehicle kept at Riverside central bus garage to cover for breakdowns became an RMC. The arrangement lasted less than a week on this occasion but it became permanent from 9th January 1968 although the RMC allocated for this purpose changed from time to time. As with the RF before it, special blinds were provided to permit the vehicle to work on all likely services. Other odd RMC allocations occurred when RMC 1480 went to Romford for a few days in November 1968 and RMC 1468 to Dunton Green for a much longer spell from April 1969 onwards. Both acted as RCL cover and it became increasingly common as time went by to find RMCs covering RCL workings, often on a loaned basis.

The Green Line network was now on a downhill slide, the next manifestation of which was the withdrawal of route 723B, already depleted in frequency, on 5th December 1968. The following year witnessed serious inroads into double deck Green Line operation, starting on 15th February when route 708 reverted to RFs after little more than a year with RMCs. East Grinstead and Hemel Hempstead both found themselves with redundant RMCs and, as there was no further work for them within the Green Line network, there was no option but to employ them as buses. Most were redeployed at Hatfield as RT replacements on the Hitchin – New Barnet 303/A run, plus odd workings on a whole variety of local Hatfield routes. A couple were sent to Addlestone to partly convert route 461A but this arrangement lasted only until May when the two vehicles were despatched to Grays' trunk bus service, the 370. An official RMC allocation on routes 370/A, plus journeys on routes 300, 328B and 371, commenced on 4th October 1969 when six more RMCs were made surplus by drastic service reductions on route 704, whereby six RCLs returned to Grays for route 723 displacing RMCs. The RMC role as buses was widened on Sundays when Grays also deployed them on local routes 300 and 328.

The London Transport era came to an end at midnight on 31st December 1969 when the entire RMC class passed into National Bus Company ownership amongst the assets of the old Country Bus & Coach Department taken over by the new London Country Bus Services Ltd. The once-proud Routemaster coaches were embarking on a decade of hard times. The close of London Transport operation found Hatfield holding the largest RMC fleet with fifteen units although, for some months following the arrival of the vehicles from route 708, this garage tended to treat its RMCs as two separate fleets, keeping those numbered in the fourteen hundreds on coach work and the fifteen hundreds plus RMC 4 as buses, a situation probably brought about by blind availability. The second largest RMC stronghold, Grays, also used a high proportion on bus work. For the RMCs, the writing was clearly on the wall.

Top **RMC 1499, overhauled in June 1967, carried brighter, almost yellow fleet names and other insignia. Several red RTs were treated similarly at about the same time and, though not perpetuated, these were without doubt more markedly visible than the customary gold ones. A Harlow-based vehicle, RMC 1499 carries plates for Windsor garage, its partner on route 718.** Alan B. Cross

Centre **Unrequired for coach use, Hatfield's RMC 1500 is one of a number transferred to bus operation on route 303 although they retained their official coach status including GREEN LINE fleet names and freedom from advertising material. It is seen at Stevenage bus station.** Tom Maddocks

Right **Addlestone's route 461A also received the attention of surplus RMCs although in this instance RTs made an early return. RMC 1464 had been drafted in for this purpose at the start of the Routemaster operation in February 1969 but departed in May to mark the start of a build up of RMCs on bus service at Grays.** Alan B. Cross

CHAPTER FIFTEEN
TOWARDS STANDARDISATION

After all the ballyhoo accompanying the final trolleybus conversion on Wednesday 9th May 1962, the London bus scene went unusually quiet for several months. The next priority was to commence replacement of the enormous RT family, a mammoth task which would obviously take many years to complete, but London Transport was convinced that, in the Routemaster, it had a vehicle so robust in construction and technically advanced in specification that it could form the basis of a new standardised fleet of double deckers for many years to come. Laudable as this aim was, it would never be fulfilled. Within a few years, events would truncate Routemaster production and, ultimately, extend the life of the RT family way beyond the wildest dreams of those who had created it so many years earlier. The rumblings of those events were already to be felt. Provincial double deck bus development was beginning to swing steadily away from the traditional front engined, rear platform vehicle and, though many in London imagined that what they regarded as their special operating circumstances would shield them from this, the reality was that, in a shrinking and fast changing industry, there would be no place for isolationism. In 1961, the London Transport Executive had itself informed the Transport & General Workers' Union that it wished to experiment with high capacity standee buses in central London as a means of easing the staff shortage as well as

helping the movement of rush hour crowds and, though it did not view this as in any way representing a significant switch away from the traditional double decker, the seeds of change were unwittingly being sown. History was to record that the great days of a fully standardised motor bus fleet, which had existed only from 1954 to 1959 when the RT family reigned supreme, would not return.

The reason that several months of inactivity occurred in the introduction of new buses over the second half of 1962 was that London Transport had become deadlocked in negotiations with the powerful TGWU which represented all London bus drivers and conductors under a closed shop agreement. Both sides were deeply worried by the continuous and worsening staff shortage although they saw the reasons for it and the means of combating it in different lights. Mistrust within the Union over management intentions was not eased when the plan for standee single deckers was revealed since this represented an abrupt about turn from the earlier stance that the 64-seat double decker was the optimum city bus. Since February, the Union had been digesting proposals by the Executive for expanding the RML fleet, the introduction of driver only operation into the red bus fleet on quieter suburban routes, and a general speeding up of schedules, fearful that these proposals would mean job losses which, though they might result in few, if any, redundancies with

the existing staff shortages, would reduce job availability for when better times returned. The adoption of such palliatives also eased the pressure away from London Transport to provide improved wages and working conditions which the union considered, not without reason, to be essential to stem the increasing staff turnover. In the spring of 1962, the Union informed London Transport that, if given a reduction in the working day to seven hours (making a 42 hour week), they would accept standee single deckers and more RMLs, but a sticking point which the Union was adamant that it would not concede was a proposal to replace RTs by RMs on the basis of nine RMs for every ten RTs even though the total seating provision would be roughly equal. The Union saw in this redundancies and a worsening of services with the consequent snowballing effect that this would produce. An offer to pay a bonus to crews working the larger vehicles failed to induce a change of mind.

Month after month, new RMs continued to arrive from Park Royal with no immediate prospect of them being put into service, and it was fortunate that part of the production between June and September consisted of RMC coaches, alleviating what would otherwise have become an acute storage problem. As it was, by the beginning of October, 132 unused RMs were languishing at a variety of locations. A large amount of surplus space had been filled up at Edmonton garage with

Facing Page **The rush to convert services from RT to Routemaster in December 1962 found the new class infiltrating route 16 immediately before Christmas. RM 1018, which had been at Cricklewood since stage 13 of the trolleybus conversion programme almost a year earlier, is seen with RT 843 during the changeover period.** Michael Beamish

Left **A tentative start was made on the RT to RM conversion programme a week ahead of the main activity with the changeover of Hounslow's small allocation on route 73. RM 1072 was one of the batch delivered for the final trolleybus conversion earlier in 1962.** Gerald Mead

Below **The first three months of 1963 were spent converting the massive 36 group of routes to RM. First to receive them were the 36A/B operated by Rye Lane, one of whose Leyland engined contingent, RM 1403, is at Marble Arch en route for West Kilburn. This vehicle stayed at Rye Lane right through to its closure in March 1969.** G.H.F. Atkins

smaller numbers of new buses in store at Willesden, Holloway, Hanwell, Hendon and Finchley. Still they continued to arrive, 19 more in October and 27 in November, causing open air storage at Walthamstow and Stonebridge to be brought into use. It had been known for some months that London Transport wished to put the first seventy into service on routes 114, 140 and 158 from Edgware and Harrow Weald garages; indeed, all the route blinds were manufactured in readiness. The commencement of the winter programme on 10th October 1962 was set as a deadline but, with the continuing lack of agreement, this could not be met. London Transport's next move was to announce that they would be introduced on 25th October. This incensed the staff at Edgware and Harrow Weald who staged a day's protest strike on Saturday 13th October in which they were supported by a number of other garages; at Edgware the stoppage lasted a further three days. In a sudden change of policy, London Transport decided to replace RTs by RMs on a one-for-one basis tackling the busiest central London routes first. It is interesting to record that, after its initial Routemaster debacle, Harrow Weald garage did not receive any of the type until a further sixteen years had elapsed while Edgware remained one of the very few garages never to be supplied with Routemasters at all.

Its squabble with the Union now at an end, at least as far as the spread of Routemasters was concerned, London Transport announced that the first services to receive the new vehicles would be the 13, 16, 36 group, 37 and 73, of which only the 37 did not pass through the heart of the West End. The first big day for RMs to replace the RT family was set for 12th December 1962 when a total of 119 scheduled workings were converted overnight on routes 37 (Stockwell 21 buses, Putney 14) and 73 (Tottenham 49, Mortlake 35). Tottenham's night service N90 was also converted. A week earlier, on 5th December, Hounslow's six bus allocation on route 73 had switched to RMs but, in this instance, the vehicles were second hand from other garages and not new ones. For the very first time, Leyland engined RMs took to the road in quantity, all of those at

Stockwell and Mortlake and all but eleven of Tottenham's being of this variety. At Stockwell, the first examples with revised interior decor omitting the polished band above the windows came into use. Except for the small Hounslow allocation, which had been RTs, all the vehicles displaced were Leyland RTLs.

Just a few days later, on 17th December, the 33 scheduled buses on route 13 were replaced overnight. The two garages involved, Hendon with 20 workings and Rye Lane with 13, were both operators of AEC-built RTs and their new Routemasters were also AEC engined. This was the first major incursion into the ranks of the RT and it heralded the start of a major onslaught on the roof-box variety which, generally speaking, were those with the oldest bodies. For many, these epitomised the traditional London bus and their steady withdrawal was met with regret. Route 13 had no Sunday operation and so the RMs were deployed differently on this day: Hendon's on

routes 113, 240 and 260 and Rye Lane's on routes 37 (joining the all-week Stockwell and Putney contingent of new RMs) and 173 (which was RM worked on Saturdays too). Hereafter, almost every conversion to RM saw a surplus of new buses on Sundays due to the lower scheduled requirements on this day and also, to a lesser extent, on Saturdays, resulting in a much wider spread of operation by RMs at weekends over routes which on Mondays to Fridays remained the exclusive province of the RT family. A night service converted to RM at this time was Rye Lane's N85.

The next scheduled conversion was route 16 which was a solo operation from Cricklewood garage requiring no fewer than 54 buses. Rather more than half the required number were available to put into service on Christmas Eve, representing the last influx of new Routemasters for 1962. The remainder were licensed on 1st January 1963. As was always

the case where a night service was operated, Cricklewood's N94 was converted to RMs as soon as they were received. On this occasion, a mixture of AEC and Leyland engined vehicles was used in the ratio of approximately five Leylands to every AEC, and the span of fleet numbers of new buses licensed for the first time was unusually wide, ranging from RM 1031 at the lowest to RM 1377 at the highest.

For the next programme, it was back to Rye Lane, this time for routes 36A and 36B. The first six RMs were due to be received on 10th January and were high-numbered buses ranging between RM 1374 and 1382 which had been allocated temporarily to other Routemaster garages hit by a bout of particularly severe winter weather. However, it is probable that these were not released to Rye Lane on the due date and that the conversion actually commenced on 15th January with the licensing of five previously unused buses. Further batches arrived up to 11th February. All the stored buses had now been used and overnight conversions were no longer possible, with the result that the next route on the list, Peckham's 36, would require a six-week span to cover the whole 33-bus scheduled operation. Also, it was not always practicable, without wholesale reallocations, to segregate AEC and Leyland engined buses, desirable though this would have been. Rye Lane's latest allocation was a case in point as, because of vehicle availability, Leylands had to be supplied although the earlier batch for route 13 had been AECs. Peckham's conversion of route 36, already mentioned, along with their night route N86 commenced on 18th February and included amongst the new vehicles licensed on that date were the first red ones in the fifteen-hundred series following on from the RMCs. The last RTs were displaced from route 36 on 1st April.

With effect from 1st January 1963, a significant change of status had befallen London Transport. Arising from the Transport Act of 1962, the British Transport Commission (the overlord of the state owned transport sector) had been abolished. The London Transport Executive had also gone out of existence, to be replaced by the London Transport Board which, without the superfluous shackles of the BTC to control its every move, had far more autonomy than its predecessor. It now reported directly to the Minister of Transport and was, in many respects, in a position similar to the much admired and similarly named London Passenger Transport Board which had ceased to exist on 1st January 1948 with the advancement of the nationalisation plans of the government of the time. The change from LPTB to LTE had been marked by an almost overnight change of wording on the legal ownership panels of all buses but the change from LTE to LTB was not nearly so quickly apparent. For some months, new buses continued to arrive with the old name and it was not until 1st June that the first new one correctly titled, RM 1601, took the road.

Within a few days of entering service, one of the latest Rye Lane contingent, RM 1414, was cleaned up and despatched on loan to Manchester Corporation who had shown an interest in hiring a Routemaster for assessment trials. Although RMF 1254 had previously been used as the preferred demonstrator, it was not appropriate for this occasion where a rear-entrance Leyland-engined vehicle was required. RM 1414 went north to Manchester on 13th February 1963, returned to London on 5th March and duly re-entered service at Rye Lane a few days later. No firm orders resulted from the demonstration hire but RM 1414 had forged a link with Manchester that was to be renewed after a lapse of some nineteen years

when the vehicle then bearing that number, no longer the original one after three intermediate overhauls had obscured the true identity, was obtained by the Greater Manchester Transport Society for preservation in the City.

The programme of RM takeovers continued with route 9 on 5th April 1963. The Mortlake allocation was tackled first and, with its completion on 14th May, a new milestone was reached; Mortlake had become the first traditional bus garage to lose all its RT family buses (in Mortlake's case these were RTLs) in favour of RMs. While this was going on, a fresh recruit to Routemaster operation came onto the scene when Uxbridge garage received a few as a spin off from a widespread reallocation scheme also involving Hanwell and Southall. Uxbridge obtained a minority working on route 207 from Hanwell, and the buses to go with it, on 8th May. Not a total newcomer to route 207, Uxbridge had previously run it on Sundays only but had used RTs. Reverting to route 9, Dalston received two batches of RMs, on 17th May and 1st June, to complete its share of the operation. The 1st June batch included RMs numbered from RM 1601 upwards, with new DYE registration letters, the first (apart from RM 1000) to forsake the LT letters which had become something of a tradition on Routemasters. Following route 9 was Hounslow's 81B which, though very much an outer-suburban operation very different in character from other recent conversions, served the fast-expanding Heathrow Airport and justified larger, more modern vehicles. The whole of the new bus production at this stage was concentrated on Leyland-engined vehicles and, in order to avoid placing these at Hounslow a selection of older RMs was used instead, drawn between 12th June and 1st July from the minority AEC-engined allocations at Cricklewood and

Below Left **Dalston's conversion to RM on route 9 used vehicles spanning the registration number changeover from the final 'LT' batch to the first 'normal' ones. One of the former category, RM 1557, is brand new on Sunday route 106A, one of a growing number of workings handed over to Routemasters on the day of the week when the requirements of their own routes were much reduced.** Michael Beamish

Below Right **Muswell Hill's route 43 had no Sunday operation at all, enabling the class to displace RTs in their entirety from the garage's other routes on this day. RM 1616 stands at Golders Green awaiting a summer Sunday trip to High Beach.** W.R. Legg

Rye Lane who received new Leylands as replacements. Route 81 was converted to RM on Sundays, taking red RMs on stage work to Windsor for a brief period. In a move which was rarely repeated, another entirely unrelated route was changed over at the same time as the 81B; generally the conversions were tackled one route at a time. This was Muswell Hill's weekdays-only route 43, whose RTs departed between 14th June and 15th July. With no Sunday work of their own, the RMs took over all of Muswell Hill's Sunday operations on routes 102, 134/A and 212.

Another large, busy, cross-town route was next on the agenda for RMs, starting on 17th July. In this case, however, the Routemaster was not entirely new as route 63 had harboured a small Highgate-based contingent for some time, but the main bulk of the operation was Peckham's, whose RTs were displaced over a period of eight weeks. RM 1662, which was one of half a dozen licensed on 9th August, was an odd man out and introduced the revised grille with V-motif as a precursor to its general application on new vehicles starting with the last of Peckham's contingent on 11th September.

On Wednesday 14th August 1963, the very first Routemaster service withdrawal occurred when the operation of route 276 was discontinued, parts of it being covered by adjustments to other services. Its loss came as no surprise; the Saturday service had already been abandoned in October 1962, only eighteen months after the service had started as a speculative venture at stage 10 of the trolleybus conversion programme, and the route had never really established a niche for itself. The displaced RMs were despatched southwestwards to Norbiton and Putney to operate route 85 plus the Putney only shuttle run on route 85A. Putney garage was again in the news on 2nd October when its entire allocation for route 14 was changed to RM overnight. Once again, the vehicles were used ones from other sources, principally AECs from Cricklewood which received new Leylands in their place but also, on a temporary basis, a few Leylands surplus from Mortlake which were replaced on 1st November by AECs. These had just started arriving new off the production line after a year of Leylands. Meanwhile, on 17th October, the last remaining new Leylands had been allocated to Holloway to complete the modernisation of route 14 and also to establish a presence on night route N92.

Next on the list for modernisation was route 24. The first half dozen RMs for this arrived at Chalk Farm in time to start work on 7th November, but it was the next group which took the road on the 12th that held the great surprise for amongst their ranks, from RM 1743 onwards, were vehicles from which the offside route number provision was omitted. Except for a falling off in wartime years, it had always been London Transport practice, where possible, to display the route number on the offside of double deck vehicles in the red bus fleet and this was also done on the Routemaster Coaches. The decision to discontinue this policy, which was taken quietly in August 1962, had not been made common knowledge and, at the time RM 1743 took the road, offside route numbers were still in full use everywhere. The instruction to remove them was not sent to garages until late in November and, in the great majority of cases, they complied immediately.

Above **RM 1212 was one of the secondhand RMs transferred to Hounslow to work the Heathrow airport route 81B in summer 1963.** Gerald Mead

Withdrawal in August 1963 of Highgate's unsuccessful route 276 permitted the transfer of rolling stock westwards for the conversion of routes 85/A. Putney's RM 458 displays the neat 'lazy' blind arrangement adopted for the short 85A. Alan B. Cross

Below **RM 1768 was one of a fleet allocated new to Middle Row for route 7 on which it is photographed at Holborn in summer 1964. As has already been recorded, two years later this vehicle suffered a spectacular fire at Marble Arch. Routemasters with the new style front grille are a common feature by this time.** David Kirk

Final conversion of route 24 was achieved on 1st December. This had been only the second RM conversion where RTWs had been deposed (the first was the Putney allocation on route 14) and it was noteworthy in marking the first real displacement of these 8ft wide vehicles from passenger service, many of them being transferred to trainer duties on which large numbers were to end their days.

The last changeover for 1963 was scheduled to be Middle Row's route 7 starting on 1st December but, in fact, only about three-fifths of the required RMs were available before Christmas and final completion did not take place until 16th January 1964. After this, a short break was planned in the forward sweep of Routemasters on to new routes; instead there was to be a catching-up period when five major routes which had been left with part-RT and part-RM allocations as a result of the trolleybus replacement programme would be converted totally to RM, the routes concerned being 18, 23, 41, 64 and 123.

By the start of 1964, there were few major areas of the metropolis that RMs did not penetrate. Their novelty value had, by now, totally worn off and, although their continued purchase represented a substantial investment in the future of the undertaking, from the travelling public's point of view they did not represent a particularly great advance over the RT and were certainly no palliative for the growing dissatisfaction with the worsening level of service which London Transport was providing. London Transport consistently failed to maximise the public relations advantage of new vehicles by plastering them with advertisements prior to entry into service with the result that they never really looked pristine and new as the RTs had done in times gone by. Because of an agreement with the company's billposting staff, vehicles were always fully posted with advertisements almost as soon as they arrived at Aldenham from Park Royal, and it was a rare occurrence indeed for a vehicle to slip through the net.

Within London Transport, a crisis was looming; the job dissatisfaction and low morale amongst bus crews which had been increasingly apparent since the long bus strike of 1958 had now reached such proportions that, by the end of 1963, the staff shortage was twice that of only a year earlier. On 20th November 1963, the Government intervened and announced the setting up of an enquiry under the chairmanship of Professor Henry Phelps-Brown with the remit to review the pay and conditions of employment of the Board's drivers and conductors, along with means to increase efficiency. The Committee of Enquiry worked speedily and was able to issue an interim report on 12th December. In due course, wages were improved though, as it transpired, not sufficiently to turn the tide. The main relevance to the Routemaster story lies in the Board's evidence to the Committee which concluded that it could reduce the current Monday to Friday fleet from 7,600 to 7,100 buses whilst increasing overall seating capacity by ten per cent through using 69- and 77-seat front-entrance buses, 4,000 being envisaged for the central area and 700 for the country bus department; this was in addition to its plans for standee single deckers and the extension of driver-only operation. Of necessity, current thinking was being forced away from the conventional type of double decker, represented by the RM, to concepts which were very different indeed.

1964 was the last full year in which the Routemaster was produced in its traditional 64-seat form. During that year came the announcement that future orders would be for 30ft-long RMLs and, ominously for the Routemaster, that fifty Leyland Atlanteans and "a few" Daimler Fleetlines were to be purchased together with a variety of high capacity AEC Merlin and Reliance single deckers. On 21st October 1964, one-man operation commenced in the central bus fleet. Although on a small scale using RF single deckers, it was the foothold which London Transport needed, and the Union feared, towards wholesale adoption of the principle in times not so far distant.

February 1st 1964 was the starting date for the replacement of Tottenham's RTWs from routes 41 and 123, and the new RMs reflected the already mixed engine position at Tottenham with the last few of the remaining AEC order and far more of the latest, and last, Leyland batch being supplied. Completion on 1st March coincided with the commencement at Barking on route 23. Alperton's share of route 18 followed immediately on 11th March. Meanwhile Croydon's route 64 had been converted from 1st February onwards by vehicles transferred in from other garages.

New RMs from 1st April onwards were allocated to Upton Park for the conversion, which took until 22nd May to complete, of the trunk east-west route 15 plus its satellite route 100 which was a short, irregular, operation beyond the 15's eastern extremity. With one exception, Upton Park's new buses were numbered from RM 1866 upwards and were notable for being the first on London Transport with suffix letters to their registration numbers (ALD 866B etc). These new-style registration numbers, using rather smaller digits than before to fit within the same space, were not completely new, having been introduced with the A suffix in 1963 but by only a few licensing authorities. Like the great majority, the London County Council did not change over to the new scheme until 1964. The exception at Upton Park was RM 1630 which was a notable late delivery ten months behind schedule. Another 'first' at Upton Park worthy of mention was RM 1902 which introduced the omission of the brake cooling grilles as the latest design modification on production vehicles.

Below Left **Barking's first Routemasters comprised some of the last to be delivered with non-suffix lettered registrations. Their main sphere of operation was route 23 but night route N95 also became RM worked as witnessed by RM 1852 crossing an almost deserted Piccadilly Circus.** LT Magazine

Below Right **Route 15's conversion in April 1964 brought its Monday to Friday Upton Park allocation into line with the small Middle Row weekend working already worked by RMs. RM 1910 rounds Marble Arch during its first week in service.** Capital Transport

Among the RMs used to convert route 30 in July 1964 was RM 1577, the prototype illuminated advert vehicle. RM 1577 was the only one with an old style front end and offside route number, although the latter remained unused on this vehicle, the change in policy abandoning this feature having been implemented before it entered service. Dennis Battams

Illuminated exterior offside advertisements were a feature of most new RMs employed on route 30 when the replacement of RTLs commenced on 1st June. Of the half-dozen new buses at Putney with which the programme commenced, one (RM 1923) was an illuminated advert bus, the first of its kind to run on service in London although this feature had been tried by a number of provincial operators before this. Included amongst the contingent received at Putney was the test bed vehicle for illuminated advertisements, RM 1577, which though over a year old had not previously been in public service. Hackney's allocation on route 30, which was changed over completely on 1st July, consisted entirely of illuminated exterior advert buses, as did future conversions right through to January 1964. After a fortnight's pause, the fleet renewal programme resumed on 15th July at Muswell Hill with routes 134/A, followed six days later by Holloway. On 17th August, the 134 was completed with the first RM allocation at Potters Bar, the central bus fleet's most northerly outpost.

Croydon's turn came next, the target being the New Addington 130 group of services. History repeated itself and, as in the earlier case of the conversion of route 64, Croydon's RMs were drafted in from other garages such as Dalston and Hendon which had received the new buses licensed in September, delivery of which took RM fleet numbers above the two

The desire to place illuminated advert buses on routes serving inner London led to a number of reallocations as earlier RMs were relegated to suburban duties. In the case of Dalston's displaced RMs, a new home was found at Croydon on the busy New Addington feeder group 130. This West Croydon scene finds a couple of ex-Dalston vehicles in their early south London days, with RM 1594 on stopping service 130B (note the interesting blind layout) followed by RM 1589 on the 130 Express. Alan B. Cross

Facing Page Upper **Conversion of route 3 towards the end of 1964 brought into service the first RMs with continuous cream bands across the heater/ventilator intakes, this being the last modification to be made to the class during its production run. RM 2103 was one of the vehicles received by Chalk Farm for this conversion.** J.G.S. Smith

Facing Page Lower **1965 was the last year of production for short length 64-seater Routemasters. The first conversion of the year embraced Bow's allocation on routes 8 and 8A and included RM 2110 seen swinging out of London Bridge station forecourt where the narrow bus islands with their quaint, illuminated cast iron columns were redolent of a much earlier age.** Ken Blacker

Above **Reallocation of route 40 to Camberwell and Poplar in January 1965 coincided with a new RM allocation although the additional vehicles required came secondhand from other garages. RM 1190 was one of several on which Camberwell painted the lower half of the heater grille cream, presumably in the forlorn hope of making them more like vehicles built with or converted to full width bands.** C. Holt

thousand mark. The Board's policy was that all buses with illuminated exterior advertisements should enjoy a high profile on routes serving inner London which certainly excluded route 130. No such qualms prevented their use at Victoria on route 137 beginning on 21st October or on route 3, the last conversion of the year, for which Norwood was equipped between 1st November and 10th December with the smaller Chalk Farm allocation being changed overnight three days before Christmas. It was during this conversion that new buses began to emerge from Park Royal with continuous cream front bands, their introduction into service starting with RMs 2063-2068/2070 at Norwood on 9th November.

The arrival of 1965 saw the programme continuing much as before, although on a slightly lower scale. New vehicles into service during the first quarter were about twelve per cent fewer than in 1964, and they were now being delivered in the knowledge that the class in its basic 64-seat form was soon to cease production. The balance of new deliveries was earmarked for two major groups of routes, the 6 and 8. This meant a major injection of new rolling stock at Willesden which worked both route 6 and routes 8/A, with smaller deliveries to Bow for their 8 and 8A, and Hackney for the 6 and 6A. At Willesden, night route N91 was also converted. The programme took very nearly five months starting with Bow on 13th January and progressing to Willesden from 17th February and, finally, Hackney from 21st April. Hackney's final pair, RMs 2213 and 2216 licensed on 6th May, brought to an end the conversion of routes using new RMs of the conventional 64-seat variety. However, one further conversion, employing older RMs remains to be recorded; this occurred on 27th

January 1965 when route 40 was revised and reallocated from Upton Park to Camberwell and Poplar and converted to RMs at the same time.

This last batch of RM deliveries had witnessed a tentative start to the changeover from the long-standing red and cream livery to red and grey. The prototype for this, RM 2128, had taken the road on 29th January as part of the Bow contingent whilst the changeover proper, which commenced at RM 2210, was evident on the last few buses delivered to Hackney. A small number of newly delivered buses were not immediately required for service and two were used for experimental purposes, RM 2196 with Automotive Products at Leamington Spa and RM 2203 at the Chiswick experimental shop, duly entering service in September and December 1965 respectively. Three others, RMs 2214/2215/2217, were nominally licensed for a single day at Hanwell on 16th June but were not used at the time. The last ordinary RM of all to enter passenger service, apart from the now legendary RM 8 which still languished for much of its time at Chiswick was RM 2214 which completed a lengthy promotional tour of Japan before finally starting to earn its keep at Riverside on 1st February 1966. From the first delivery in May 1959 to the last in May 1965, the RM had progressed to a creditable total of 2120 and, in the process, had overcome the majority of its teething pains to become one of the most robust and long lived urban buses ever conceived. Apart from a few unavoidable casualties, the class was destined to remain complete right through the next decade and a half before obsolescence rather than fatigue was to dictate the first withdrawals in 1982.

CHAPTER SIXTEEN

THE RCLs

The success with which the 24 RMLs built in 1961 had operated at Finchley on route 104 made it inevitable that, in due course, many more thirty-footers would be purchased and it came as no surprise when the announcement was made in 1964 that production of standard length RMs would cease in the following year in favour of the longer version. Rather more unexpected was the news that the first of the longer vehicles to roll off the production line would be a batch of 43 Green Line coaches. Full details of the forthcoming new vehicles emerged towards the end of the year. They were to be called the RCL class and would be 65-seaters powered by the AV690 11.3 litre engine; their sphere of operation would be at Romford on routes 721, 722 and the summer seasonal 726, and at Grays on routes 723/A/B, and at both they would oust RTs which would, thereafter, no longer be scheduled for regular Green Line work.

In ordering comparatively expensive new double deckers for this network of services, London Transport was taking what can only be regarded as a calculated gamble. Once very heavily patronised, they had been losing trade to a worrying extent with the swing away from coaches to the competing suburban electric railway services becoming ever more apparent as the road approaches into London from the east became increasingly congested. London Transport pinned its hopes on the appeal of new vehicles reversing or at least stemming the trend and emphasised the "private car comfort" as a major part of their attraction.

Construction of the RCLs continued straight on from the last of the standard RMs, resulting in a break of almost two months in deliveries to the central bus fleet whilst the coaches were being built. Allocated fleet numbers RCL 2218–2260 (CUV218C–260C), they were classified as 8RM10 with unit numbers R2RH/3 2175–2217. The first to arrive, RCL 2218, did so on 5th May 1965; the remainder following in a steady flow between 11th May and 28th June.

Apart, of course, from their length, the new coaches closely resembled RMC 1469 in its revised form except that the words GREEN LINE were carried in the traditional position on the lower deck panels and not adjacent to the various bullseye transfers. External handrails had, however, been omitted with handles being sited instead on the insides of the doors. Unlike the RMLs, they had no emergency window fitted into the offside of the lower deck as the one on the rear platform met the legislation. Internally, they were immediately distinguishable from RMCs, apart from the obvious difference of length, because the polished moulding above the windows was omitted in line with the current practice and a plain yellow strip took its place. On the lower deck, a more fundamental difference lay in the whole appearance of the front bulkhead. Whereas on the RMC the panels over the windows on either side of the heater ducting were covered in a light brown coloured plastic material, on the RCL they were enamelled white, the same as the main ceiling panels. The duct itself was also very different in that the heater control was now sited vertically at window level, a modification introduced to coincide with the introduction of the illuminated advertisement panel although the RCLs did not carry these. On the RMCs the heater control was placed horizontally just below the ceiling and it remained there even after those on the entire central bus RM fleet had been resited to the lower position. An additional row of seats on each deck meant that 36 passengers were accommodated upstairs and 29 downstairs.

Left **The revised frontal style introduced as standard with the RCLs, giving a continuous sweep to the bottom line of bonnet and grille, the latter unimpeded by the registration plate, brought the Routemaster frontal design to its final and very satisfactory conclusion after years of trial and error. The first of the class, RCL 2218, waits in the sunshine at Aldgate on its very first day of operation, 2nd June 1965. A new base colour of yellow was adopted for the indicator blinds which also replaced the amber used hitherto on the RMCs.** Capital Transport

Facing Page **The RCL upper saloon did not differ much from that of the RMC, apart from the plain band above the windows replacing the polished strip and, of course, the extra length.** Capital Transport

Above **The lower saloon front bulkhead looked quite different from that of the RMC due to the repositioning of the heater control to a lower, vertical position.**

At a weight of 8–0–0, the RCL class was the heaviest Routemaster variant yet, and the more powerful 11.3 litre engine was deemed necessary because of this and to improve acceleration. As with the RMC, transmission was semi-automatic but, in the case of the RCL, the gearbox was not readily convertible to fully automatic, this now being considered an unnecessary option. The same axle ratio of 4.7:1 was used. This had proved ideal on the RMC, as indeed it had also done on the RFs used for Green Line work and, coupled with the higher power of the RCL, it gave a very fast ride. To cope with the extra weight, the front tyres were increased in size, but the rear ones remained unaltered. The suspension arrangement of the RMC, coil front and air rear, and the use of SCG transmission and Lockheed brakes was repeated but the electrical equipment and control panel differed from the RMC in being of CAV and not Simms manufacture.

As initially planned, Romford was to receive 29 RCLs and Grays 14, and Romford did indeed receive the 29 precisely as scheduled. Eighteen were available for conversion of route 721 from RT to RCL on 2nd June 1965, ten for route 722 a fortnight later on 16th June, and the last on 14th July for route 726. The only vehicle to be licensed ahead of the main 2nd June batch was RCL 2223 which was to be found out and about from 21st May onwards on driver familiarisation work. As already recorded in the RMC chapter, the plans for Grays were amended at the last

moment from 14 vehicles to 9, it having been found prudent to use RMCs on route 723B. The nine vehicles on routes 723/A started work from Grays on 1st July whilst, on the same date, the five no longer required for route 723/B were found employment at Hertford on route 715A.

Green Line Routemasters meet at Golders Green in 1966. Addlestone's RMC 1516, now almost three years old, contrasts with the shining newness of Romford's RCL 2230. Changing leisure patterns mean that a single Routemaster now copes with the Whipsnade traffic on route 726 whereas, a few years earlier, a small convoy of utility Daimlers may have been required. Michael Beamish

RCL 2244 speeds past one-time RT 925, now in the pale blue livery of Super Coaches who created interest by establishing a small network of local services in the Upminster area. As so often on route 722, and particularly on its outer end, the RCL is almost empty. Grays based RCL 2254 presents a fine sight at Aldgate on route 723A on 13th July 1965, as does Hertford's RCL 2249 at Marble Arch on the 715A. Unfortunately neither route experienced a rise in patronage as a result of these fine new vehicles; they came too late. Hertford's RCLs sometimes strayed on to the much longer and busier 715 as witnessed by RCL 2260, highest numbered of the class, as it heads for Guildford in February 1966.
Alan B. Cross

The RCL was, unquestionably, a smooth riding and most comfortable vehicle, its added length and weight giving what appeared to be a greater stability in motion than the RMC; with its deep and comfortable seats, speed and superb handling it could be claimed to mark the zenith in Routemaster development but, of course, it came too late to revive Green Line's

ailing fortunes. Being built in Park Royal's works at the same time was the batch of XA Leyland Atlanteans which, numbering fifty in all, was a larger class than the RCLs. Though having little in common with the RCLs in quality of construction and refinement of finish, the XAs appeared to point to the future, leaving the uneasy feeling that the RCLs, and the RMLs that were to follow, were heading for obsolescence in concept even as they were being built.

As was fully anticipated, the declining trade on route 715A was totally insufficient to support the RCLs but they lasted on it for nearly a year until 12th June 1966 when RFs returned. A similar position applied on route 722 which reverted to RT operation on the same date. The sixteen RCLs thus displaced were distributed, eight each, to Windsor and Tunbridge Wells for operation on route 704. At the tiny Tunbridge Wells garage, they comprised the entire vehicle complement and, at Windsor, the RCLs gained their first scheduled bus operation by taking over journeys on route 457D latterly covered by RMCs. On the very last day of 1966, route 709 was drastically pruned,

leaving just four journeys on Monday to Friday (two in each peak) and a Sunday trip principally to serve hospitals. This called for an allocation of two RCLs at Godstone, provided by service reductions at Grays and Romford releasing one vehicle each. The vehicle from Romford was of interest in having spent a month at Hertford prior to being required at Godstone. It had been the only RCL at Hertford at this time, all others having departed to route 704 some months earlier. The Grays service reductions saw the complete withdrawal of route 723A, the third sphere of operation from which the RCLs had been deposed in their young lives, for they were still not eighteen months old.

1967 was a year of comparative stability for the RCLs and it was not until the last month that any further changes took place. The saddest was the closure of Tunbridge Wells garage on 2nd December. That this tiny outpost of the empire had survived for so long was, perhaps, a little surprising but its closure was inevitable when space at Dunton Green became available to accommodate the 704s. These were not the only RCLs to arrive at

Both classes of Green Line Routemaster meet at Windsor, each now in the modified livery. The two RCLs on the left, both on route 704, are Windsor based RCL 2254 and Dunton Green's RCL 2247. Next to the latter stands Windsor's RMC 1456 on the 718. Alan B. Cross

Near the south eastern extremity of the Green Line network, RCL 2257 loads up for a scheduled Dunton Green working on route 431D even though it is a Windsor vehicle. The dents now left untreated in the front dome are a sign of declining standards.
E. Shirras

Dunton Green on 2nd December; its own Green Line service 705 was converted on a reduced frequency on the same date, with Windsor garage, at the other end of the route, receiving additional RCLs at the same time. The single deckers displaced from route 705 were the almost new RC class AEC Reliance 36-footers whose entry into service on 28th March 1965 had been much heralded with particular emphasis on their power and ability to travel at 65mph. Unfortunately, they did not display an ability to run reliably and their temporary withdrawal from service on arrival of the RCLs provided an opportunity to reassess the reliability problem. In order to provide the RCLs for route 705, the entire allocation was withdrawn from Grays garage whose 723 was converted to RMC operation. Slightly earlier in 1967, RCL 2250 at Grays had been modified to a 63-seater by the remo-val of the two-passenger offside longitudinal seat to provide more luggage accommodation, this feasibility study having been carried out in anticipation of diverting routes 704 and 705 via Heathrow Airport Central, a scheme which never came to fruition in double decker days. RCL 2250 was reclassified as 8RM10/1 and entered service in its modified form on 25th August, passing to Dunton Green with the RCL clearout from Grays on 2nd December. On 5th October 1968, it was de-licensed for reconversion to its original state, being officially reclassified back to 8RM10 on 8th November.

1968 was only a few days old when a repainting programme commenced with Romford's RCL 2220 going first. As was only to be expected, its emergence from Aldenham on 10th January was marked by the loss of its light green window surrounds. Gradually, the whole class was dealt with in the same way, though in a rather leisurely fashion which meant that the last in the old livery, RCL 2258 at Windsor, did not enter the works until 13th November. No RCLs ever received a full over-haul during their period of LT ownership which meant that body swapping never took place and the vehicles retained their true identities throughout. There is little more to record as having taken place during the London Transport regime and such items as there were represented further negative moves for the Green Line network. Romford's well known seasonal service 726 ran to Whipsnade Zoo for the last time on 6th September 1968 and, a little over a year later on 4th October 1969, route 704 was much reduced enabling six RCLs to return to Grays for route 723, demoting an equivalent number of RMCs to bus operation.

CHAPTER SEVENTEEN

THE MAIN RML BATCH

The final phase of Routemaster construction for London Transport marked a return to the RML class, the orders for which finally totalled exactly five hundred vehicles, RML 2261-2760. They began to roll off the production line immediately after the completion of the RCLs; RCL 2260 was delivered on 28th June 1965 and RML 2261 was handed over three days later on 1st July. The London bus world into which they emerged pristine from Park Royal was bracing itself for an era of great change and, because so much was beginning to happen, the arrival of the new RMLs went largely unremarked. Their thunder had

been stolen by the appearance just beforehand of the first of London's 'off-the-peg' double deckers, a batch of fifty Leyland Atlanteans with bodies from the same Park Royal stable as the Routemasters but exhibiting little similarity in subtlety of design or quality of finish, the passenger seats being just about the only substantial area of commonality between the two. XA 2 had been ceremonially displayed to the press at Stockwell garage on 17th June and plans had already been divulged for comparative trials between the two entirely different types of bus.

Experience in day to day operation was

quickly to show that, in terms of reliability, the Routemaster was streets ahead. Even after the lapse of two decades, the performance of the Atlanteans remains legendary for the abnormally high levels of lost mileage and lost sleep which it caused. On a purely statistical level, the RML was superior in returning an average fuel consumption of 7.8mpg on central London service whereas the Atlantean, which was also a 72-seater but approaching a ton heavier, managed only 6.6mpg. The mechanical problems which beset the Atlanteans seemed at times almost insurmountable and, whilst unfamiliarity on the part of Lon-

Facing Page **A meeting of extremes. London Transport buses all, but apart from livery and a few other minor things, the Routemaster and Atlantean had precious little in common. The solid aluminium alloy construction of the Routemaster exuded quality; the steel framed Atlantean gave the appearance of little care having gone into its design and it looked cheap. Events were to prove that, in London operating conditions, it would be quality that counted. RML 2264 stands alongside XA 6 and XA 7 at Park Royal just prior to delivery.** Lens of Sutton

Above **The first green Routemasters for country bus work (with the exception of prototype RM 2) were the fifty-strong batch RML 2306-2355. Livery was simplified compared with the red fleet as the mudguards and lifeguards were not picked out in black, giving a slightly more drab effect. The matching green radiator badge can be seen on RML 2308 at AEC's Southall works.** Colin Brown

don Transport's engineering staff has been cited as a contributory factor, it has to be remembered that Leyland's own staff were also usually in attendance and sometimes at their wits' end to provide enough vehicles for service. Eight green liveried Daimler Fleetlines, the XF class, performed somewhat better in comparative running, resulting in this model being selected in due course as the double deck generation to follow the RMLs. But the DMSs niche in London bus history has been far from happy and, even with the much improved Metrobuses, Titans and Olympians of later years, no family of double decker has

yet succeeded in matching the performance levels set by the RML back in 1965.

The 500 new RMLs closely resembled their 1961 predecessors mechanically, and AEC engines were specified for the whole batch. The AV590 continued to be deemed adequate despite the larger size of the vehicle but, apart from about the first 26, all were fitted for improved performance with a redesigned fuel pump which, not being of the normal in-line type, required a revision to the fuel feeds. The DPA (Distribution Pump type A) pump, rotating to distribute fuel to each injector at the required moment, had first been tried experi-

mentally in January 1962 on RMs at Cricklewood and Stonebridge, and had proved its worth. Engines with this fitment often strayed in later years onto ordinary RMs depending on availability. RML 2368 achieved a form of notoriety early in its life when, even before it entered service, its AEC engine was exchanged for a Leyland unit in March 1966. This was a requirement for a promotional trip to Oslo and the vehicle remained in this unique form afterwards, retaining a Leyland engine with two successive overhauls when it changed identity to RML 2397 in December 1972 and RML 2295 in November 1979.

The new RML batch introduced the bus version of the revised bonnet and wing treatment first seen on the RCLs, the difference being that the RML had only a single headlamp on each side whereas the RCLs had twin fitments. This marked the culmination of London Transport's strivings to achieve aesthetic perfection for the front end of the Routemaster, and it certainly eliminated much of the fussiness of the first standard production design of six years earlier. It was only a pity that, with wing and grille units of various styles in use, garages soon managed to mix them up, sometimes producing a lop-sided effect through having different depth wings on either side. The RMLs were not immune from this confusion and it soon became possible to see older style front end units fitted to them. In other respects, the design features of the RMLs, both inside the body and out, followed the most recent batch of RMs. It appeared at first as if the fitment of an illuminated bulkhead advertisement panel had now been adopted as standard and it came as something of a surprise that the 110-vehicle batch RML

2351-2460 did not have them. One of these, RML 2368, the Oslo vehicle mentioned above, was fitted with an illuminated panel for this same trip; the remaining 109 were brought up to standard between April and September 1968. Exterior offside illuminated panels were a feature of one hundred vehicles (RML 2561-2660).

Whereas the 24 earlier RMLs had been given the same R2RH chassis coding as the

shorter RMs, the new batch was differentiated by the designation R2RH/1 with the numbers running in order with the bonnet numbers as R2RH/1 2275-2774. Multi-sourcing of mechanical and electrical components continued on from the pattern established by the RMs, lending a fair degree of complexity to the internal type designations of which there were seven variants for the 500 vehicles. These can be summarised as follows:—

7RM7/1	RML 2267-2291	CAV electrics, Lockheed brakes.
1/7RM7/2	RML 2261-2266	Simms electrics, Lockheed brakes.
	RML 2292-2310	
2/7RM7/3	RML 2311-2350	Simms electrics, Clayton Dewandre brakes.
	RML 2461-2560	
2/7RM7/4	RML 2351-2460	As 2/7RM7/3 but without exterior illuminated advertisement panel.
2/7RM7/5	RML 2561-2610	As 2/7RM7/3 but with exterior illuminated advertisement panel.
3/7RM7/6	RML 2611-2660	CAV electrics, Clayton Dewandre brakes. Exterior illuminated advertisement panel.
3/7RM7/7	RML 2661-2760	As 3/7RM7/6 but without exterior illuminated advertisement panel.

Internally the production RMLs closely resembled the final deliveries of RMs except, of course, for the additional bay and the extra row of seats which the greater length provided. LT Museum H/16315

Left The exterior illuminated advert panel sat more pleasingly on the side of an RML compared with an RM, the extra length of the vehicle enabling it to be centred in relation to the windows. RML 2577 was one of 100 RMLs so fitted and is seen at Brixton in May 1968. Gerald Mead

Right Lifting the Routemaster in an emergency. RML 2691 is used to demonstrate the means by which the front end could easily be lifted to permit a suspended tow after removal of the grille and the securing of special attachments to the front frame. LT Museum

The classification 2/7RM7/4 became redundant in 1968 with the fitment of illuminated interior advertisement panels to this group of vehicles which then became 2/7RM7/3; further classifications introduced in later years as a result of modifications are mentioned in the next volume.

Six years into the Routemaster programme, the design had reached a definitive stage at which few modifications proved necessary during the production cycle. From May 1966 onwards, the figure shown on the nearside legal panel and also signwritten in the driver's cab changed from 7-12-0 to 7-15-0, current practice being to round off to the nearest 5cwt. A few months earlier, in October 1965, a rear end modification was approved whereby the offside direction indicator was taken out of the rear frame and resited in the corner panel some inches to the right of its former location, a modification evidently required to comply with revised Ministry of Transport regulations. It is not known exactly where the changeover came but it has since spread through much of the earlier fleet including very many ordinary RMs as a result of rear end replacements.

By 1965, it was becoming rare to find new buses still being constructed with old-style tungsten internal lighting systems, except for the Routemasters. Elsewhere, it was almost universally recognised that better illumination was required on urban buses and fluorescent lights were now the norm. Even London Transport was belatedly coming around to this way of thinking, though too late for the RMLs. However, as a step towards a brighter environment, RMLs built from August 1966 onwards, starting with RML 2561, were given white (officially magnolia) lower saloon ceilings which, although undoubtedly brighter, seemed to match the Routemaster decor less well than the traditional sung yellow. Several years were to elapse before older Routemasters were similarly treated but, in due course, white was applied whenever ceilings needed complete repainting. However, upper deck ceilings remained yellow for fear of nicotine staining. In May/June 1967, three vehicles, RMLs 2674-2676, went even further by introducing an

entirely new decor of light grey window surrounds and side panelling, white ceilings and a blue and green seat moquette. The ensemble looked very fine when new and was later adopted as standard on many rear engined single deckers and other subsequent types; unfortunately, the moquette, which was also used fairly extensively on the Underground, quickly lost its attractiveness as the colours faded more rapidly than with many earlier designs, and light grey panelling, although very popular for a while, made for a cold looking environment. These three buses survived an overhaul with their grey interiors, becoming RML 2678, 2676 and 2679 respectively in August and September 1974, but at the next overhaul the grey rexine was repainted in the customary Routemaster burgundy and the seats were retrimmed in standard moquette. The last to keep its grey interior was RML 2679 (ex RML 2676) in October 1981.

The RMLs started arriving just after a major upheaval had hit London with the coming into office of the Greater London Council on 1st April 1965 as a result of the Local Government Act 1963. Unlike the London County Council before it, the GLC included amongst its wide ranging powers over an enlarged London, a responsibility for public transport, the subsequent exercise of which was to bring a fresh approach to the capital's public transport, marred alas by instability and potential infighting. This was the start of an era of great change, shortly to be compounded by Barbara Castle's far reaching measures to inject new life into the transport world, which were to spell doom for crew operated buses in most environments, and heralded the end of production for the Routemaster. It was duly decided that RML 2760 would be the last, though the final ones to be delivered were RML 2754 and 2756 on 8th February 1968. The Routemaster production lines at Park Royal were dismantled and many workers, who had regarded the Routemaster as their meal ticket for several years, were laid off.

The final 30-month production run of RMLs had included the first Routemasters in green Country Bus (as distinct from Green Line

coach) livery since RM 2. The hundred buses concerned, RML 2306-2355 and 2411-2460, were modified to run in semi-automatic mode. Although they injected a degree of modernity into an otherwise rapidly ageing fleet, the wisdom of purchasing them was not universally accepted. As with the RTs many years earlier, the need for such high specification vehicles on country bus work was questioned. Even more in doubt was the long term benefit to the fleet of so many vehicles which had to be crew operated at a time when the economy of driver-only single deckers was becoming widely established and the industry was confidently expectant of obtaining authority for single manned double deckers in the not too distant future. Furthermore, the RMLs on country work quickly accumulated complaints from conductors and passengers alike that the lower saloons were colder and more draughty than on RTs despite the heating system fitted. Tests carried out with temperature measuring probes proved that this was indeed the case. It was concluded that the probable explanation lay in the additional vehicle length altering the aerodynamics and causing a stronger in-draught not noticeable on slower central area work. Nothing more could be done about it.

By the end of the nineteen-sixties, the future of the Routemaster looked bleak as hordes of rear engined single deckers, followed by similarly engined double deckers, took to the road. It looked very likely at one stage that the RMLs would not be required for long enough to see out their intended lifespan. This was before the now well known vagaries of the infamous Merlins, Swifts and Fleetlines brought chaos to a once well-ordered scene, and before the perfidious changes in political climate rendered it unwise, and restrictions on capital investment made it well-nigh impossible, to dispense with the RMLs until much later.

Below **The last RML to be built, seen in Hyde Park during a special department store promotion in May 1968.** Capital Transport

CHAPTER EIGHTEEN

MID-SIXTIES AND RESHAPING

Chapter 15 ended with the closing down of production of standard length Routemasters at RM 2217. The light had dawned that longer, higher capacity buses were both commercially desirable and operationally feasible so, henceforth, all new production for London Transport was to be of 30-footers. The enormous task of replacing the RT family was well in hand with the first priority being to dispose of the Leylands, both RTLs and RTWs, and those AECs not fitted with saloon heaters. A short pause occurred to enable the RCLs to be built for Green Line but, with the delivery of RML 2261 from Park Royal on 1st July 1965, what was destined to be the last phase of the Routemaster programme began in earnest.

Included within the first batch of one hundred were fifty green buses for country area operation but the first scheduled delivery was of red buses. However, the central bus department was not yet ready to place these into service. Their plans were to run comparative trials between the RMLs and the fifty XA class Leyland Atlanteans now being delivered, the initial scheme being to allocate RMLs to Middle Row and Highgate for routes 7 and 271 respectively, and the XAs to Chalk Farm and Stamford Hill for routes 24 and 67, swapping them over later in the trial. Middle Row was later ruled out as unsuitable because

of the tight access and Tottenham substituted with routes 76/34B but, in any event, no start was likely to be made until November. The country bus department, desperate for modern double deck rolling stock required new buses ahead of this.

The busy jointly-scheduled network of trunk routes centred around Godstone, 409/410/411, plus the Thursday and Sunday hospital service 482, were earmarked for RML operation from 3rd October 1965. The vast majority of the operation was the responsibility of Godstone garage requiring an allocation, including spares, of 28 buses, but a one bus allocation existed at East Grinstead for route 409 and, similarly, at Reigate for routes 410 and 411. On 10th August, the first of the new RMLs to be licensed, RMLs 2278/2279, were dispatched to Godstone for training drivers at all three garages, joined afterwards by RML 2280. By the start date of 3rd October, green RMLs had been arriving on the scene, starting with RML 2306 on 17th September, but by no means enough existed to enable the changeover to take place unaided. No fewer than seventeen red RMLs started their working lives at Godstone (RMLs 2278-2280, 2287, 2288, 2293, 2295-2305) working alongside eleven green ones; the single vehicles at East Grinstead and Reigate were also green.

The green RMLs made a welcome addition to the Routemaster scene and they looked very handsome, when new, in their livery of Lincoln green, including wings and lifeguards, with Chiswick cream relief. Their central area counterparts were in traditional red livery with pastel grey middle band; when the next delivery commenced at RML 2356, the relief band had darkened to mist grey. Seven of the red RMLs departed from Godstone ready to take up duty at Tottenham on 1st November, new green replacements having arrived, and the remainder were released for service at Stamford Hill on 1st December.

The central bus department's RML versus XA trials were now ready to commence with the receipt of 31 RMLs at Tottenham to replace RTWs on 1st November. On 7th November, the first Atlanteans entered service at Chalk Farm on route 24, displacing RMs to Putney and Riverside to release RTWs from the 74 group. Somewhat earlier than

Above **Country Routemasters in their heyday. A line-up of some of the many RMLs which entered service from Garston garage on 20th March 1966. Unfortunately Garston's standards were not of the highest and these vehicles did not stay pristine for long.** Capital Transport

The first work for the main batch of RMLs was the conversion of country area routes 409, 410 and 411. In October 1965, prior to being needed for the RML/XA comparison trials, brand new red RML 2304 is among those helping out until enough green ones became available, and it makes a colourful contrast with 'native' RML 2309 inside Godstone garage. Capital Transport

It was a rare occurrence indeed for Routemasters (with the exception of Green Line ones) to enter service without advertisements already in place. One which escaped the net and proudly exhibits its newness is Tottenham's RML 2273. Route 76 was linked in the comparative trials with XAs on route 24 commencing in November 1965. Fred Ivey

this, back in September, two other routes had become RM operated through redeploying surplus vehicles, namely the 46 at Willesden and the 33 at Upton Park, of which the latter was a surprising choice being a somewhat low key operation which ceased entirely on 31st December 1966. A further changeover had occurred on 3rd October when route 55 received RMs consequent upon its reallocation from Southall to Hanwell, the smaller Turnham Green allocation also being converted at the same time.

An interesting experiment carried out during 1965 was the blanking out of the entire rear destination and route display, except for the route number itself, on all of Tottenham's and Mortlake's RMs working on route 73 (and also on RTs working from Garston on route 321). The idea was to test whether any information other than the route number was needed at the back of double deckers; no such information was carried on the low-height RLH class, nor was it specified for the new Atlanteans and Fleetlines. It was eventually decided to retain the destination display but to dispense with the via points. The experiment ceased offically on 29th November but the new standard display had already been introduced with the Godstone fleet on 3rd October and the RMLs carried just a large route number in the rear upper box. This arrangement was somewhat illogical because the display above the platform remained unchanged. Two sets of blinds now had to be printed and garage stockholdings were made more complex. The new type blinds duly spread throughout the fleet but, quite often, side blinds including via points were fitted in rear boxes without causing any obvious harm.

The second stage of country conversion occurred on 21st November 1965 when nineteen new green RMLs started work at Northfleet to cover eighteen scheduled workings, primarily on the very busy route 480 but with odd journeys on a variety of routes including 480A, 487A, 488/A, 495A and 496A. Together with the earlier Godstone area conversion, this used up 49 of the 50 green RMLs in the 2306-2355 batch and, with the 2411-2460 batch not due to come on stream until the new year, emphasis reverted to the central area. Here it was the turn of Stamford Hill on 1st December, more than half of its allocation for route 67 being ex-Godstone buses supplemented by the first eight new ones (RML 2356 upwards) from the second red batch. The displaced RMs went to Walworth for route 45, displacing RTWs whose demise was now running at a very fast tempo.

Top **The onward march of RM 64-seaters in place of RTs continued unabated even after manufacture had ceased, but now employing used vehicles deposed from busier services by new RMLs. Upton Park's RM 1896 rounds a corner in a typical Silvertown setting on short lived route 33.** Alan Nightingale

Centre **The 1965 experiment with reduced rear blind displays at Mortlake and Tottenham was meant to cover only route 73. However RM 1260 escaped the net when transferred from Mortlake to Riverside in early October, its new garage failing to remove the masking for a while afterwards.** Ken Blacker

Right **RML 2345 was one of Northfleet's contingent of new green RMLs placed into service in November 1965. It is seen passing through Dartford at the start of its country career, all ten years of which were to be spent at Northfleet.** Alan B. Cross

1966 was probably the RMLs' finest year as they entered service in droves, making their presence felt in many new areas of London and, in the process, eliminating the RTW class except for those which managed to cling on as driver training buses. However, for London Transport as a whole, things were looking bleak and the undertaking was reaching its worst crisis since the disastrous bus strike of 1958. A ban imposed by almost all central bus garages on working rest days or overtime began on 23rd January and lasted through to 26th February. It was a sign of extreme frustration at the continuing staff shortages and service reductions which, amongst the January cuts, included a 9% reduction in Sunday mileage. The effect of the ban was catastrophic and brought a sharp management response with the total suspension of some forty routes from 30th January. Consent was given to private operators to break London Transport's monopoly and provide temporary cover over 34 sections of route and, although most services resumed operation later, there were two (98B and 235) which did not and these continued to be covered by private operators. In such a depressed atmosphere, the introduction of new buses was by no means the staff morale booster that it had been in earlier years.

The final eighteen Atlanteans from the batch of fifty were delivered in time to enable the conversion of Highgate's route 271 to take place on 1st January 1966, RMs heading for Chalk Farm to complete the removal of RTWs from route 45. From 17th April, the whole of the eight strong XF class of Daimler Fleetlines was drafted into Highgate from East Grinstead, still in green livery, to operate alongside Atlanteans on route 271, thus broadening the scope of the comparative trials with RMLs. In the meantime, RMLs had been used to inaugurate Finchley's new Monday to Friday route 104A from 24th January. With the formation of the GLC in 1965 and the cessation of vehicle licensing by the old Metropolitan District Councils, their registration marks had passed to the GLC, and Finchley garage had the honour of displaying the oddity of an ex West Ham registration on a London bus in public service for the first time with the licensing of RML 2407 on 21st January and RML 2405 just afterwards. The batch began with JJD364D, and, coincidentally, many of the earlier ones in it started their working lives at West Ham.

An incursion of some 40 RMLs into east London was the next plan for the central fleet. Most of the action centred on West Ham garage as the main provider of the routes due for

Top **Stamford Hill garage was destined to enjoy three separate spells of RML operation, the first of which was on route 67 in December 1965. RML 2298 left when the class moved away in July 1966 to make way for Atlanteans.** Ron Lunn

Centre **The first new central bus route — as distinct from a trolleybus conversion one — to use RMLs from the start was Finchley worked 104A in January 1966. One of the original 30-footers, RML 898, stands at the Golders Green terminus.** Michael Beamish

Left **West Ham and Poplar, the two garages which had introduced Routemasters on trolleybus replacement, received RMLs together in February 1966 for the 5 group of routes. RML 2263 was among those allocated to West Ham.** E. Shirras

Although RMs with non-opening front windows had appeared at a few locations other than the original ones, this really gained impetus when Poplar and West Ham received their RMLs. RM 203, which moved to Riverside, was one of many older Routemasters which provided a low key modernisation for route 11. C. Holt

conversion which were the 5 group and the 249/A. Poplar had a minority allocation on the former and Walthamstow on the latter. West Ham received part of its requirement and Poplar its full quota on 1st February, followed by Walthamstow on 13th February and the rest for West Ham on 1st March. The many RMs displaced by this conversion, the last involving the central fleet for a while, found their way to Dalston and Riverside for the most famous of London's routes, the 11, which had held on to its RTWs longer than most. Riverside's night route N89 was also converted at this time.

The RTWs even suffered at the hands of the next batch of green RMLs although indirectly as a result of surplus green RTs being repainted red. The first recipient of the new series was High Wycombe on 20th February 1966 where the larger buses enabled a saving of two scheduled buses on route 363. As with so many country area operations, the 363 schedule was not totally self-contained and RMLs would also work journeys on routes 305, 326, 362 and 455. The same applied to Garston where an ambitious conversion embracing all of routes 306/A, 311, 347, and new route 347A on 20th March also took in journeys on routes 318 and 346/C/D. Hemel Hempstead had a small allocation on routes 347/A and thus gained two RMLs for these. Finally, on 15th May, it was the turn of Windsor and Harlow which received ten and nine buses respectively. The main object of the conversion at

Windsor was the Slough Trading Estate group of routes 446/A/B but linked to them were a whole range of journeys on routes 353, 400, 417, 445, 460 and 484. At Harlow, a wide scale interworking of New Town and country routes found RMLs on routes 396, 397/A/B, 804/A, 805/A/B and 806 but here the total operation required twenty scheduled buses so RTs remained active alongside the RMLs and were, in fact, slightly in the majority. With the completion of the second batch of green RMLs, nine country garages were now custodians of the class with holdings ranging from one bus right up to 28. Vast political changes just over the horizon were to mean that these would be the last new double deckers to be delivered to London Transport for country area operation.

Back in the centre, an event had occurred on 18th April 1966, the ripples from which were to spread far and wide. The pioneer Red Arrow service, 500, had commenced operation introducing the concept of driver-only high capacity buses to one of the busiest parts of the network and, though the inevitable comments about 'cattle truck' travel were heard, the experiment was perceived to hold great promise. Amongst other repercussions, it heralded the end for Routemaster production. A month later, on 15th May, the entry into service of new red RMLs was resumed with the busy south suburban route 37 as their target. The Putney allocation was dealt with first, releasing RMs to Brixton where they took over route 95 from the last few RTWs still in passenger

service. The first of the major post-war classes had succumbed to the advance of the Routemaster; next in line were the RTLs whose numbers were fast diminishing.

On 1st June, Stockwell's share of route 37 was three-quarters converted to RML, the remainder following on the 12th. The RMs not required after the 1st were temporarily delicensed but revived on the 12th, some to remain where they were replacing RTLs on route 88 whilst others departed to Victoria for route 52. Willesden's share of route 52 had already been converted on the 15th of the previous month using an assortment of spare RMs gathered from various garages. Night service N87 worked by Stockwell and Brixton was another operation to receive RMs. 12th June also saw the first total reallocation of a garage's RMLs when Chalk Farm received the Tottenham contingent from routes 76 and 34B to work on route 24, the XAs moving in the opposite direction as part of the ongoing comparative trials. On 10th July, which was the next but one major date for RML moves, Highgate gained Stamford Hill's RMLs for route 271 but lost its Atlanteans and Fleetlines, the latter going back to the country area although they later made a return trip to the centre. In these cases, Chalk Farm's gain was Tottenham's loss and Highgate benefited at the expense of Stamford Hill. The RMLs were performing almost faultlessly whereas the rear engined buses were becoming a nightmare to operate and maintain.

Service reliability on route 24 improved immeasurably in June 1966 when RMLs arrived from Tottenham in exchange for XAs. RML 2270 speeding along Whitehall represents one of Chalk Farm's first RML intake. On the other hand route 76 deteriorated and RMs, and later even RTs, were often called upon to help out where Atlanteans had failed. RM 1818 and XA 33 meet at the Victoria terminus. G.H.F. Atkins/ Michael Beamish

A long established feature of interest concerning Garston's workings was its large number of school and works journeys. RMLs participated in these as witnessed by RML 2420 at Bushey schools along with RT 2940.
J.G.S. Smith

Many RMLs went into Upton Park on 1st July 1966, including the unique Leyland engined RML 2368 back from its overseas tour, followed by another batch on the 10th, all to work on route 15 and its subsidiary route 100. The ousted RMs went both east and west: to Shepherds Bush to complete route 88 and to Hornchurch for route 165 and nearby North Street for route 174, the last two giving a small network of Routemasters out in the far eastern suburbs based on Romford.

A whimsical experiment carried out at this time was the fitting of advertisements to the roof of Holloway's RM 1977 on route 134. Colour-fast stove enamelled advertisements on aluminium sheet with an adhesive backing were applied along the roof on either side of the bus, extolling Gordon's Gin. There must have been a large latent market of customers wishing to look down on the roofs of buses for RM 833 at Cricklewood and RM 1166 at Walworth were also subsequently treated, following which a contract requiring a further 47 was undertaken in February 1967. Newly overhauled RMs were selected from fourteen garages endowed with roof gantries and whose buses served central London. The advertisements were carried for three years, unseen by the average man in the street, until the contract expired in 1970.

The 6 group was chosen for the next intake of RMLs, Hackney's on 1st September and Willesden's on 1st October. Included amongst the Hackney intake were the first RMLs to run in service with illuminated offside advertisements. Hackney's displaced RMs were sent to Hendon for route 113 whilst Willesden's made the trip to Alperton for route 83. 1st November saw Putney receiving its second batch of RMLs, this time for route 14 which was where the programme halted temporarily. After the manufacture of RML 2598, a break in production had been agreed to allow an order from British European Airways for Routemasters to be progressed and no further RML deliveries were expected until March 1967. However, Routemaster activity for 1966 had not quite ceased. Putney's RMs from route 14 were shared between Norwood and Stockwell for route 2B. The year 1966 ended on an unhappy note with many service cuts implemented on the very last day of the year in both central and country departments. As a result, Poplar's requirement for RMLs ceased and they moved across as a batch to Leyton for whom they were the first Routemasters of any sort, it being a rare occurrence for an RML

Top **The central fleet's two most easterly garages both received RMs on 1st July 1966, and the class suddenly took on a high profile in and around Romford. Seen a few days later, Hornchurch's RM 1869 has already had its new garage letters applied.** Michael Beamish

Centre **Due to a long standing restriction agreed between London Transport and the union, examples of interworking between routes within the central bus fleet were rare. A famous exception to the rule was route 100 which worked off from route 15, one of whose newest Routemasters, RML 2521, is seen at Barking in its first month of operation, July 1966.** Capital Transport

Right **September 1966 found Hendon in receipt of its second allocation of RMs, this time for route 113. The Sunday use of RMs on route 240 was already well-established but RM 2200 was one of the later, route 113 batch. Alongside it at Edgware are Enfield's RT 3465 and Edgware's RF 412.** Michael Beamish

garage not to have had RMs first. Here they inaugurated new route 262, which was a side effect of the withdrawal of RT worked route 26, and they also appeared at night on route N96. Upton Park's route 33 was another 31st December 1966 casualty, but its number immediately reappeared at the opposite end of London on what was in effect a localisation of the western end of route 73 to which most of the Mortlake allocation was transferred. In the country department, four RMLs surplus through cuts established a second foothold at Windsor garage on Slough circular service 400.

With a working surplus reduced from £5.5 million to £1.1 million, and an overall loss of £5.9 million, plus a 7.2% drop in passengers, 1966 had been a very bad year but, out of ill had come a five-day week and two pay increases for staff which, it was thought, might help reliability and, much more importantly, a new vision of the future had been unveiled. September had seen the publication of the famous, wide-ranging, report entitled 'Reshaping London's Bus Services'. It advocated a big extension of driver only operation, with single deckers replacing a large number of double deckers and the ultimate elimination

of all conductor operation, greater use of flat-fare buses in the centre and on suburban satellite services, standee buses on new short and heavily used routes, and new fare collection methods. Some trunk routes with large double deckers were envisaged as remaining for some time though many would be shortened and, in addition to flat fare operation, there would also be some conventional one-man operation on suburban services. In the country area, the route pattern was not expected to change much but there would be a big expansion of one-man operation. The report, which was backed soon afterwards by an initial £1m order for 150 Merlin single deckers as a firm confirmation of the Board's intent, left no doubt that the present contract for Routemasters would be the last.

RML deliveries were resumed in March 1967 but there seemed to be little haste to put them to work. Holloway was the first recipient, between 1st May and 1st June, resuming the conversion of route 14 where it had been left off after the Putney allocation six months previously. Putney came next with its third RML intake commencing on 1st June and destined for route 74, the RMs from these two conversions passing to Stockwell and

Cricklewood for route 2. On the minus side peak hour service 293 which Middle Row had operated since the January 1962 trolleybus conversion ran for the last time on 16th June. 1st July found RMLs taking over route 74B at Riverside in a clean sweep, resulting in Plumstead getting its first ever RM intake, for route 53. The New Cross share of this route had to await the arrival of RMLs for routes 207/A. This major west London trunk service first obtained RMLs on 1st September at both Uxbridge and Hanwell but, whereas the smaller Uxbridge contingent was completed by 1st October, Hanwell's requirement took until 15th November to be fulfilled. Numbered amongst its intake were the three with experimental grey interiors (RML 2674-2676) whilst on 1st October the first vehicles in the 2700 series took to the road. It was now known that this was almost as high as the Routemasters would go and that RML 2760 would be the last. During the final few months, little interest had attended the entry into service of new RMLs; new and more exciting machines were now on the production lines.

During October, a start had been made in placing RMs from Hanwell into Hackney for route 22, even though route 53 was not quite

complete. Full conversion of these allocations, and also of Battersea's share of route 22 and Peckham's route 173, had to wait until 11th November, when the final RML allocation began. Croydon garage was to be the recipient for the 130 group of services to New Addington and, on the same date as its first RMLs arrived, it lost its eleven bus RM allocation on route 64 to Thornton Heath. Though fast initially, conversion of the 130 group slowed after mid-December in line with a slowing down of RML deliveries as production edged towards a close. At the end of 1967, Croydon was short of ten RMLs although two were in stock ready to be licensed on 1st January. At the start of 1968, nine Routemasters remained to be delivered from the manufacturer: RMLs 2751/2752/2754-2760. The last pair, 2754/2756, were taken into stock on 8th February, without ceremony, marking the close of an era. The last to enter service were 2754/2755 at Croydon and the highest numbered of the class, RML 2760, which was allocated as a one-off at Upton Park, all on 1st March. The very last of all were two overseas tour buses, RML 2756 which went into service on 22nd May at Putney and RML 2548 at Chalk Farm eight days later.

A very quiet period now followed, effectively the lull before the storm when the first of the suburban satellite schemes would commence on 7th September 1968 with the start of Reshaping. The only new Routemaster allocation during this time was a small Clapton share on route 257 for which it received its first RMs on 23rd March 1968.

The unusual quietness was broken on 31st May by the emergence from an Aldenham repaint of Highgate's RM 523 without its grey relief band, the first bus in a small-scale study to test the feasibility of going to an all-red livery to save costs. RMs 494, 496, 508, 514 and 520 followed, also at Highgate, and the overwhelming opinion was that they did not look at all good. Fortunately, officialdom took the same view and all were restored to normal livery in September 1968.

New Merlins were now flooding in and the climax came on 7th September when 22 new one-man services were introduced by the central bus department, including Red Arrows, suburban flat-fare satellite schemes and conventional one-man operations. Especially notable were the large OMO networks at Wood Green and Walthamstow. Numerous other changes took place throughout the fleet and many Routemasters were made redundant. Consequent rearrangements saw the transfer of all of Walthamstow's RMLs plus some of Willesden's to Hornchurch to take over from RMs on route 165. Services converted to RM for the first time included route 29 (Wood Green and Highgate garages), 35 (Camberwell and Hackney) and 171 (Tottenham and New Cross). Reallocations brought Kingston onto route 85 with its first RMs and, similarly, Enfield on route 127 whilst Leyton, which already had RMLs, now gained RMs for route 69. A new RM route, the 8B, gave additional work for the class at Cricklewood, but Wood Green's route 269 was withdrawn.

On 29th November, the RTL class ran in service for the last time, the final few being at Willesden. Two of the three post-war classes had now gone, though the hastening in recent months of RTL withdrawals had been more the result of the influx of Merlins than of

Croydon's route 130 and its various offshoots marked the end of an era in being the last upon which new RMLs were placed, production now being on its final run down. A very dirty RML 2744 is seen at East Croydon. *Alan B. Cross*

The all-red livery tried out on half-a-dozen RMs at Highgate was fortunately short-lived. RM 514 was dealt with at an Aldenham repaint in June 1968 and was photographed at work in Whitehall soon afterwards. *Capital Transport*

Routemasters. Next day, the final ignominy hit Highgate's route 143 when it was shortened and its RMs replaced by MB class single deckers. At the same time, RM worked route 55 from Turnham Green and Hanwell garages was withdrawn, being replaced in part by flat-fare MBSs on the Ealing based E route network and partly by new RT route 274. The RMs from all three garages were employed to convert route 180 at Abbey Wood and Catford garages from 1st December. Another 29th November change involving Hanwell was the transfer of a few of its RMLs to Southall along with route 207A. Shortly before Christmas, a number of unlicensed RMs were revitalised at Poplar and Hackney to permit the ousting of RTs from route 106.

With more than four hundred Merlin single deckers already in stock by the end of 1968,

the London bus scene was going through a transition more rapid than ever before as old traditions were swept away and new ones instituted. So, too, was the bus industry as a whole, and the repercussions of this were to bear heavily on London Transport in times to come. The first hint of impending change had been the shock announcement by the BET group in November 1967 that it had accepted an offer from the Transport Holding Company for its substantial bus interests in the United Kingdom. The vast majority of stage carriage services outside the municipal sector were thus under state ownership, leaving the way clear for a major revision from which London Transport would not be insulated. The Government's clear concern over public transport as evinced by the most forceful of Transport Ministers, Barbara Castle, and by her

Route 171 was one of a number of RT services converted to Routemaster on the first day of Reshaping. RM 1743, newly received at Tottenham, prepares to depart from the garage on the long run to Forest Hill. Michael Beamish

Southall's holding of RMLs commenced in November 1968 with duties on the 207A but ceased with its withdrawal in May 1971 in favour of augmentation on parallel services 49 and 207. RML 2707 did not move far — only from Hanwell to nearby Southall — to continue its service on the Uxbridge Road. E. Shirras

successor, Richard Marsh, was manifested by the new Bus Grants scheme which, after 1st September 1968, provided encouragement for operators to renew their fleets with approved types of bus by giving 25% grants towards the cost of purchase. Needless to say, the approved types did not include buses of Routemaster configuration. October 1968 saw the registration by the Transport Holding Company of London Country Bus Services Ltd with a nominal capital of £100, to be used, if necessary, to take over the Country Bus & Coach Department of London Transport. The Greater London Council, with wide transport powers which it was anxious to exercise to the full, had produced its own White Paper on Transport in London, advocating that it should take over control of London Transport's business within its territory. The Government was

known to be sympathetic to this idea, hence the formation of London Country Bus as a repository for the operations beyond the scope of the GLC. Meanwhile, the far reaching Transport Act 1968 had received Royal Assent on 29th October and, on 14th November, Richard Marsh announced that the vesting date for three new state-owned transport authorities created under its powers would be 1st January 1969. These were the National Bus Company, the National Freight Corporation and the Scottish Transport Group, the first of which would hold all the bus assets in England and Wales formerly with the Transport Holding Company including, of course, the embryonic London Country Bus. In metropolitan conurbations, Passenger Transport Authorities would be set up with a statutory duty binding both them and the National Bus

Company to co-operate with each other. Whilst no formal PTA was to be set up in London, the central bus and Underground operations would pass to the GLC which would carry out a similar function. When 1969 came, the London Transport Board as a reasonably autonomous body had only a year left to function.

There was not much Routemaster activity in 1969. 15th March saw the introduction of Autofare equipped Merlins on all the Slough local services. A few RMLs remained at Windsor to work jointly with RTs on routes 407/A, 417 and the 457 group (plus odd journeys on 353, 446/A/B and 484) but the majority of the allocation moved to Northfleet. Here, service reductions on route 480 had latterly found an RML scheduled alongside RTs on routes 497 and 498; now they were to complete these routes and also to take over route 487. On 22nd March, the onward sweep of MBSs reached the Harlow town service 804 group but the RMLs remained in the locality to increase their share on other operations at the expense of RTs. In the central area, this same date was chosen for the closure of Rye Lane garage, a modern property less than twenty years old, its RMs transferring to Peckham and Camberwell. A further garage to gain RMs for the first time was Palmers Green which took a number from Walthamstow along with a new, self contained, northern leg of its route 123. On 23rd August, the final RT to RM conversion of the 1960s took place when surplus Routemasters were employed on routes 81 and 81C at Hounslow.

On 21st October 1969, a statement was issued jointly by the Minister of Transport (Fred Mulley had now replaced his more dynamic predecessor) and the Leader of the Greater London Council (Desmond Plummer) that agreement had been reached for transfer of the responsibilities for London Transport to the Council as provided for in the Transport (London) Act 1969, to take place on 1st January 1970. A new London Transport Executive responsible to and appointed by the GLC would be responsible for day-to-day operation but overall policy and control would rest with the GLC. The future was now clear; the great organisation was to be split between municipal control for the red buses and Underground, and continuing state ownership, through the National Bus Company, for the green fleet.

The last move involving Routemasters under the auspices of the old London Transport Board was the repainting into red livery of three green RMLs, the first colour change ever to befall any standard Routemaster. On 3rd December, RML 2441 arrived in red at Uxbridge after its inter-overhaul repaint, followed by RML 2443 at Upton Park on the 10th and RML 2321 at Willesden on the 17th. These three were, in effect, exchanged with the country department for three XA class Atlanteans which, in turn, released three XF class Fleetlines for repainting into an attractive blue and silver livery for the Blue Arrow service at Stevenage which commenced only days before London Transport surrendered responsibility for country operations. The three RMLs came from Windsor, indirectly in two cases, leaving only one member of the class still resident there when the London Transport era drew to a close and 209 Routemasters passed into the ownership of London Country Bus Services Ltd.

CHAPTER NINETEEN

NORTHERN GENERAL

'Routemasters available for all' read the heading in one of the trade magazines in November 1962 when the news finally broke that London Transport was relinquishing its exclusive rights to the Routemaster. At last it was on offer to all comers and in a variety of options: 27ft or 30ft long, rear or forward entrance, coil or air rear suspension, Leyland or AEC engine, plus a range of transmission options. In order to demonstrate some of these features, the unique RMF 1254 had figured prominently on the Park Royal stand at Earl's Court and was available for demonstration if required but the big question in many minds was: who was likely to want the Routemaster? Generally regarded as expensive and over-complicated, it did not have an obvious niche in a market dominated by operators faced ever more urgently with the need for financial stringency, many of whom could foresee even harder times ahead. The rear engined, high capacity double decker was rapidly gaining

favour and, for those who preferred to stick with the more conventional layout, a wide range was already available from a number of manufacturers. The outlook for provincial sales of Routemasters was not good, especially as service trials with the Liverpool, Manchester and Halifax municipalities, as well as East Kent, all failed to result in the placement of an order.

When an order finally came, it was from a completely unexpected source and took the whole industry by surprise. The Northern General Transport Co Ltd of 117 Queen Street, Gateshead had long held a reputation for individuality and, in the past, had even designed and built some of its own vehicles, but those days were reckoned to be gone. In more recent times, this BET-owned company had settled down with a workmanlike fleet of trusty Guy Arabs and, latterly, appeared to have decided to standardise on the Leyland Atlantean of which, by the end of 1963, eighty-seven were

in service excluding those owned by Northern's various subsidiaries. Without so much as trying a demonstrator in service, Northern approached the manufacturers in 1963 with a view to buying no fewer than fifty Routemasters.

Faced with the need to re-equip some of its longer distance services with new vehicles, Northern adopted a plan to obtain fifty double deckers of extra quality in acknowledgement that passenger comfort was of special importance on this type of operation. Several of the main services were worked jointly with the Tilling-owned United Automobile Services Ltd which was standardising on the group's

A sparkling new 2098 pays a visit to Aldenham from Park Royal for tilting prior to delivery. The radiator badge specially produced for Northern can be seen, as can the contrast in shades of red livery comparing the dark Northern colour with the lighter paintwork on newly overhauled RT 2966. W.H.R. Godwin

No.2098 again, this time in Northern service early in its career. Also in view is one of the company's numerous AEC Reliances.
Ken Blacker

70-seater FLF version of the Bristol-ECW Lodekka: Northern clearly aimed to go one better than this by specifying the Routemaster. Negotiations for their purchase were conducted during 1963, as a result of which two orders were placed, comprising an initial batch of 18 buses followed by a second batch of 32. The first vehicles began to arrive from Park Royal in March 1964.

Northern's specification was clearly influenced by RMF 1254 in following closely its general layout but with numerous modifications to suit the Company's requirements. The seating capacity was higher than on RMF 1254 and totalled 72, 41 upstairs and 31 down. Northern's standard two-piece destination display was fitted only at the front and the canopy route number blind was omitted. Sliding ventilators were fitted in place of quarter-drop windows and the driver's windscreen was a one-piece sealed unit. The conductor's coat locker was omitted and the saloon lighting was by fluorescent tubes. Northern's preferred Deans Beta tubular seat frames were used in place of London's Beaton variety. Leyland engines were specified, as was a four-speed Monocontrol, semi-automatic gearbox which had no provision for fully automatic conversion. Manual brake adjustors were fitted. The biggest break of all from London Transport standard was the use of a conventional worm driven rear axle in place of the Routemaster's unusual spiral bevel type. This was probably a wise move on Northern's part, for the spiral bevel axle, though theoretically more efficient, was less trouble free and long lasting than the old-fashioned worm design. The rear axle ratio was 5.2:1 and the vehicle's unladen weight was 7-14-0.

It was convenient that Northern's current livery was very similar to London Transport's with only a central cream band for relief, although the red was much darker, and it was applied in much the same way as in London except that the mudguards and lifeguards were not separately picked out in black. The traditional underlined NORTHERN gold fleet name was carried, and the equally traditional 'SHOP AT BINNS' legend was applied to the fronts of the buses before they entered service. Internally, the finish was somewhat plain with cream ceilings, window surrounds and side lining panels, red beading and red patterned moquette covered seats trimmed at the edges with red hide. Fleet numbers 2085-2102 and registration numbers RCN685-702 were allocated; unit numbers ran in sequence and were 3R2RH 2157-2174. They were known officially as Leyland-Park Royal Routemasters.

Wisely, Northern maximised its publicity advantage by giving the local press full access to the Routemasters prior to their entry into service, including a display of several buses on the Team Valley Trading Estate, and they produced a handy and not over-technical handout. The first buses entered passenger service on 1st May 1964, at which time all except the last two of the first batch of 18 were in stock. Divided between the depots at Bensham and Chester-le-Street, they began their working lives on the longer, interurban routes linking Newcastle with Hartlepool, Middlesbrough, Crook and Darlington. Some of these, such as the 40 mile long Newcastle-Durham-Stockton-Middlesbrough service, were fast busy runs and the Routemasters immediately found favour all round. On services run jointly with United, such as this, they inevitably

attracted favourable comparison with the mundane Lodekkas. Much of Northern's operating territory was subject to subsidence because of mining activities and maximum benefit was therefore gained from the independent coil suspension. A tendency soon evident on bad roads was for the Routemasters to pitch a little more than leaf-sprung buses but the absence of roll was very noticeable. Some drivers were unhappy at first with the feel of the Lockheed hydraulic brakes but the general handling characteristics and power assisted steering quickly made them very popular vehicles.

Delivery of the second, larger batch of 32 buses was scheduled to take place towards the end of 1964 running into the early months of 1965. Because Park Royal was anxious to display one of them on its stand at Earl's Court, all the stops were pulled out to complete the first vehicle ahead of the remainder. The fleet numbers for the new batch followed on immediately from the earlier delivery; they were 2103-2134. The show bus, 2103, which was licensed in October, carried an out of batch registration number BUP249B; 2104-2107 of December 1964 were EUP404-407B and the remainder, licensed between January and April 1965 except for 2131 which was delayed until June, wereFPT578-604C Though a single batch of 'chassis' numbers were allocated, they were not applied in strict sequence but in the order 3R2RH 2525/26/38-40/27-37/41-49.

Although fundamentally the same as the first batch, the new buses were superficially different in a number of ways and immediately distinguishable both inside and out. The outward changes reflected London Transport's own developments of the time in that the front

Swinging into Chester-le-Street is one of the second, larger batch, No.2127. This series was easily distinguishable from the first by the continuous cream band across the heater intake and the omission of brake cooling grilles. A larger, rectangular nearside mirror has also been fitted to this bus since delivery. Ken Blacker

Park Royal used No.2103 in a 1965 advertisement through which it hoped to stimulate further Routemaster sales, but to no avail. No.2103 was one of those which carried a plainer style of NORTHERN fleet name when new. Ken Blacker collection

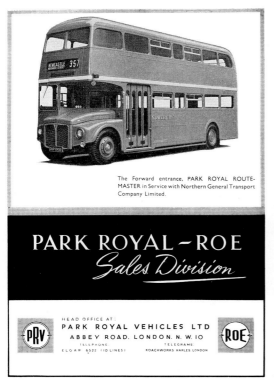

The Forward entrance, PARK ROYAL ROUTE-MASTER in Service with Northern General Transport Company Limited.

PARK ROYAL – ROE
Sales Division

cantrail band was now continuous with a consequent reduction in the size of the air intake, and the brake cooling grilles were omitted. A minor change instigated by Northern themselves was the use on some buses of a plainer and less attractive fleet name transfer, in which there was no underlining, which was positioned forward of the customary position. The internal changes were totally related to decor and were both startling and controversial; whether or not they were an improvement on what had gone before was a matter of some debate and very dependent on personal choice. Northern had decided to abandon the traditional internal colours and had enlisted the help of a leading design consultant, John Reid who had wrought changes with a vengeance. The results of his labours were ceilings in a Swedish plastic laminate in beige with a doodles design of criss-cross lines, matt black window surrounds and lower saloon rear end doors, brown side lining panels again with doodles and the same for seat backs, front bulkhead and lower saloon partitions, and a tartan type seat moquette supplied by Firths with light beige Bridge of Weir hide edgings and squab tops. Unlike some avant garde designs, Reid's did not date quickly and the materials used withstood the ravages of time very well. On the technical side, the second batch was fitted with DPA distributor pumps instead of the in-line type.

With fifty Routemasters in stock, the class became a familiar sight throughout the area between Tyne and Tees. The initial allocation of the complete class was spread between four depots. The two originals, Bensham and Chester-le-Street ended up with 13 and 18 respectively while new allocations comprised 8 at Consett and 11 at Sunderland. However,

the allocations in themselves were not straightforward; all the buses in the first batch were transferred on delivery of the second and ended up at Consett and Sunderland depots, the latter being noteworthy in never having an official allocation of any second batch buses. In mid-1965, the number of Routemaster services per depot was Bensham 8, Chester-le-Street 4, Consett 5 and Sunderland 8, ten services being recorded at the time as exclusively Routemaster worked, at least as far as their Northern share was concerned for several were joint operations. Though many were the longer trunk runs for which the Routemasters had been purchased, this was not exclusively the case and at Sunderland, for instance, four short local services shared with Sunderland Corporation were generally worked by Routemasters. Generally speaking, the Routemasters remained at these four locations throughout their lives with Northern, the only notable exception being that six of the Bensham stock moved to Washington when the new depot opened there in September 1968.

In complete break from the usual routine, No. 2111 (FPT581C) made a trip to Gütersloh in West Germany between 21st September and 3rd October 1965 as part of a British Trade Week. This type of event was fairly common at the time and London Transport normally provided buses when required but it is reported that they were unable to do so on this occasion. A much more substantial link with London Transport occurred in the following year when, on 25th November 1966, Northern purchased RMF 1254, a natural move since it was more akin to Northern's Routemasters than any of London Transport's own. Fitted with a reconditioned Leyland

engine in place of its original AEC unit prior to its journey north, RMF 1254 was subjected to further alterations by its new owners prior to entering service as their 51st Routemaster.

Most noticeable amongst the modifications carried out at Bensham works was the removal of the London Transport destination blind gear, the offside and rear indicators being replaced by plain panels, and a standard Northern two-piece unit, behind a single glass, fitted at the front. The seating capacity was increased to the Northern standard of 72 and a prominent plaque was installed on the staircase panel, immediately facing the entrance door, giving the history of the vehicle. When painted in Northern livery as its 2145, the bus blended well with the rest of the fleet although its drop windows, including the front ones which were retained, opening windscreen and later-style headlamp panels rendered it easily distinguishable from the remainder. On 1st January 1967, the new 2145 entered service at Bensham, starting its first ever prolonged spell of stage carriage operation.

Northern's Routemasters saw out the nineteen-sixties in fine fettle with repainting on an approximate two year cycle ensuring that their appearance remained smart; though subtly changed with modern style Northern fleet name, in trendy lower case lettering and revised fleet number numerals to match, and also a new-image 'SHOP AT BINNS'. In 1969, thirteen buses were repainted in the livery normally reserved for the subsidiary Gateshead and Tynemouth fleets with cream window surrounds and roof which suited them extremely well for the two years that it lasted; unfortunately the standard livery returned at the next round of repainting.

The former RMF 1254 retained its London style radiator badge as Northern 2145 as well as various other original features. It is seen crossing the Bowes Railway at Wrekenton in 1968. Capital Transport

CHAPTER TWENTY

AIRPORT ROUTEMASTERS

About a month after the last of Northern General's Routemasters were placed into service came the announcement that a batch of 65 vehicles had been ordered by another non-London Transport operator, in this case British European Airways Corporation. The order did not come as a complete surprise as London Transport was BEA's contractor for the provision of its town to airport service in the capital, on which RMF 1254 had been running experimentally since August 1964 complete with luggage trailer in tow. The backbone of the operation had traditionally been special deck-and-a-half coaches with large luggage capacity beneath the raised saloon floor, initially Commer Commandos but more recently a fleet of 74 AEC Regal IVs, designated 4RF4 by London Transport, with a seating capacity of 37. These vehicles were still in good condition but the rapid development of air travel had now rendered them too small, just as it had done with the Commers a little over a decade earlier. Larger aircraft were now being employed, notably the Vickers Vanguard which could accommodate up to 130 passengers. BEA's answer to the capacity problem was to contemplate the use of double deck coaches, and trial operation had been under way for some time with 220CXK, an AEC Regent V carrying a supremely ugly Park Royal body built in December 1961 at the

An airport Routemaster at Gloucester Road air terminal. The general similarity to RMF 1254 and the Northern General vehicles is readily apparent despite the vastly different livery, but the shorter length somehow makes the overall effect less impressive. Just visible behind BEA 10 is one of the Lansing Bagnall tractors used in connection with the baggage trailers. D-registered like the Routemaster itself, these tractors were purchased at about the same time. V.C. Jones

The bus which proved the feasibility of double-deck operation on the airport run, with the aim of gaining greater seating capacity than was available on single deckers with a raised rear compartment, was this ill-proportioned AEC Regent V. It did not long outlast the arrival of Routemasters. G.F. Walker

With the trailer detached, it is possible to see the towing gear and the removable panel within which it is mounted. These, together with the rear registration plate, were not usually visible when in service because the trailer hid them from view.

time when this company's standards of design and finish had plumbed the depths. However, this vehicle was traditional in the sense that passengers' luggage was carried on board; internal BEA thinking now favoured the use of a separate luggage trailer, hence the trial with RMF 1254.

BEA's method of operation was one which particularly lent itself to the use of trailers. At its West London Air Terminal in Gloucester Road, passengers were able to check in for their flight and hand over their luggage which they could then forget until arrival at their destination. Each departing coach was linked to a specific flight, and it was a simple matter to detach the luggage trailer at Heathrow and take it straight to the aircraft, thereby eliminating much luggage handling at Heathrow itself. With some forty to sixty percent of all aircraft passengers availing themselves of the coach service, a worthwhile saving in time and labour at Heathrow was achievable.

The trial with RMF 1254, which was carried out under special dispensation, was successful in obtaining legislation for PSVs to tow trailers, but a Ministry of Transport requirement that those doing so should not exceed 27ft 6ins in length meant that BEA's new fleet marked a return to the manufacture of short Routemasters. The choice of Routemaster was clearly influenced by London Transport's pref-

erence for running, maintaining and over-hauling vehicles similar to its own standard, but it was rumoured at the time that there were those within BEA who would have preferred something a little less expensive. In ordering the Routemaster, one particular tradition was maintained in that Park Royal was the bodybuilder as it had been with the earlier generations of Commandos and Regal IVs.

Construction of the BEA contract started in September 1966 and ran through to April 1967. The Routemaster production line at Park Royal had been reduced in capacity and, in order to meet BEA's requirements within existing resources, it was agreed with London Transport that manufacture of vehicles for the latter would be temporarily suspended. The break between delivery of RML 2598 in November 1966 and RML 2599 in March 1967 was the first and only one which occurred in London Transport's Routemaster programme. The 65 airport Routemasters were licensed as KJD601-625D/NMY626-665E and carried unit numbers R2RH/2 2807-2871 which ran in sequence. Though owned by BEA and officially numbered 8208-8272 in their road vehicle fleet, they were referred to internally by London Transport as BEA 1-65 (or, in the case of garage operating and engineering staff, by their registration numbers) and given the type coding 9RM12.

The first newly completed vehicle, BEA 1, was delivered from AEC on 18th October 1966 and straight away made a very favourable impression, notably in demonstrating how handsome the traditional Routemaster lines could appear, even when carrying a livery totally different from the one for which the model was designed. Only a few months ear-

lier, in July 1966, BEA had introduced a new image which was already a familiar sight on a fleet of eight Executive Express Willowbrook bodied AEC Reliances now working alongside the Regal IVs. Forsaking its previous grey, a handsome new blue, black and white style was applied to the Routemaster with blue on the lower half and white above, the colours being separated by a black band. The wheels, mud-guards and lifeguards were also black, and the impressive effect was lessened only by the omission of polished wheel trims which would have put the final touch to the whole ensemble. The BEA logo, consisting of its initials on a panel adjacent to an outline of an aircraft, was carried all round, those on the sides being slightly raised and illuminated at night to good effect. The Company's full title was also signwritten on each of the main side panels. For the purist, an unfortunate omission was that of a front destination display, the logo taking its place, it apparently being considered unnecessary to show the flight destination which the Regal IVs had always done. Internally, the colour styling was less attractive, and was indeed rather clinical with grey panelling, white window surrounds and ceilings, and the same grey seat moquette as used on the Green Line Routemasters. Parcels racks were fitted above the seats, of which there were 24 downstairs and 32 up.

Speed was of the essence on the M4 Motorway and the new coaches were designed to run at 70mph and frequently did so even though regulations officially restricted them to 50mph while towing trailers, as they always did. The AEC AV690 engine developed 175bph at 2200rpm and, with a rear axle ratio of 4.08:1, ensured that even though there was no

Interior view of RMA lower deck in original condition.
LT Museum 24731

improvement over a normal Routemaster at low speed, top speed performance could be some 55% better. Gearbox operation was of the semi-automatic type, and suspension was by coil at the front and air at the rear. The electrically operated double jack-knife doors, situated in the forward position as on the RMF, were controlled from a waist level switch on the nearside panel of the driver's cab where a red warning light indicated to the driver when the doors were open; internal and external emergency switches were located as on RMF 1254 and the Northern General vehicles which the BEA batch closely resembled in appearance apart from their shorter length. A particularly non-London Transport feature was the fitment of a paraffin heater under each rear seat, from which hot air was ventilated into the saloons whilst exhaust from the burners was led outside through ducts in the bodywork. Necessary to keep the interiors warm whilst the vehicles were waiting for

passengers, these were an admission, if ever one was needed, that the Routemaster's normal heating system alone was less than totally adequate. A fixed, one-piece windscreen was fitted, resembling the Northern General buses in this respect, although the specification differed in that BEA favoured opening windows at the front of the upper saloon in preference to plain ones. Twin, rear view mirrors were provided on each side to assist in manoeuvring with a trailer, and double headlights were provided in the latest style frontal assembly as used on the RCLs. Unladen weight was officially quoted as 7-14-0 but the vehicles carried the legend 7-10-0.

Eighty-eight drawbar trailers (numbered N101-188) were purchased to accompany the 65 Routemasters which seldom appeared in public without one in tow. The design was very similar to the prototype which RMF 1254 had hauled around for two years, and they were built by Marshall of Cambridge (Engi-

neering) Ltd on Rubery Owen single-axle running gear. Access to the body was by means of hinged double doors at the rear as well as a single sliding door on each side. Two kick-down support jacks with spring-loaded quick release mechanism were provided at the rear of the trailer, and a jockey-wheel type of landing gear at the front was brought into use by a manually operated hydraulic pump, a release valve allowing the jockey wheel to be retracted quickly once the trailer had been attached to a bus. A warning buzzer in the bus cab informed the driver if the trailer handbrake had not been released, this manually operated brake being supplementary to the main mechanical overrun brake. Lancing Bagnall tractors were used at termini to position the trailers. The lifespan of the trailers was comparatively short and, in 1972, they were replaced by a batch of seventy new ones (numbered J001-070) which were built by Locomotors Ltd of Andover.

The first coach to be licensed for service was BEA 2 on 28th October 1966. As was generally the case with the Routemaster construction programme, delivery ran late and BEA's hopes that the Regal IVs would all be replaced by the end of February 1967 were quickly thwarted, the final entries into service not coming until 1st May when BEAs 62, 63 and 65 were licensed. These did not totally eliminate the 4RF4s as originally planned, as a lone example (MLL740) survived alongside the Routemasters right through to May 1973. BEA's were the last Routemasters to be built for an operator other than London Transport and it was sad, though perhaps inevitable, that, despite ample advertising, only two customers had been found, taking a total of 115 vehicles between them which, by Routemaster standards, was not a large number. An indication of where operators' preferences lay was given by British Overseas Airways Corporation, BEA's partner in the publicly owned airline sector, who placed their own first new double deckers on London to Heathrow shuttle operation in the very same month as the new Routemasters. BOAC turned to the rear engined Leyland Atlantean, without trailers. The MCW bodies on these carried wrap-round front windscreens upstairs and down, Alexander style, and anyone other than the most

ardent Routemaster fan would acknowledge that they projected a far more modern and luxurious appearance than the now dated half-cab Routemaster.

BEA 1-65 started their lives operating from the old Chiswick tram depot which was enjoying its first spell of regular operational use for many years. After the end of the trams, it had been put to several uses, none of them permanent, including short spells as a bus garage and trolleybus depot, as an overhaul works, and as a storage place for surplus vehicles. The allocation to it of 65 brand new buses proved to be but a prelude to the full scale rehabilitation which, in due course, put it back in the mainstream of public transport operation as today's Stamford Brook garage. Though based at Chiswick, a few vehicles inevitably found themselves stabled overnight at Heathrow and, though the main focus of their work was the Gloucester Road to Heathrow corridor, they were sometimes found to be straying elsewhere. This normally occurred when weather conditions forced the diversion of flights to other airports and, for the same reason of adverse weather, it was sometimes necessary to make trips, particularly at night, direct to hotels which were often in central London.

In sharp contrast to the bus industry and its

state of steady decline, air travel was developing fast in a regulated but nonetheless competitive environment. Only two years after the last of the Routemaster coaches was built, BEA felt it necessary to update its image yet again and, in April 1969, coach BEA 56 was taken to the authority's own workshops for a livery trial to take place. It emerged in June, minus its illuminated side panels which no longer fitted the required image, painted in a predominantly orange (officially tangerine) livery with white upper works. Larger, new-style, sloping BEA logos were carried. At the same time, trailer N119 was painted orange to match. BEA must presumably have been proud of the result as they decided to adopt it as standard but, in truth, it was the complete antithesis of the previous colour scheme. The effect was both cheap and garish, and the paintwork had a finish more akin to the surface of 'Dayglo' posters than the quality gloss normally associated with coachwork. Repainting of the remaining 64 vehicles into the orange hue started with BEA 16, which emerged from Aldenham on 14th January 1970, and ended with BEA 55, the last blue one to go in for repainting on 12th May. The trailer fleet was repainted between January and April.

The new livery for BEA's Routemaster fleet, which first appeared on BEA 56 in June 1969, cheapened the appearance of these coaches considerably. John Fozard

CHAPTER TWENTY ONE

ALDENHAM AND THE ROUTEMASTERS

Although it is now a thing of the past, London Transport's vehicle overhaul factory at Aldenham played an important part in the rejuvenation and recertification of the Routemaster fleet for very many years. Conceived in the days when London Transport had complete faith in its own invincibility and in the permanence of London's unified transport monopoly, Aldenham was awe-inspiring in its scale and was the only bus overhaul works of its magnitude ever attempted anywhere in the world. Although used in a smallish way as a bus maintenance depot from April 1949, its famous mass production overhauls on impressive assembly lines began only after the first prototype Routemaster had been built. Its heyday was short and, by the late nineteen fifties, a run down had already begun, reflecting the fleet reductions which were being made and a widening of periods between overhauls on economy grounds. By the time the first production Routemasters went into overhaul in 1962, part of the 17.5-acre site had already been declared redundant and in 1964 a third of it was leased to Leyland Motors Ltd as its London depot.

The Routemaster was designed with Aldenham in mind and must have been one of the very few instances where the opportunity has occurred in designing a bus to ensure that it complies fully with the requirements of the operator's overhaul facilities. Its complete interchangeability of parts was the key feature in suiting Aldenham's flow line system.

As with all types of new bus, London Transport ran a series of pilot overhauls on the Routemasters before embarking on the full programme. By this means, general levels of wear and tear, and the level of work required for rectification could be established whilst, for work study purposes, the average length of time for individual tasks could be assessed

and agreed with the Trade Unions. Thus the first few RM overhauls were carried out individually, generally taking up to three months per vehicle to start with and speeding up to two months after the first four had been cleared. West Ham's RM 53 was the first into Aldenham on 18th April 1962, a full year ahead of the projected start date for the main programme. Also dealt with in 1962, with intake at approximately six week intervals were, in order of overhaul, RMs 66, 59, 70, 19 and 125. In the early months of 1963, RMs 83, 6, 9, 11, 24 and 14 were dealt with on a similar basis but by April the full Aldenham process was set to commence. This required the establishment of a works float of a size approximating to the number of buses of the type expected to be in for overhaul at any one time. It was this float system, inherited from the old London General Omnibus Company, which ensured that most Routemasters changed their identity a number of times during their life span. On entering the works, each vehicle was stripped of its public identity which, on the same day or soon afterwards, would reappear on a different vehicle fresh from overhaul. This interchanging of identities had the advantage of saving a considerable amount of money on road fund tax since, with each bus theoretically never off the road for more than a few days, the administrative and fiscal costs of delicensing and relicensing were saved. It also meant that the total number of fleet vehicles requiring road fund tax was reduced according to the size of the float. As a result, some buses disappeared for long periods of time because the identities which they had carried made up the float. The first bus into Aldenham to form the float was RM 5 on 10th April 1963 and a further 24 followed up to the end of May. Some of these early float Routemasters remained unseen for the rest of

the decade, with RMs 5, 7, 10, 15, 16 and 17 being absent from the streets of London until June and July 1972 whilst RMs 18, 23, 25, 26, 27, 29 and 30 were not seen again until the final three months of 1978.

As is well known, each bus body kept its own particular number, visible under the driver's canopy, enabling its origin to be ascertained easily. Likewise, it had been the practice to issue chassis with a unit number which enabled them to be traced for internal purposes even though their outward identity was changed; on the Routemaster there was no conventional chassis but the front and rear sub-frames were given numbers coinciding with the original bus number. Thus RM 72 in its first life carried body number B72, A-frame number A72 and B-frame B72; after overhaul in September-November 1963, body B72 appeared as RM 159 whilst units A72 and B72 went under body B69 which was now identified as RM 166. In a number of cases, perhaps half, running units were reunited with the body from which they had originated although the use of bus bodies built as floats (another LGOC practice) meant that, even if it had been the wish to keep original body and units together, this could not have happened. As it was, float body 9985 became RM 162 using A and B frames from RM 144 whilst body 9986, in the guise of RM 90, took the units of RM 96. When the A and B frames were removed for overhaul, they were kept in their original pairs except that, in a few cases of A frames and many more B frames, replacements were constructed 'in house' numbered from ALD1 upwards. The original pair of home produced sub-assemblies was tried out on RM 61, it is believed in June 1963. The remainder were used when required: thus RM 67, which after its first overhaul carried body B21, had A-frame A21 and B-frame ALD4.

The most famous memory of Aldenham will always be the impressive hall where rows of bodies were dealt with in adjustable stilts served by the overhead gantry crane which carried them at a great height. J. Wyndham

The first overhaul cycle resulted in several early type bodies with non-opening front windows straying beyond their original batch, but it was at the second cycle in 1968 that things really went awry. When RM 1522 was overhauled to Peckham in February 1968 it was only the second of this type to be numbered above 1000 and was a great novelty; over the years many more followed. Jeffmac Films

The very first RM to emerge from overhaul with a different identity was RM 36, with body B42, on 15th May 1963. Thereafter, except in a few special cases, all overhauled Routemasters changed identity. This meant that the edges between usually different types became blurred, which was most noticeable with the early plain front window batch, the first of which appeared out of number sequence at Walthamstow in December 1963 as RM 273 (body B158). After the second cycle of overhauls was commenced in January 1968, it was inevitable that these early bodies would also intermix with newer bodies going through their first overhaul, giving plain window bodies on buses numbered well into the thousands, the first being RM 1422 (body B59) at West Ham on 21st February 1968. This had a marked effect on specialised batches such as the original RM 22 – 130 series which, because of being fitted with alkaline batteries, were always kept at Poplar and West Ham. These special batteries still remained even after the second cycle overhaul but, by then, the bonnet numbers were dispersed between RM 12 and RM 1618.

In most major respects, the overhaul process itself was very similar to that carried out on the RT family. The first task on a bus entering the works was to remove the body from the chassis. On the Routemaster, this meant disconnecting the propellor shaft, controls, fuel and brake lines and removing the pins holding the A and B frames. To get the steering column clear of the A-frame required the disconnection of the front attachment points first of all, the vehicle then being lifted so that the frame hinged down from the rear attachments until the column had cleared the cab floor. As Aldenham was designed to handle separate chassis, the two subframes were then converted into chassis form using steel links, about four feet long, with hinged sections which folded over and clamped down with screw bolts onto the ends of the subframes. The coupled units then moved through the chassis shop to receive the same treatment as given to conventional chassis which included brushing down to remove all loose dirt, washing and then the stripping and replacement of units as necessary prior to being painted with silver protective paint. The items stripped down were safety ones such as axles and steering gear, which were then sent to Chiswick Works for overhauling; engines and gearboxes were not normally dealt with at Aldenham as these were changed in garages when the need arose.

Meanwhile, the dismounted body would be hoisted onto one of the nine giant cradle-like invertors, three of which had been modified to carry Routemasters. Special adaptors on the front beam of the cradle matched the forward pick-up points of the bus body and new beams at the rear took the RM's rear pick-ups. When turned to its side in the invertor, the underside of the body would be thoroughly cleaned, a task more difficult than on the RT because the gearbox was attached to the body with a tendency for oil, dirt and grease to accumulate around it. The normal high pressure hot water jets were insufficient to remove this deposit without first spraying the area with an emulsified paraffin to act as a solvent. Cleaning completed, one of the works' six travelling overhead cranes would lift the body to an adjacent invertor for the underside to be inspected and repaired as necessary, then on to one of many stilts which could pick up the normal body mounting points and hold the body in one of two positions for the remaining inspection and repairs to be carried out, gantries giving access to the upper deck and roof.

In due course, the overhauled body was lifted on to an overhauled 'chassis' in the body mounting section of the factory, and the various connections between the two were completed. Unlike the RT whose air systems could be tested for leakage by high pressure compressed air prior to mounting the body, the Routemaster could not be tested until the two were together. Having a mixture of high pressure oil pump for the brakes and power assisted steering together with a compressor for the air operated gearbox, the RM could best be tested by running the vehicle engine but this was not feasible within the shop because of noise and fume problems. Special compressed air motor drives were thus devised to drive these items through the gearbox via a belt drive. At this stage, it was found essential to have fitters both inside the cab and under the vehicle and, because of the noise of the equipment, they had to be provided with a simple microphone and loud speaker system to communicate with each other.

After road testing within the works' grounds, the bus was painted in a three-coat spray process, each put on while the previous one was still wet, finishing with two coats of sprayed varnish and a three hour spell in the drying oven. Spray painting requires much window masking and, on the RM, this was less straightforward than on the RT. Special wooden masks could quickly be secured to the RT by metal blades which fitted between the glass and the rubber seal. The RM's windows, being sealed on the inside, required a three stage process which began by placing pre-cut, radiused self-adhesive corner pieces on the glass; self-adhesive tape was then fitted around the perimeter of the window, covered finally with a special formula paste. When painting was completed, the corner pieces were removed and the masking came off in one piece. When the overhaul was complete, each bus was submitted for testing by the resident Ministry of Transport vehicle examiner for its Certificate of Fitness. So thorough was the overhaul, and so robust the vehicle, that RMs frequently obtained a seven year CoF which, outside London, was a most uncommon occurrence. Elsewhere, a seven year old vehicle being presented for its first CoF would normally rate only a five year certificate, these becoming shorter as the vehicle aged.

When the RM overhaul programme first began it was on a four year cycle, but later this frequency was deemed to be unnecessary and in 1967 a revised system was brought in to save costs. This gave a seven year gap between overhauls with an intermediate body repaint which was also carried out at Aldenham.

CHAPTER TWENTY TWO

QUIETENING THE ROUTEMASTER

In June 1963, Ernest Marples, then Minister of Transport, published draft regulations forewarning bus and commercial vehicle operators that they should plan for the introduction of quieter vehicles, quoting 1st January 1968 as the projected deadline date. A noise level of 88 decibels was proposed as the maximum limit for existing vehicles, and 86dB for new ones, although these were hotly contested by vested interests on one side and environmentalists on the other, with the Road Haulage Association actively seeking a relaxation to 89dB, and the Noise Abatement Society a tightening to 80dB. Whatever the eventual outcome was to be, London Transport was quick off the mark in instituting, early in 1964, a series of tests aimed at quietening the Routemaster. Noise is, of course, largely a matter of personal perception and the majority would probably not consider the Routemaster particularly noisy. Compared with some passenger vehicles around at the time, notably the Foden two-stroke and the Commer TS3, it was positively quiet. However, some

of the Leyland engined examples had been known to exceed 90dB and London Transport's decision to experiment in noise reduction was prudent. It was perhaps ironic that Routemasters had replaced trolleybuses which were environmentally perfect in being noise and fume free, but environmental considerations were then very much subservient to commercial priorities.

Under the direction of K.G. Shave, who had replaced the much respected A.A.M. Durrant as chief mechanical engineer, discussions took place in the latter part of 1963 with Ricardo & Company Engineers (1927) Ltd, who undertook to examine the noise problem. On 8th January 1964, Leyland-engined RM 1719 was delivered to their works at Shoreham-by-Sea where, over the next few months, it was the centrepiece for trials examining various designs and materials centred principally around encapsulating the engine as far as practicable to reduce noise emission. At this stage, no particular regard was paid to practical factors such as ease of accessibility for

maintenance, or ground clearance. When returned to the Chiswick experimental shop on 13th August, RM 1719 carried a large engine undertray, a sound deadening panel below the bonnet to the nearside of the engine, various deadening shields particularly around the radiator, and insulation under the bonnet top and along its cabside edge. Experiments in materials had resulted in an aluminium undertray rather than the slightly more effective glass fibre alternative on the grounds of ease of manufacture, and polyurethane foam sound deadening in preference to various other types. An air intake silencer was also added, and the overall result was very impressive with the maximum sound level reduced to about 81.5dB. RM 1719 stayed at Chiswick undergoing further tests for several months before being returned to normal condition and put back to service in March 1965. Meanwhile another Leyland engined vehicle, RM 1980, had been commandeered in September 1964 for further experiments to be undertaken, this time by London Transport

Facing Page **RM 738 at Warren Street in 1966 while working from Edmonton garage.** Capital Transport

RM 1719, the original Leyland-engined Routemaster on which Ricardo conducted its experiments, is seen with the sound proofing equipment partially removed and laid out for display. Ricardo Ltd

themselves, building on the experience gained from the Ricardo conversion. Like RM 1719 before it, RM 1980 had notched up only a few weeks' passenger service before being earmarked, and quite coincidentally, Holloway garage had been the operational base for both. London Transport had been sufficiently encouraged by the results with RM 1719 to want to mount a larger scale experiment using buses in active passenger service. They wished to manufacture and fit the conversion kits themselves, and RM 1980 was used as the guinea pig for this. Some changes were made to the Ricardo specification, notably a revision to the undertray which, in order to meet statutory ground clearance requirements, had to be raised to the degree that there was no gap whatever between the tray and the bottom of the sump. It was found that the rear portion of the undertray could be omitted with little detrimental effect, and sound absorbant material on the driver's side was also omitted. PVC foam was used as sound deadening material on the bonnet top etc. Various experiments were carried out with an air intake silencer fitted and removed; with it in position the results achieved were very similar to the Ricardo kit.

For service running, it was decided to convert 24 buses as they passed through overhaul, starting in late September but mostly in October 1965. Numbered between RM 736 and 768, these were all AEC engined buses to which the fitment of air intake silencers did not apply. They were, however, equipped with sound deadening kits similar to that on RM 1980 and some produced maximum readings below 80dB. One of their number, RM 738, went one stage further and was fitted with a revised radiator grille in which baffles replaced the conventional mesh, a modification which was clearly visible and did nothing for the appearance of the vehicle. This particular modification was not a great success as it achieved less than one decibel of sound reduction while sometimes proving detrimental to the cooling system. Nevertheless, RM 738 ran in this condition from Edmonton garage from October 1965 through to May 1968 inclusive and, after a spell when it was delicensed, appeared unaltered at Abbey Wood for a period from December 1968 onwards.

Although the Aldenham produced conversion parts were designed for easy removal, they inevitably led to increased maintenance time and costs. With pressure to reduce noise levels below those of the Routemaster no longer imminent, interest in the experiment waned and it was discontinued in due course. Thereafter, the familiar sounds of the Routemaster, be it the mellow tones of the AEC or the throatier roar of the Leyland, were left untampered with to become a classic feature of the London traffic environment.

Centre **RM 1719 again, showing the nearside acoustic panel ready to be dropped into position.** Ricardo Ltd

Left **A close-up view of the front baffles which distinguished RM 738 from the remainder of the fleet for three years.** John Gascoine

CHAPTER TWENTY THREE
THE FRM

It is a strange fact that many of the bus designs remembered with the greatest nostalgia have been one-offs or types which have had only a small production run and were, therefore, failures from a strictly commercial point of view, even if features of their design may have influenced subsequent development in a positive way. A notable inclusion in the much loved one-off category is FRM 1. Like so many other pioneering designs which failed to make the grade, it remains the subject of tantalising conjecture over what might have been if only things had been different.

Above **FRM 1's entry into service on 26th June 1967 occurred without any of the publicity which the vehicle deserved. It is seen on arrival at Enfield garage on its very first journey, having worked up from Tottenham in readiness for its first 34B peak run to Walthamstow.**

Right **FRM 1 under construction at the works of Park Royal Vehicles.** LT Museum 24732

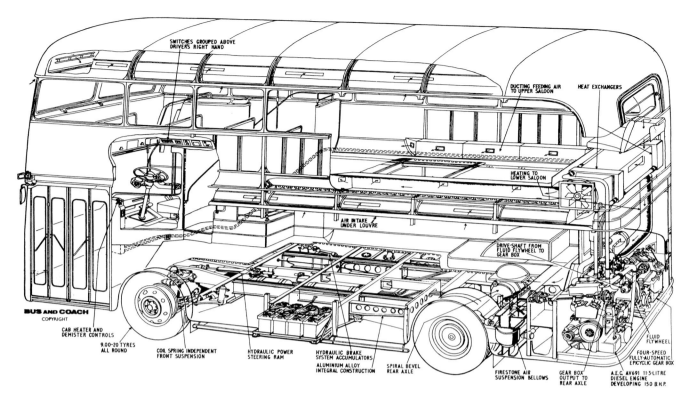

SWITCHES GROUPED ABOVE DRIVERS RIGHT HAND

DUCTING FEEDING AIR TO UPPER SALOON

HEAT EXCHANGERS

HEATING TO LOWER SALOON

AIR INTAKE UNDER LOUVRE

DRIVE-SHAFT FROM FLUID FLYWHEEL TO GEAR BOX

BUS AND COACH COPYRIGHT

CAB HEATER AND DEMISTER CONTROLS

9.00-20 TYRES ALL ROUND

COIL SPRING INDEPENDENT FRONT SUSPENSION

HYDRAULIC POWER STEERING RAM

HYDRAULIC BRAKE SYSTEM ACCUMULATORS

ALUMINIUM ALLOY INTEGRAL CONSTRUCTION

SPIRAL BEVEL REAR AXLE

FIRESTONE AIR SUSPENSION BELLOWS

GEAR BOX OUTPUT TO REAR AXLE

A.E.C. AV691 11·3-LITRE DIESEL ENGINE DEVELOPING 150 B.H.P.

FLUID FLYWHEEL

FOUR-SPEED FULLY-AUTOMATIC EPICYCLIC GEAR BOX

The trouble with FRM 1 was that it came too late. London Transport's ill considered edict that the optimum urban bus should be a 64-seater crew worked vehicle with open rear platform meant that a decade of movement towards the high-capacity, rear-engined bus was largely ignored. When the inevitability became too strong to ignore, construction of a rear engined version of the Routemaster was put in hand during 1964 but lead times are always long on prototypes and events were moving so rapidly that standard Atlanteans and Fleetlines had to be purchased in 1965. Questions were already being asked about the wisdom of London Transport designing and

commissioning the construction of its own specialist buses, and the pressure to abandon this policy became even stronger once London Transport began buying manufacturers' standard products. Failure to respond sooner to trends within the industry and to update the Routemaster sounded the death knell for the rear engined Routemaster even before it was born. As late as October 1965 the Chief Mechanical Engineer (Road Services), K.G. Shave, was quoted as saying that, so far as he was concerned, if operation of the Atlanteans and Fleetlines was successful, buses of similar layout but based on Routemaster principles would be built, but few believed him.

Having decided to proceed with a rear-engined Routemaster as a joint venture between London Transport, AEC and Park Royal the partners decided to construct five sets of parts. A good deal of secrecy surrounded the project in its early stages but, by February 1965, the trade press had got wind of the news that something was going on, although they could not gain confirmation. A strong hint that developments were afoot was dropped by R.M. Robbins, London Transport's Chief Commercial & Public Relations Officer at a talk to the Omnibus Society in June 1965 when he said that he believed the possible permutations on the original Routemaster concept had still not been exhausted. Thereafter, a cat and mouse game was carried out between the trade press who tried to obtain pictures and details of the design, and the development team who seemed determined that they should not. Official information was sparse but the news came in November 1965 that design work was well advanced with a prototype expected to be on view at Earl's Court in the following September. A strong suggestion was that it would be shown in a provincial livery (most likely the attractive blue and cream of Sheffield Corporation), leading to the speculation that the model was being developed as AEC's alternative to the Atlantean and Fleetline. Production, it was suggested, could begin early in 1967.

KGY 4D

LONDON TRANSPORT

Above **A general arrangement drawing of FRM 1 published in** *Bus & Coach.* **This shows the air ducting system, suspension arrangements and the layout within the engine compartment.**

Left **The bonnet lid lifted open within the built-in rear aperture to reveal the engine compartment which was particularly well thought out, many components being far more readily accessible than on very many other types of rear engined bus built before or since. The whole of the surrounding panelling could also be quickly removed in sections if required.** LT Museum 3405/6

By mid-1966, the lucky few had gained glimpses of the FRM in Park Royal's factory, and the completed bus was officially taken into London Transport stock on 4th July 1966. Even so, it remained elusive to the extent that the first photograph of it gained by the trade press did not appear until *Commercial Motor* secured a scoop on 2nd December. The Earl's Court show had by now come and gone but, to the disappointment of many, the FRM failed to appear and no explanation for its absence was given. Its first public appearance finally came just before Christmas 1966 when members of the technical press were invited to inspect the vehicle at Victoria garage. Far from being introduced with a fanfare, the affair was very low key and it was immediately clear that any hopes of putting the design into production had already been abandoned. London Transport frankly admitted that the new bus had been overtaken by events. Its own new vehicle plans now hinged on high-capacity single deckers, 150 of which had been called for in 1967 with a similar number in 1968, and no immediate demand for new double deckers was foreseen. Both of its partners in the new design were now members of the Leyland combine whose development strategy was leading towards the Leyland National in the mistaken belief that the double decker had little or no future, so plans for interesting provincial operators in the design were abandoned. Since neither funds nor willpower existed to promote the FRM, the other four intended prototypes remained unbuilt. Sadly, after so very many years of classic co-operation, there would be no more new double deck designs for London from the AEC stable.

FRM 1 (FRM standing for Front entrance RouteMaster) proclaimed its Routemaster ancestry from all angles despite its total break from tradition in engine and entrance configuration; indeed some sixty percent of its body parts were common with the Routemaster. This meant that, in general appearance, it differed considerably from the general run of Atlantean/Fleetline body styling. The use of standard shallow Routemaster windows with a depth of only 21 inches gave a heavy appearance, accentuated by the length of the vehicle which, at 31ft 3ins, was the longest of the Routemaster family. Although the first impression was of a dated outline, the avoidance of gimmicky features such as wraparound front windows and peaked domes produced a shape which has proved timeless and, two decades on, looks less dated than some of the more modern, upmarket body styles of the time.

Sensibly, well proven Routemaster design features were perpetuated wherever possible but major modifications were obviously called for, both at the front where the entrance layout required the wheels to be set back, and at the rear where the engine and gearbox were situated. With the engine mounted at the back, there was no longer any need for the traditional Routemaster A frame, extension members being adequate to support the entrance area, driver's cab, steering column and pedal gear. Conventional Routemaster units bolted to the body structure formed the front 'axle', and standard coil suspension was provided at the front. At the rear, the customary Routemaster B frame arrangement was retained but the sub-frame was modified so

that the axle sat on it rather than passing through and was therefore changeable without removing the sub-frame. The usual spiral bevel axle was employed but coil suspension could not be accommodated so Firestone rolling diaphragm air bellow units were used. The engine was vertically mounted transversely across the back of the bus as on the Atlantean and Fleetline, occupying the nearside half of the frame with the gearbox on the offside. However the power pack idea of the Atlantean with its flywheel disastrously sandwiched between the engine and gearbox was abandoned, and on the FRM the gearbox and flywheel could each be removed independently of the other. The 11.3 litre AV691 engine, closely related to those on London's large fleet of single deck AEC Merlins, marked a reversion from Routemaster back to RT practice in having dry rather than wet liners; its output was 150bhp at 1800rpm. The drive line, through a fluid flywheel to the favoured electro-pneumatically operated epicyclic gearbox, incorporated a revised design of shaft drive. Developed in conjunction with Self Changing Gears of Coventry, it was taken over the top of the gearbox, to the end of which was fitted a transfer gear permitting a lower mounting of the box with take-off for the brakes and air suspension system at the transfer stage. In order to carry the weight of the engine etc, the normal Routemaster rear bulkhead structure was considerably strengthened although whether this would have been adequate for the long hard working life to which Routemasters were subjected remains a matter for doubt.

Two offside fuel tanks were fitted, giving a total capacity of 46 gallons. CAV electrics were fitted. A wheelbase of 16ft 10ins, 7ins longer than on the Atlantean, promised a

reduction in the pitching at speed normally associated with rear engined double deckers. At 7ft 2ins, the front overhang was only fractionally less than the Atlantean but a lower step height was achieved at 1ft 3ins as against the Leyland's 1ft 4ins. The rear axle ratio was 5.22:1.

Internally, FRM 1 was pure Routemaster in its decor and fitments, and a total of 72 seats were fitted, 41 up and 31 down, the same number as on the RML, Atlantean and Fleetline for comparison purposes. Fluorescent lighting was provided, London Transport having belatedly conceded that even the Routemaster could benefit from modern illumination techniques. A major, and many would say detrimental, deviation from Routemaster practice was the elimination of opening windows in both saloons, and also of the conventional engine cooling radiator. Gone was the Routemaster's normal fresh air heating and cooling system. Taking its place were two Clayton 'Compass' Still-tube heat exchangers, fitted with hydraulically driven reversible fans and housed in the upper saloon under the rear seat, forming a sealed pressurised system in connection with the engine header tank. Each fan had its own grille, visible on the outside of the bodywork, from which warm air was forced into the saloons under thermostatic control through slots over each of the main side windows, and stale air was ejected. In addition, a direct air intake was provided at the front of the upper deck through slots identical to those on production RMs up to RM 353, the front dome having the same type of external lip as on these early models. The 'Compass' system, which depended on the engine running, soon proved less than satisfactory and the vehicle could become very stuffy at termini when the engine

Below **An official photograph of FRM 1 taken prior to its entry into service, whilst still very much hidden from the public eye, shows its general outline which benefits compared with the RMLs through having even window spacing, although in the absence of opening windows the sides look rather plain. The intake louvre for the forced air system is prominent above the lower deck windows. Visible in this view are the rearward facing staircase and the single step into the lower saloon which marked an improvement over RMF 1254 where there were two.**

Facing Page **Interior views of FRM 1, showing its unmistakably Routemaster parentage.** LT Museum

was switched off. The platform and staircase arrangement followed very closely the design employed by Park Royal on the XA and XF classes which had itself been inspired by a Stockton Corporation requirement on an earlier batch of Park Royal Atlanteans which the London buses resembled in many ways. The platform doors were electrically operated. An interesting feature of the design was that, unlike other rear engined double deckers, the lower saloon side windows extended right to the rear of the bus, a neat curved arrangement of the partition above the engine making this possible. The rearmost offside window was a push-out emergency exit and, very unusually, there was also a full height emergency door on the offside just behind the staircase.

Although the engine compartment had an inset recess above it, the rear end treatment of the FRM was much neater than many of its contemporaries. At the front, a totally conventional Routemaster blind display was fitted but, somewhat surprisingly, there was none on the nearside, not even a route number aperture, whilst at the rear the destination box was surmounted by a route number box to form an inverted T layout. FRM 1 was classified 10RM11 and it carried body number A88 in a new series started in 1965. The 'chassis' number was FR2R001. Its livery was standard central area red and grey but embellishments included gold LONDON TRANSPORT side transfers in a new plain style without underlining, contrasting with white outline bullseyes, carrying a black fleetname across the bar, which were situated centrally on the lower panels front and rear and were the same as those already familiar on the Strachans bodied Red Arrow single deckers. Fleet numbers were in the minuscule and tasteless white characters that were to characterise the huge Merlin fleet still to come.

The rear offside aspect of FRM 1 can be seen as it pauses between trips at Victoria garage sidecourt alongside Muswell Hill's RM 1962. An unusual feature was the provision of emergency exits at both ends of the lower saloon. Alan Nightingale

All who have driven the FRM will probably agree that it was outstanding in terms of performance and handling compared with other rear engined double deck designs. The high seating position inherited from the standard Routemaster gave excellent forward vision, noise levels within the vehicle were low, the high powered engine was very responsive, the automatic gear change was jerk-free, the power assisted steering required just the right level of effort, and the hydraulic brakes were of the usual high Routemaster standard. Even with a full load, the vehicle was very lively. At an unladen weight of 8-10-0, it had a weight per passenger ratio of 264lbs compared with 275lbs on the Atlantean and was, therefore, more economical on fuel consumption. London Transport's engineers' view was that, being a one-off, it was about 3cwt heavier than a production model would be, on which a still better fuel return would be achieved. However, it was on the matter of fuel consumption that an early disappointment was experienced. Early service running indicated that the vehicle was returning about half a gallon per mile worse than might have been predicted from normal Routemaster experience, and it was thought that the culprit might have been the hydraulic drive for the two heat exchanger fans which was operative whenever the engine was running, and inevitably absorbed a fair amount of power. The idea was promulgated that hydraulic operation of the fans might be abandoned altogether and substituted by suitable electrics with the aid of a second alternator.

A hope that FRM 1 would enter service in February 1967 alongside Atlanteans on route 76 and its peak period satellite 34B proved over-optimistic. By the time of its demonstration run for the press in Christmas week 1966, it had notched up only about 3,000 miles of trial running and much more proved necessary. It was not until 23rd June that the vehicle was finally dispatched to Tottenham garage for its working life to begin. Three days later, FRM 1 entered service without prior notice and without ceremony. Most drivers fell in love with it immediately but teething troubles prevented it from appearing as regularly as might have been hoped. Calamity struck on 31st August when, because of leaking flywheel oil, the engine compartment caught fire in Princes Street, close by the Bank of England. The whole bus filled with smoke and, as no windows could be opened, glass had to be smashed by the fire brigade who were quickly on the scene. A hasty return to Chiswick was organised, and the next three months were spent back in the hands of the experimental shop staff.

The Princes Street fire which put the FRM temporarily out of action was promptly dealt with by the fire brigade. The front window smashed by them to release the build up of smoke and the scorching of the rear are evidence of what has occurred. Opening windows were fitted before the vehicle returned to service. A.D. Hurley

Back at Tottenham, FRM 1 sports a full set of opening windows in this view at Waterloo taken in October 1968 where Metro-Cammell bodied AEC Merlin MBA 178 represents the new generation of bus which killed off FRM 1's development.
Alan B. Cross

Centre A photograph taken in the same year as the one above shows London Transport's thinking at the time the first large-capacity single-deck omo buses were entering service. A partially completed mock-up of a double-deck omo design with four axles shows a radical shift from the FRM of just a few years earlier and presages the XRM project of the 1970s. According to the mock-up, passengers would have entered the bus by the centre doors and paid by means of automatic turnstiles before alighting via the front door. Boarding times of large capacity omo vehicles were causing concern and the lower steps made possible by the four small-wheeled axles coupled with the use of 'stored fare' tickets validated on entry were considered as the means to overcome the problem. The single-door FRM concept was clearly out of date so far as LT was concerned just one year after the vehicle had entered service. LT Museum 24733

When it returned for service at Tottenham on 1st December, FRM 1 had taken on a rather different, but improved, appearance. Standard Routemaster quarter drop winding windows were now clearly evident, with three on the lower deck and six upstairs, including a pair at the front. The opening windows took away much of the heaviness of the appearance of the vehicle and were an acknowledgement of failure for the original heating-cum-ventilation concept. Thereafter, the vehicle operated fairly steadily on routes 76 and 34B for the next twenty months although it was by no means always in service, some periods of enforced idleness being unavoidable because of difficulty in obtaining spare parts. On 1st August, FRM 1 returned once again to Chiswick, its short career as a crew worked bus on busy in-town work having come to an end.

Decisions about future employment had had to be made. The XA class Atlanteans had been found unsuitable for heavy city work because of overheating and other problems, and were due to be transferred to quieter duties in the suburbs as one-man operated vehicles. It would clearly have been pointless to have FRM 1 as the only rear engined, front-entrance bus on route 76, hence its removal. The majority of the Atlanteans were destined to work on flat fare routes at Croydon and Peckham, whose method of fare collection required the use of 'Johnson' fareboxes, but the FRM was not adaptable for this because of its high driving position. The work chosen for it was on the short West Croydon to Round-shaw shuttle service 233 which had been Atlantean operated since 22nd November as the Central Bus Department's first double deck omo service. FRM 1 was allocated to Croydon on 19th December 1969 and took up a quiet, suburban, existence hardly suited to such a splendid and expensive bus.

FRM 1 kicks its heels on the undemanding outer suburban 233 on which it cruises through West Croydon bus station where XA and RT types are also in evidence. The advertisements which the vehicle now carries, albeit in-house rather than commercial ones, somehow lighten the previously rather heavy appearance. M. Dryhurst

CHAPTER TWENTY FOUR
AMBASSADORS ABROAD

One of the most famous emblems of London, in the eyes of people of other nationalities, is the red double deck bus. In the years between 1950 and 1957 this close link between London and its bus fleet was successfully exploited through a series of eight overseas journeyings by vehicles of the RT family in connection with trade fairs and festivals in many European countries and even as far afield as the USA. Wherever they went the RTs were a huge success, giving rides to hordes of eager passengers most of whom had never seen and certainly never ridden upon a double decker. The goodwill value of these tours was enormous and yet, apart from the cost of providing the vehicles, no financial burden fell upon London Transport as each trip was fully sponsored.

The final trip of the old era which lasted from August to October 1957, saw an RT and an RTL flying the flag in Finland. After this came a pause of more than three years before the next venture when RM 546 departed in January 1961 for Switzerland. So successful was this initial overseas trip by a Routemaster that many more followed in fairly quick succession. At their peak the foreign journeyings by Routemaster were so frequent that the co-ordinators of these events within London Transport began almost to regard them as a

matter of course. Between 1961 and 1975 London Transport supplied Routemasters and their crews for no fewer than 41 overseas tours, and a staggering 52 RMs and RMLs carried the famous GB plates – some on more than one occasion – as London's Ambassadors Abroad to thirteen countries in three continents.

RM 546 earned its spurs as London's first GB Routemaster by undertaking not just one, but three tours prior to settling down to a more prosaic life serving the streets of London. Delivered as a new vehicle for service at Hanwell garage on 1st December 1960, it was soon set aside for its first overseas trip for which it was specially prepared at Hanwell, and later at Chiswick, during January 1961. Departing London on 28th January with a complement of three London Transport staff, a spare parts kit and some dolly stops, RM 546 travelled via Dover and Boulogne to reach the Swiss city of Basle on 2nd February where it was due to be star performer at the British Fair week. Four drivers from the local transport undertaking, Baseler Verkehrsbetrieb, were taught to handle the vehicle and to give rides to an eager local populace throughout the duration of the Fair from 6th to 18th February. Arriving back in London on 24th February, RM 546 returned to Hanwell on 1st March but was soon com-

mandeered once again, this time for a trip to Holland and France. Departing on 25th April, the vehicle spent a couple of weeks supporting campaigns featuring British goods in Rotterdam and The Hague before heading for Paris to take part in a publicity campaign centred upon the opening of a new office for British Overseas Airways Corporation in the Champs Elysees. After returning to England on 25th May, RM 546 was retained at Chiswick for almost a full year before its third and final venture overseas, which found it departing on 11th May 1962 for a trade fair in the Swedish capital of Stockholm. Arriving back on 20th June, RM 546 was stored at Aldenham for several months, presumably in case any further overseas excursions cropped up. However, when they did, other vehicles were specified and on 7th December 1962 RM 546 was relicensed at Hanwell to take up its bus career in earnest, its days of glory at an end.

Above **Although polished wheel fittings were taboo for service at home, they were still thought desirable for prestige trips overseas. RM 1804, photographed in Grosvenor Place before its 1964 trip to Dusseldorf, has also acquired a nearside wing mirror.** David Kirk

For the next overseas venture a Leyland-engined Routemaster was required. RM 1272 was one of many Routemasters stockpiled during the management versus union battle of 1962 over the future employment of the class, and though delivered in June it saw no service prior to departure for the docks on 20th September in readiness to sail the next day. Once again Switzerland was the goal, but on this occasion the host city was to be Geneva where, from 1st to 13th October 1962, the Routemaster was to carry passengers on a circular tour as part of British Fortnight sponsored by the Board of Trade. Back at Aldenham on 19th October, RM 1272 then remained out of use until commissioned for service at Mortlake in April 1973.

There was a second overseas tour in 1962 of an altogether more ambitious nature when RML 898, unused since delivery in December 1961, was selected for a 6,000-odd mile trip to San Francisco at the behest of the British-American Chamber of Commerce for its London Week, scheduled from 12th to 17th November. RML 898, which left London on 26th September in the hold of the *Dongedyk* was by no means the first London double decker to visit San Francisco, the famous cross-USA trip by RTs 2775/6 and RTL 1307 in 1952 still being fairly fresh in the mind. Nor was its achievement quite as great, for whereas the RTs had driven from coast to coast RML 898 proceeded direct as deck cargo via the Panama Canal. However, its impact in the beautiful Californian city was just as great and was undoubtedly the catalyst for further Routemaster trips to the USA in the years to come. Indeed, before entering passenger service in London, RML 898 was itself destined to cross the Atlantic yet again. After reaching London in early January 1963 it remained in store through to 26th August when a couple of British festivals in the American Deep South called it back. First stop was New Orleans, Louisiana, to which RML 898 sailed direct from Liverpool for a fortnight's operation along the length of the city's famous Canal Street. Then came a 400-mile drive to participate in British Week at Memphis, Tennessee. RML 898 returned to England from Houston, Texas, reaching Aldenham on 27th November and finally entering service at Finchley in May 1964.

While RML 898 was being prepared for its second stint in the USA, another member of the class was flying the flag in Europe. The fact that there were more 30-footers than required for route 104 made them obvious candidates for trips abroad at this time, as they would otherwise only be standing idle. Furthermore the additional passenger-carrying capacity helped clear the crowds which these vehicles inevitably attracted wherever they went, the great majority of whom wanted to sample the novelty of travelling on the upper deck. A British Week scheduled to take place in Munich between 8th and 16th June 1963 led to RML 902's departure for West Germany on 1st June. Arriving back home on the 21st, the vehicle was held in store for another journey into Europe planned for two months later. On 26th August RML 902 was again aboard the Dover-Boulogne ferry, this time with Zurich in Switzerland as its destination where, at the request of the Board of

With the famous bay as a backdrop, and one of the traditional cable cars sharing a steep incline, RML 898 makes an impressive sight in San Francisco on its tortuous mile long circular route. The blinds for London's famous route 11 were specially made for the trip, the 'real' 11 still being in the hands of RTWs at the time.

Trade, circular tours were given from 2nd to 14th September in support of British Fortnight. 20th September found RML 902 back home with a further spell of storage lying ahead prior to taking up service, like RML 898, àt Finchley on 1st May 1964.

The RML overseas tours saga of 1963 was not yet complete. A third as yet unused member of the class, RML 903, was destined to be the second Routemaster to set off with the USA as its destination. The departmental store chain John Wanamaker Inc was holding an 'Exposition Britannia' in Philadelphia from 14th October to 6th November which RML 903 was to support in the customary way by providing free rides. It was away from England from 12th September through to 20th November 1963 during which appearances were also made at other Wanamaker branch stores in the States of New Jersey and Delaware. Back home, RML 903's future itinerary followed that of the other two GB RMLs with initial entry into revenue service at Finchley commencing in May 1964 by which time it was well over two years old.

The 1964 overseas touring season commenced with the departure on the Dover-Boulogne ferry of not one, but two Routemasters

on 15th May. Now past their first blush of youth, the RMLs were no longer in vogue and newer standard length RMs were selected in the shape of RMs 1804 and 1806. Both had been licensed for passenger service at Tottenham on 1st February but were quickly retrieved and prepared at Aldenham with a trip to West Germany in mind. The venue was Dusseldorf, much rebuilt after its wartime destruction, where a new style British Week was due to be opened by the Minister of Trade & Industry, Edward Heath, on 23rd May. The same two vehicles, after arriving home on 5th June, were put aside for a visit to Denmark departing on 16th September. British Week in Copenhagen was their first destination beginning on the 25th, followed by visits to Aarhus and other Danish towns before being finally delivered back to Chiswick on 21st October.

Meanwhile two others of the same batch – both of which had also been briefly licensed at Tottenham on 1st February 1964 – were earmarked for two separate transatlantic trips. RM 1809 sailed for New York on 21st August to take part in a British Fortnight in Cincinatti, Ohio commencing on 21st September, after which came a long run westwards for a 'Hail Britannia' fortnight in Omaha,

Expected at Yokahama on 1st September, RM 2214 was due to participate in the British Exhibition in Tokyo from 17th September to 3rd October. Arranged by British Overseas Fairs Ltd in conjunction with Seibu, a large Tokyo departmental store, the itinerary for RM 2214 included various passenger-carrying trips into Tokyo from the suburbs using Japanese ladies as conductors. Before the event opened on the 17th RM 2214 was put on show near the Seibu store and generated an enormous amount of interest, no doubt much to the delight of the sponsors. The across-the-world trip was concluded when RM 2214 arrived back at Aldenham on 2nd December; it was later allocated to Riverside to take up normal service on 1st February 1966.

Meanwhile the USA remained high on the agenda for goodwill missions, and 27th August 1965 saw the departure from Bristol docks on the Bristol City Lines ship *Northold* of RML 2261, the first of the main production batch of RMLs. A busy two-month schedule lay ahead once the vessel docked at Rochester, NY in support of trade fairs in Rochester itself and also in New York City, progressing southwards thereafter to Richmond, Virginia, and finally Charlotte, North Carolina. The fair at the last port of call, Charlotte, coincided with another at Toledo, Ohio which commenced on 4th November and closed, like its more southerly counterpart, on the 13th. Had they been staggered, RML 2261 could have perhaps proceeded northwards to Toledo, but as it was a second Routemaster was called for to complete the 1965 USA programme. RML 2262 – delicensed since delivery in July – departed on 12th October, again on a Bristol City Lines vessel but this time the *Halifax City*, via the St Lawrence Seaway and Lake Erie direct to Toledo. RML 2261 was the first of the two to arrive home, on 3rd December, some five weeks ahead of RML 2262 on 10th January 1966. The former entered service at Poplar on 27th January but RML 2262's first role in the UK comprised seven months on trainer duties, a very unglamorous existence compared to heady earlier days as a focus of public attention in the northern USA.

April 1966 found Routemasters flying the flag in the tenth 'new' country, Norway. Two RMLs were required to ferry passengers from the centre of Oslo to the suburban grounds where the British Trade Fair & Fortnight was due to take place between 29th April and 15th May. RMLs 2368 and 2396 were selected more or less straight from the production line although in the case of RML 2368 a couple of modifications were carried out prior to shipment. One was to fit a Leyland engine in place of the original AEC unit, which, though resulting in a vehicle non-standard from the rest of its class, was required by the organisers who wished to show both makes of engine. Additionally RML 2368 was fitted with an illuminated advertisement panel on the lower deck

Nebraska from 19th October. Following quickly on its heels was RM 1808 which left Surrey Commercial Docks on 28th August to retrace the steps formerly taken by RML 898 to New Orleans. The goal this time was a 'Best of Europe' festival commencing on 20th September followed by a similar event in Birmingham, Alabama from 11th October. Though the further travelled of the two, RM 1808 arrived back in England on 20th November a month ahead of RM 1809 which was home just in time for Christmas. Of the four overseas tourers for 1964, RMs 1804/6/8 resumed normal passenger service in January 1965 at Croydon, Barking and Dalston respectively, leaving RM 1809 idle until required for service at Hackney in April.

Tilbury was the departure point on 10th May 1965 for RMs 2158 and 2159 for Rotterdam, en route to British Week in Amsterdam from 15th to 22nd of the month. These two

previously unused Routemasters were stored upon returning home on 28th May in readiness for a slightly more ambitious trip to Italy later in the year. The venue on this occasion was British Week in Milan from 9th to 17th October for which the two crossed from Dover to Calais on 30th September aboard the *Free Enterprise I*. This involved a drive through France and back and was concluded when the two buses reached Aldenham on 28th October. Both entered service at Walworth on the first day of 1966.

Journeyings into Europe were by now becoming fairly commonplace, but RM 2214's overseas tour in the latter part of 1965 was a different scale of venture altogether. The Asian continent beckoned when the vehicle left Chiswick on 26th July for the Royal Victoria Dock to be loaded upon the Ben Line's MV *Bengloe*, which sailed on the 30th via Singapore on the 11,000 mile voyage to Japan.

bulkhead to bring it into line with RML 2396 which was so equipped from new. The two buses left England on 22nd April and returned on 31st May, after which RML 2368 entered passenger service at Upton Park still with its Leyland engine. For RML 2396 a further, more exotic trip lay ahead for which it left Chiswick on 25th August at the start of the eighth Routemaster visit to the USA. First stop on the itinerary was New York City from 12th to 24th September followed by a fortnight in Baltimore, Ohio from 26th September to 8th October. Back at Chiswick on 26th October, RML 2396 finally found its way into service at Putney in November.

RML 2543 made the only sortie into Europe of 1966. The famous Galeries Lafayette department store on the Boulevard Haussmann in Paris was host to the fortnight long 'Les Britanniques' trade show and a Routemaster was required to operate a shoppers' service from Clichy in the north-western suburbs to the store via Avenue Wagram, the Arc de Triomphe and the Champs Elysees. RML 2543 was just six weeks old when it was despatched on 22nd August. The trade show lasted from 26th August until 10th October and RML 2543 got home two days later, entering service at Willesden on the 1st of the next month.

When Leyland Atlantean XA 50 was selected for a trip to Leipzig in East Germany in the early months of 1967 there was speculation that perhaps the role for Routemasters as Ambassadors Abroad was drawing to a close in favour of more 'modern' (if less worthy) vehicles. However this turned out to be but a minor aberration and the Routemasters' jaunts continued undiminished. Not surprisingly, since these and not Atlantean-like creatures were what most people overseas regarded as the typical London bus. The 22nd Routemaster trip was sponsored by Brooke Bond Tea Ltd and saw RMLs 2548 and 2560 departing on 22nd March for Toronto en route to EXPO 67, a grand exhibition in Montreal to mark Canada's centenary as a Dominion. With marker lights on front and rear domes to comply with local traffic laws, the two RMLs operated in Canada for a full six months from 28th April to 24th October carrying passengers from downtown Montreal to the exhibition pavilions on islands in the St Lawrence river, a 3½ mile trip. Multi-lingual ladies in London Transport uniform – modified with a miniskirt to add glamour – acted as 'clippies'. Not until 11th December did the two buses arrive back at Chiswick, and even then further plans for them meant that there was to be no entry into passenger service yet awhile. After some preparation work at Hanwell garage and in Chiswick they were destined to leave for Denmark on 18th April 1968 to sponsor British goods in Esbjerg. Back at Chiswick on 9th May, both were at last placed into service later in the month, RML 2548 at Chalk Farm and RML 2560 at Upton Park. However for RML 2548 the overseas wanderings were not yet at an end and on 5th September it was withdrawn to be made ready to travel to Basle in Switzerland on 16th September where it was required for the 20th. Back at Chiswick ten days later, it returned to Chalk Farm during October, its overseas wanderings now complete.

Meanwhile, reverting to 1967, RML 2661

The inevitable queue forms to take advantage of a free trip on RM 1756 during its 1969 visit to Vienna. After so many overseas tours the enthusiasm for fitting polished wheel rings seems to have vanished and, apart from posters and blinds, the vehicle looks much as it would have done in London service. R.F. Mack

had left Felixstowe for Rotterdam aboard the *Gaelic Ferry* on 18th August for a three week tour of Holland in conjunction with the Board of Trade to promote British foods at the many stores run by the De Gruyter chain. Between 21st August and 8th September trips were given in Amsterdam and The Hague, and also in Rotterdam, upon completion of which RML 2661 returned to Chiswick on 13th September and was allocated to Hanwell next day.

RML 2661's trip to Holland was overshadowed by an event which occurred just afterwards when, in the greatest show of Routemaster power to date, no fewer than seven vehicles (RML 2662-2668) were despatched on 25th September to take part in British Week in Brussels from 29th September to 7th October. This was the first Routemaster incursion into Belgium and was on such a scale that the convoy was met upon docking at Antwerp by a British Military Police escort who saw it to the Brussels city limits where Brussels tramways staff took over. The seven-strong contingent arrived back at Chiswick on 11th October, but it was again to Belgium that the first Routemaster excursion of 1968 headed. On this occasion the destination was Bruges for a trade fair from 20th April to 3rd May. RML 2756 was allocated to Hanwell to be made ready for departure on 17th April, finally commencing its working career at Putney on 22nd May, just on a fortnight after arriving back from its Belgian jaunt.

The highest numbered RML, 2760, had its working life at Upton Park interrupted in June 1968 when a trip to British Week in the French city of Lille beckoned. Although the week's events were not due to start until 11th October, ample time was allowed for Chiswick staff to prepare the vehicle in readiness for departure on the 8th. It was accompanied on the venture by a Daimler Fleetline carrying the attractive green livery of Leeds City Transport and looking as totally different from the Routemaster as it was possible to be. The tour finished back at Chiswick on 24th October after which RML 2760 resumed its service career, but this time at Chalk Farm.

The great success of the 1965 journey by RM 2214 to Japan was repeated, albeit on a far larger scale, in 1969 when no fewer than eight Routemasters crossed the globe by cargo boat. This largest and presumably costliest of all Routemaster goodwill trips, with all the tremendous amount of organisation which it entailed, was carried out solely to support a week's British trade fair in Tokyo from 26th September to 5th October. The joint sponsors of the expedition were Blue Funnel, Glen Line and McGregor Swire Air Services, all members of the Ocean Steamship group on whose Blue Funnel steamer *Patroclus* the party left from Birkenhead on 1st August. Routemaster production having now ceased, London Transport adopted the next best course in selecting eight newly-overhauled vehicles which, having emerged from the Aldenham paint shops between 12th and 22 May, were held back from re-entering service and were sent instead, some to Chiswick and some to Hanwell, to be prepared for the forthcoming trip. The vehicles selected were RMs 1590, 1599, 1613, 1619, 1674, 1680, 1682, 1700. As a precaution RM 1635 was also set aside after overhaul but in the end was not needed. It was not until 15th December that the party arrived back at Chiswick, concluding what was to be the final Routemaster goodwill mission to the Asian continent.

Two European trips in the autumn of 1969 brought the number of Routemaster trips abroad to over thirty. Again, newly-overhauled RMs were employed, RM 1757 and 1758 departing on 22nd September and arriving back on 9th October from a week's stint in Hamburg lasting from 26th September to 4th October, whilst RMs 1756, 1759, 1761, 1767 were the first of the class to travel to Austria for a week in Vienna from 10th to 18th October. These four sailed on 3rd October and were back home on the 27th. Theirs was the final tour of the decade, and with none at all scheduled for the following year a notable dwindling of interest in such trade promotional ventures was evident in the nineteen-seventies.

Appendices

APPENDIX 1
ORIGINAL REGISTRATION NUMBERS OF ROUTEMASTERS

RM 1/2	SLT 56/57	RM 1001-1253	1-253 CLT	RM 2001-2105	ALM 1-105B
RML 3	SLT 58	RMF 1254	254 CLT	RM 2106-2217	CUV 106-217C
CRL 4	SLT 59	RM 1255-1452	255-452 CLT	RCL 2218-2260	CUV 218-260C
RM 5-300	VLT 5-300	RMC 1453-1520	453-520 CLT	RML 2261-2363	CUV 261-363C
RM 301-879	WLT 301-879	RM 1521-1600	521-600 CLT	RML 2364-2598	JJD 364-598D
RML 880-903	WLT 880-903	RM 1601-1865	601-865 DYE	RML 2599-2657	NML 599-657E
RM 904-999	WLT 904-999	RM 1866-1999	ALD 866-999B	RML 2658-2760	SMK 658-760F
RM 1000	100 BXL	RM 2000	ALM 200B	FRM 1	KGY 4D

NORTHERN GENERAL		BRITISH EUROPEAN AIRWAYS	
2085-2102	RCN 685-702	BEA 1-25	KJD 601-625D
2103	BUP 249B	BEA 26-65	NMY 626-665E
2104-2107	EUP 404-407B		
2108-2134	FPT 578-604C		

APPENDIX 2
ROUTEMASTER UNIT NUMBERS

R2RH 001	RM 459	R2RH 461-468	RM 449-458	R2RH 1716-1806	RM 1720-1810
R2RH 002	RM 341	R2RH 469-474	RM 466-471	2R2RH 1807-1981	RM 1811-1985
R2RH 003	RM 398	R2RH 475-495	RM 479-499	R2RH 1982-2156	RM 1986-2160
R2RH 004-251	RM 5-252	R2RH 496-627	RM 500-631	3R2RH 2157-2174	NGT 2085-2102
R2RH 252-258	RM 333-339	2R2RH 628	RM 632	R2RH/3 2175-2217	RCL 2218-2260
R2RH 259	RM 340	R2RH 629-865	RM 633-869	R2RH 2218-2274	RM 2161-2217
R2RH 260	RM 464	2R2RH 866	RM 870	R2RH/1 2275-2524	RML 2261-2510
R2RH 261-340	RM 253-332	R2RH 867-875	RM 871-879	3R2RH 2525/2526	NGT 2103/2104
R2RH 341-344	RM 342-345	R2RH 876-899	RML 880-903	3R2RH 2527-2537	NGT 2108-2118
R2RH 345/346	RM 447/448	R2RH 900-1004	RM 904-1008	3R2RH 2538-2540	NGT 2105-2107
R2RH 347/348	RM 457/458	2R2RH 1005	RM 1009	3R2RH 2541-2556	NGT 2119-2134
R2RH 349-352	RM 460-463	R2RH 1006-1249	RM 1010-1253	R2RH/1 2557-2806	RML 2511-2760
R2RH 353	RM 465	3R2RH 1250	RMF 1254	R2RH/2 2807-2871	BEA 1-65
R2RH 354-360	RM 472-478	2R2RH 1251-1448	RM 1255-1452	FR2R 001	FRM 1
R2RH 361-412	RM 346-397	R2RH 1449-1516	RMC 1453-1520		
R2RH 413-460	RM 399-446	2R2RH 1517-1715	RM 1521-1719		

Unit numbers were not allocated to the four prototypes

ROUTEMASTER-WORKED SERVICES IN THE COUNTRY BUS DEPARTMENT AT 5TH OCTOBER 1968

Routes	Allocation			Also worked
	MON-FRI	*SAT*	*SUN*	
306/A, 311	Garston 12 RML	Garston 7 RML	Garston 3 RML	346/C/D
335			Windsor 1 RML	
			Garston 1 RML	
347/A	Garston 9 RML	Garston 9 RML	Garston 5 RML	318, 346, 385C
	Hemel Hempstead 2 RML	Hemel Hempstead 2 RML		
363	High Wycombe 6 RML	High Wycombe 5 RML	High Wycombe 1 RML	362
396, 397/A/B	Harlow 3 RML (+ 3RT)	Harlow 1 RML (+ 5RT)	(1 RT)	339, 393A, 804, 805
400	Windsor 3 RML	Windsor 3 RML	Windsor 1 RML	407, 417, 446
				457/A/D, 484/A/B
407/A, 417	Windsor 1 RML (+ 3RT)	Windsor 2 RML (+ 1RT)		335, 353, 441
				446/B, 457A, 460
409, 411, 482	Godstone 15 RML	Godstone 9 RML	Godstone 6 RML	410, 428
	East Grinstead 1 RML	East Grinstead 1 RML		
	Reigate 1 RML	Reigate 1 RML		
410	Godstone 10 RML	Godstone 4 RML	Godstone 2 RML	
446/A/B	Windsor 5 RML	Windsor 3 RML	Windsor 1 RML	353, 400, 484
457/A/C/D	Windsor 2 RML (+ 4RT)	Windsor 5 RML	Windsor 4 RML	446
460	Windsor 1 RMC (a)			
480	Northfleet 14 RML	Northfleet 14 RML	Northfleet 5 RML	495, 496A
484/A/B	Windsor 3 RML	Windsor 2 RML		417, 446/A/B
487			Northfleet 2 RML	
495			Northfleet 1 RML	
496			Northfleet 1 RML	
497, 498	Northfleet 1 RML (+ 2RT)	Northfleet 1 RML (+ 2RT)	Northfleet 2 RML	
804/A/B	Harlow 1 RML (+ 4RT)	Harlow 2 RML (+ 4RT)	Harlow 1 RML	339, 393, 396
				397/A, 805, 806
805/A/B, 806	Harlow 5 RML (+ 4RT)	Harlow 5 RML (+ 1RT)	Harlow 2 RML	339, 396, 397/A, 804/B
GREEN LINE				
704	Dunton Green 7 RCL	Dunton Green 7 RCL	Dunton Green 7 RCL	441
	Windsor 7 RCL (b)	Windsor 7 RCL	Windsor 7 RCL	
		1 RMC (c)		
705	Dunton Green 5 RCL	Dunton Green 4 RCL	Dunton Green 4 RCL	431, 493
	1 RMC (d)	1 RMC (d)	1 RMC (d)	
	Windsor 3 RCL	Windsor 3 RCL	Windsor 3 RCL	
708	East Grinstead 4 RMC	East Grinstead 4 RMC	East Grinstead 4 RMC	334, 435
	Hemel Hempstead 3 RMC	Hemel Hempstead 3 RMC	Hemel Hempstead 3 RMC	
709	Godstone 2 RCL	No service	Godstone 1 RCL	
715	Guildford 7 RMC	Guildford 7 RMC	Guildford 7 RMC	331, 415
	Hertford 7 RMC	Hertford 7 RMC	Hertford 7 RMC	
716/A	Addlestone 7 RMC	Addlestone 7 RMC	Addlestone 7 RMC	303, 420, 461/A
	Hatfield 5 RMC	Hatfield 5 RMC	Hatfield 5 RMC	463, 800, 801
	Stevenage 4 RMC	Stevenage 4 RMC	Stevenage 4 RMC	
718	Harlow 5 RMC (e)	Harlow 4 RMC	Harlow 4 RMC	417, 804
	Windsor 4 RMC	Windsor 4 RMC	Windsor 4 RMC	
721	Romford 13 RCL	Romford 13 RCL	Romford 10 RCL	
723	Grays 9 RMC (e)	Grays 9 RMC	Grays 7 RMC	367, 371

(a) Also serves as late running coach for route 704. Main Mon-Fri allocation on route 460 is RF ex Staines
(b) Plus 1 x RMC late running coach which also works route 460
(c) Late running coach
(d) Duplicate
(e) Including one late running coach

A service operated by RMLs — and other types — just a few days per year was the 406F Epsom racecourse special. RML 2315 is seen at Epsom station on bank holiday 28th August 1967. A special allocation of vehicles, drawn from a number of garages, was provided for each occasion.
Gerald Mead

APPENDIX 4

MONTHLY SUMMARY OF LONDON TRANSPORT ROUTEMASTERS
INTO PASSENGER SERVICE AND INITIAL ALLOCATIONS

February 1956	RM 1 (W)
May 1957	*RM 2* (RG)
October 1957	*CRL 4* (RE)
January 1958	RML 3 (AC)
June 1959	RM 5, 7, 24 (AC), RM 14 (R), RM 18 (B), RM 19 (W)
July 1959	RM 22, 25, 28 (AC), RM 29, 32, 33, 34, 37 (R), RM 30, 31, 35, 39, 42 (W)
August 1959	RM 10, 41 (W), RM 36 (V), RM 43 (H)
September 1959	RM 38 (W), RM 40, 47, 54, 55 (H), RM 44, 45, 48, 49, 51, 56, (AR) RM 52 (R), RM 57, 75 (V)
October 1959	RM 86 (AC), RM 89, 94-96, 101 (V), RM 99 (H)
November 1959	RM 6, 9, 11-13, 15, 20, 21, 23, 27, 58, 64, 70, 137 (WH), RM 26, 50, 53, 59-63, 65-69, 71-74, 76-85, 87, 88, 90-93, 97, 98, 100, 102-110, 112-117, 119-123, 125, 130 (PR), RM 111 (V)
December 1959	RM 118, 124, 126-128, 131-135 (PR)
February 1960	RM 129 (PR), RM 136, 138, 186-207, 216 (WH), RM 139-141, 143-146, 148-185, 218, 219 (WW)
March 1960	RM 16, 17, 210, 238, 249, 250, 253 (WH)
April 1960	RM 142, 208, 209, 211-215, 217, 220-237, 239-241, 243, 244, 246-248, 305, 306, 309, 310 (WW), RM 147, 242, 245, 251, 252, 254-260, 262-293, 295-304 (WH)
June 1960	RM 307, 308, 312, 314-318, 320-322, 352 (WH)
July 1960	RM 313, 323-351, 353, 355-362, 365-372, 377, 380, 389, 394, 395, 402 (S), RM 364, 373, 374, 376, 378, 379, 381-388, 390, 391 (HT)
August 1960	RM 392, 396 (S)
October 1960	RM 398 (PR)
November 1960	RM 261 (WW), RM 319 (WH), RM 375, 393, 397, 399-401, 403-421, 423-429, 431-452, 454-459, 461-480, 483, 486, 488-491, 498, 501-506, 522, 526 (HL)
December 1960	RM 525, 527-574 (HL)
January 1961	RM 604, 607 (HL)
February 1961	RM 422, 430, 453, 460, 481, 482, 484, 485, 487, 492-497, 499, 500, 507-509, 511, 513-517, 519, 520, 523, 575-599, 601-603, 605, 606, 608-610, 612, 613, 615, 616, 618-620, 622, 623, 626-631 (HT)
March 1961	RM 510 (HT)
April 1961	RM 518, 521, 524, 600, 621, 624, 625, 633-646, 648-659, 668, 671, 673, 675, 677-682, 688, 691, 694 (WN), RM 611, 614, 647, 661-663, 666, 667, 730, 732-735, 737-745, 747 (HT), RM 617, 669, 670, 672, 674, 676, 683-687, 689, 690, 692, 693, 695-729, 731, 736, 746, 748-752, 758-772, 775 (EM), RM 753-757 (WG)
June 1961	RM 632, 660, 665 (HL)
July 1961	RM 311, 354, 363, 512, 773, 774, 776-781, 802-813, 815, 818, 824, 834, 841, 842, 844-848 (EM), RM 664 (HT), RM 782-801, 814, 816, 817, 819-823, 826, 828-833, 835-840, 843, 849-861 (SF)
August 1961	RM 46 (WW), RM 827 (EM), RM 862, 864 (SF)
September 1961	RM 870 (HL)
November 1961	RM 294 (HT), RM 876, 878, 879, 904-908, 910, 912, 922-925, 935, 965, 976-979, 981-984, 986 (FY), RM 909, 911, 915-921, 939-941, 943-945, 955-964, 966-969, 972-974 (WN), RM 926-934, 936-938, 942, 946-954 (NX), RM 970, 975, 980, 985, 987-991 (WH)
	RML 880-894 (FY)
December 1961	RML 895-897 (FY)
January 1962	RM 825, 913, 914, 998, 1001, 1002, 1004, 1006, 1008, 1012, 1026, 1029, 1030, 1033 (X), RM 868, 869, 871-875, 877 (FY), RM 971, 1007, 1010, 1011, 1014-1017, 1020-1023, 1025, 1036, 1038, 1039, 1051-1057, 1059-1070, 1075, 1080, 1082-1084 (SE), RM 992, 999, 1018, 1032, 1035, 1037, 1041-1050 (W), RM 1071 (AR), RM 1072 (HL), RM 1076 (HT), RM 1077, 1079 (SF), RM 1078 (WH)
	RML 899 (FY)
February 1962	RM 1074, 1081, 1097-1099, 1103, 1108 (SE), RM 1085, 1094 (NX), RM 1096 (FY)
March 1962	RM 994, 1005 (HT), RM 1000 (WH), RM 1003 (SF), RM 1009 (HL)
April 1962	RM 1163 (AR), RM 1166 (FY), RM 1168, 1169, 1177, 1178, 1195, 1196 (NX)
May 1962	RM 863, 866, 867, 993, 995-997, 1013, 1019, 1024, 1027, 1028, 1159-1162 (SE), RM 1040, 1158, 1164, 1165, 1167, 1174, 1181, 1183-1187, 1197-1200, 1202, 1205, 1209, 1210 (NB), RM 1058, 1086-1093, 1100-1102, 1105, 1106, 1113-1133, 1135-1137, 1139, 1142 (FW), RM 1073, 1095, 1104, 1107, 1109-1112, 1134, 1138, 1140, 1141, 1143, 1145-1154, 1212 (AV)
June 1962	RM 1170 (NX)
July 1962	RM 1144 (SE)
August 1962	*RMC 1453-1455, 1457-1459, 1466-1471* (HG), *RMC 1456, 1460-1465, 1472* (GF)
September 1962	RML 900 (FY)
	RMC 1474 (HG), *RMC 1477* (GF)
October 1962	*RMC 1473, 1475* (HG), *RMC 1476* (GF), *RMC 1478, 1480-1484, 1487, 1490-1492, 1494, 1496* (EP), *RMC 1479, 1485, 1486, 1488, 1489, 1493, 1495* (WR)
November 1962	*RMC 1497* (GF), *RMC 1499-1506, 1509* (GR)
December 1962	RM 865, 1155, 1156, 1171, 1175, 1176, 1179, 1182, 1192, 1193, 1226, 1227, 1229, 1246, 1248-1253 (AE), RM 1031, 1034, 1230-1235, 1257, 1335-1340, 1358, 1368, 1369, 1371, 1372 (W), RM 1157, 1180, 1188-1191, 1194, 1201, 1203, 1204, 1206-1208 (RL), RM 1211,1213-1225 (AF), RM 1228, 1236-1238, 1240-1245, 1247, 1256, 1274, 1277, 1286, 1288-1290, 1292-1303, 1305, 1307, 1308, 1310, 1315, 1319-1323, 1327-1334 (AR), RM 1255, 1260-1263, 1266, 1267, 1269-1271, 1278-1285, 1287, 1291, 1304, 1306, 1309, 1311-1314, 1316-1318, 1324-1326, 1341 (M), RM 1342-1346, 1348-1354, 1356, 1357, 1359-1365 (SW)
January 1963	RM 1172, 1173, 1258, 1259, 1264, 1265, 1268, 1273, 1275, 1276, 1347, 1355, 1366, 1367, 1370, 1373, 1375-1377 (W), RM 1374, 1378, 1379 (SE), RM 1380 (FY), RM 1381 (FW), RM 1382 (AV), RM 1383-1407, 1409-1411 (RL)
	RMC 1498, 1508, 1512, 1515-1520 (WY), *RMC 1507, 1510, 1511, 1513, 1514* (SV)
February 1963	RM 1239 (AF), RM 1408, 1412-1432, 1523 (RL), RM 1433-1437, 1439-1441, 1521, 1522 (PM)
March 1963	RM 1438 (W), RM 1524, 1533 (NX), RM 1525, 1532, 1534-1537, 1540, 1541 (PM), RM 1526 (RL), RM 1527 (SW), RM 1528, 1530 (WN), RM 1529 (AR), RM 1531 (EM)
	RML 901, 903 (FY)

April 1963	RM 1272, 1450, 1538, 1539, 1543, 1549-1554, 1558-1562, 1564 (M), RM 1442-1449, 1451, 1542, 1544-1548 (PM), RM 1452, 1555, 1565, 1568 (AR), RM 1563 (NX)
May 1963	RM 1556, 1589-1594 (D), RM 1566, 1569, 1570, 1572, 1573 (AR), RM 1567, 1571, 1574-1576, 1579, 1580, 1582, 1584 (RL), RM 1578, 1581, 1583, 1585-1588 (M)
June 1963	RM 1557, 1595, 1596, 1598-1602, 1604, 1606 (D), RM 1603, 1605, 1607 (RL), RM 1608, 1610, 1624, 1628 (W), RM 1611, 1613-1623, 1625 (MH), RM 1612 (SW)
July 1963	RM 1597 (M), RM 1626, 1632, 1633, 1645, 1647, 1650 (W), RM 1629, 1631, 1634-1644, 1646, 1648, 1649, 1652 (MH), RM 1651, 1653-1660, 1669 (PM), RM 1668 (NX)
August 1963	RM 1661-1664, 1666 (PM)
September 1963	RM 1665, 1674, 1679, 1683, 1684 (M), RM 1667, 1670-1673, 1675-1678, 1680-1682 (PM)
October 1963	RM 1685, 1687-1703 (W), RM 1686 (AF), RM 1704-1719 (J)
November 1963	RM 1627 (SW), RM 1720, 1725, 1737-1740 (W), RM 1721, 1728-1734, 1736, 1741-1750, 1752, 1754, 1755 (CF), RM 1722-1724, 1726, 1727, 1735 (AF)
December 1963	RM 1751, 1753, 1756-1758, 1760-1762 (CF), RM 1759, 1763-1778, 1780, 1781 (X)
January 1964	RM 1779, 1782, 1785, 1787-1789, 1793 (W), RM 1783, 1784, 1786, 1790-1792, 1794, 1798, 1799, 1801-1803 (X), RM 1795 (WH), RM 1796 (WN)
February 1964	RM 1797, 1800, 1804-1833, 1837-1839 (AR)
March 1964	RM 1834-1836, 1840, 1841, 1843, 1844 (AR), RM 1842, 1845-1847, 1849-1856, 1858, 1859, 1861 (BK), RM 1848, 1857, 1860, 1862-1865 (ON)
April 1964	RM 1630, 1866-1874, 1877-1888, 1890 (U), RM 1875, 1876 (ON)
May 1964	RM 1889, 1891-1899, 1902, 1905, 1908-1911 (U), RM 1900, 1901, 1903, 1904, 1906, 1907 (TC)
	RML 898, 902 (FY)
June 1964	RM 1577, 1912-1921, 1923-1934 (AF)
July 1964	RM 1922 (AF), RM 1935-1940, 1942-1949, 1952-1956 (H), RM 1941, 1950, 1951, 1957-1973, 1978 (MH), RM 1975, 1977, 1979, 1980 (J)
August 1964	RM 1974, 1976, 1981-1992, 1994-1996 (PB)
	RMF 1254 (BEA)
September 1964	RM 1993, 1997-2001, 2003 (D), RM 2002, 2004-2015, 2018, 2021 (AE)
October 1964	RM 2016, 2017, 2019, 2020, 2022-2030, 2032, 2034-2037, 2039-2041 (GM)
November 1964	RM 2031, 2042-2045, 2047-2049, 2051-2053, 2056 (GM), RM 2033, 2046, 2050, 2054, 2055, 2057-2070, 2072-2075, 2077 (N)
December 1964	RM 2038, 2071, 2076, 2078-2090, 2092, 2096, 2097, 2099, 2101 (N), RM 2091, 2093-2095, 2098, 2100, 2102-2105 (CF)
January 1965	RM 2106, 2108, 2109, 2111, 2112, 2115-2117, 2121, 2122, 2124, 2127, 2128, 2132, 2133 (BW)
February 1965	RM 2107, 2110, 2113, 2114, 2118-2120, 2123, 2125, 2126, 2129, 2134-2137, 2139-2145 (BW), RM 2130, 2131, 2138, 2146-2150, 2152, 2156, 2157 (AC)
March 1965	RM 2151, 2153-2155, 2160-2176, 2178 (AC)
April 1965	RM 2177, 2179, 2181-2184, 2187, 2188, 2190-2195 (AC), RM 2180, 2185, 2189, 2197-2199, 2201, 2202 (H), RM 2186 (D)
May 1965	RM 2200, 2204-2213, 2216 (H)
June 1965	*RCL 2218-2245* (RE)
July 1965	*RCL 2246, 2249, 2258-2260* (HG), *RCL 2247, 2250-2257* (GY), *RCL 2248* (RE)
August 1965	RM 1609 (MH)
September 1965	RM 2196, 2215, 2217 (AC)
October 1965	RML 2278-2280, 2287, 2288, 2293, 2295-2305, *2307, 2309-2317, 2319* (GD), *RML 2306* (EG), *RML 2308* (RG)
November 1965	RML 2263-2277, 2281, 2283, 2285, 2286, 2289-2292, 2294 (AR), *RML 2318, 2320-2328, 2337-2345* (NF), *RML 2329-2332, 2334-2336* (GD)
December 1965	RM 2203 (SF)
	RML 2333, 2346-2354 (GD), RML 2356-2363 (SF)
January 1966	RM 2158, 2159 (WL)
	RML 2282, 2405, 2407 (FY)
February 1966	RM 2214 (R)
	RML 2261, 2366, 2373, 2377, 2380, 2386, 2393, 2394, 2399, 2400, 2402, 2404, 2408 (WH), RML 2367, 2370, 2376, 2378, 2383, 2387, 2388, 2390 (WW), RML 2379, 2384, 2389, 2398, 2401, 2403, 2406, 2409, 2410 (PR), *RML 2411, 2412, 2415-2419* (HE)
March 1966	*RML 2355, 2413, 2420-2425, 2427-2435, 2437-2441, 2443* (GR), RML 2369, 2372, 2375, 2381, 2382, 2391, 2392, 2395 (WH), *RML 2414, 2426* (HH)
April 1966	RML 2385 (WH)
May 1966	*RML 2436, 2447, 2457* (WR), *RML 2442, 2444, 2445, 2448-2450, 2453, 2456, 2458* (HA), *RML 2446, 2451, 2452, 2454, 2455, 2459, 2460* (NF), RML 2461 (AR), RML 2462-2464, 2468, 2471 (FY), RML 2465-2467, 2469, 2470, 2472-2475, 2477-2480, 2483 (AF)
June 1966	RML 2371, 2476, 2481, 2482, 2484-2495, 2497, 2498, 2502, 2506 (SW), RML 2496, 2500, 2501 (FY)
July 1966	RML 2368, 2499, 2503-2505, 2507-2528, 2530-2538, 2540 (U)
September 1966	RML 2397, 2529, 2539, 2541, 2542, 2544-2547, 2549, 2550, 2552, 2553, 2555-2557, 2561-2567 (H), RML 2554 (SW)
October 1966	RML 2284, 2543, 2551, 2558-2560, 2568-2574, 2576 (AC)
November 1966	RML 2262, 2364, 2365, 2374, 2396, 2575, 2577-2592 (AF), RML 2593, 2594 (AC)
December 1966	RML 2595-2598 (U)
May 1967	RML 2599-2614, 2619, 2620, 2622-2626, 2628-2633 (J)
June 1967	RML 2615-2618, 2621, 2627 (J), RML 2634-2637, 2639-2643 (AF)
	FRM 1 (AR)
July 1967	RML 2638, 2645-2649, 2651-2655, 2657 (R), RML 2650, 2656 (HL)
September 1967	RML 2644, 2658, 2659, 2692, 2693, 2704 (UX), RML 2660, 2661, 2669-2691, 2694-2699 (HL)
October 1967	RML 2663, 2700-2703, 2705-2708, 2711-2715 (HL), RML 2709, 2710 (UX)
November 1967	RML 2662, 2664-2667, 2716-2723, 2725-2727, 2729-2733 (TC), RML 2668 (CF), RML 2724, 2728, 2734-2738 (HL)
December 1967	RML 2739-2747, 2749 (TC)
January 1968	RML 2748, 2750-2753 (TC)
February 1968	RML 2757-2759 (TC)
March 1968	RML 2754, 2755 (TC), RML 2760 (U)
May 1968	RML 2548 (CF), RML 2756 (AF)
March 1976	RM 8 (SP)

Vehicles shown in italics were in green livery

SERVICES WITH ROUTEMASTER ALLOCATIONS, CENTRAL BUSES, AT 31ST DECEMBER 1969

Route	Garage	Mon-Fri	Saturday	Sunday
1	TL	18 RT	–	–
	NX	11 RT	15 RM	–
1A	NX	–	–	5 RM
2	W	13 RM	15 RM	7 RM
	SW	12 RM	8 RM	13 RM
2A	SW	14 RM	–	–
2B	N	14 RM	8 RM	6 RM
	SW	15 RM	13 RM	6 RM
3	CF	10 RM	7 RM	6 RM
	N	19 RM	19 RM	9 RM
5	WH	13 RML	9 RML	–
	PR	–	–	6 RM
6	H	23 RML	14 RML	11 RML
	AC	16 RML	16 RML, 4 RM	13 RML
7	X	32 RM	18 RM	–
8	BW	24 RM	24 RM	14 RM
	AC	16 RM	15 RM	8 RM
8A	BW	13 RM	–	–
8B	W	9 RM	–	–
9	D	20 RM	12 RM	–
	M	17 RM	13 RM	5 RM
	PR	–	–	7 RM
10	BW	22 RT	12 RT	8 RM
11	D	27 RM	13 RM	9 RM
	R	13 RM	12 RM	7 RM
	GM	–	15 RM	5 RM
12	TC	8 RT	15 RT	–
	ED	47 RT	29 RT	27 RT
	PM	25 RT	18 RT	–
	S	11 RT	7 RM	–
13	AE	17 RM	19 RM	–
	Q	15 RM	–	–
14	J	33 RML	25 RML	20 RML
	NB	–	–	9 RM
	AF	24 RML	7 RML	6 RML
15	U	43 RML	13 RML	11 RML
	X	–	17 RM, 10 RT	12 RM
16	W	51 RM	34 RM	25 RM
17	HT	20 RM	11 RM	5 RM
	WL	–	–	14 RM
18	ON	8 RM	–	8 RM
	SE	37 RM	37 RM	7 RM
	X	6 RM	–	–
22	B	14 RM	10 RM	5 RM
	CT	17 RM	13 RM	8 RM
23	BK	14 RM	–	14 RM
	WH	8 RM	12 RM	–
	PR	–	–	8 RM
	U	–	9 RML	–
24	CF	28 RML	23 RML	13 RML
25	BW	31 RT	25 RT	7 RM
	WH	20 RT	8 RM	14 RM
27	J	14 RT	17 RT	7 RT
	R	11 RT	8 RT	6 RML
	V	6 RT	–	7 RT
28	X	15 RT	16 RT	8 RM
	WD	18 RT	17 RT	13 RT
29	HT	22 RM	16 RM	6 RM
	WN	24 RM	17 RM	6 RM
	AD	–	–	6 RM
	PB	–	–	7 RM
30	H	26 RM	23 RM	14 RM
	AF	12 RM	9 RML	7 RML
31	B	17 RT	14 RT	7 RM
	CF	8 RT	13 RT	9 RM
33	M	22 RM	14 RM	–
34B	AR	RM/XA (ex 76)	–	–
35	Q	18 RM	21 RM, 1 RT	14 RM
	H	13 RM	5 RML	6 RM
36	PM	30 RM	19 RM	16 RM
36A	PM	16 RM	6 RM	–
36B	PM	31 RM	24 RM	9 RM
	NX	–	9 RM	–
	Q	–	–	9 RM
37	AF	16 RML	8 RML	6 RML
	SW	20 RML	20 RML, 18 RM	10 RML
	PM	–	–	6 RM
40	PR	11 RM	11 RM	–
	U	--	–	12 RML
	Q	–	–	7 RM
40A	Q	7 RM	7 RM	–
	PR	8 RM	7 RM	–
41	AR	18 RM	18 RM	10 RM
43	MH	26 RM	10 RM	–
45	CF	10 RM	7 RM	–
	WL	21 RM	19 RM	–
47	TB	12 RT	–	–
	TL	17 RT	19 RT	22 RT
	D	12 RT	21 RM	8 RM
52	X	11 RM	7 RM	5 RM
	AC	25 RM	20 RM	13 RM
53	NX	41 RM	26 RM	12 RM
	AM	8 RM	–	5 RM
58	WW	5 RM	8 RM	2 RM
	WH	19 RM	22 RM	7 RM
59	TC	–	–	15 RML
	AK	–	–	6 RT
63	PM	33 RM	21 RM	10 RM
	HT	8 RM	–	–
64	TH	23 RM	15 RM	7 RM
66	NS	10 RT	11 RT	5 RM
67	SF	17 RM	21 RM	–
68	CF	9 RM	5 RM	4 RM
	TC	19 RM	6 RML	5 RML
	N	7 RM	10 RM	5 RM
69	T	5 RM	5 RM, 6 RT	–
	WH	27 RM	14 RM	13 RM
72	R	18 RT	9 RM	8 RM
73	AR	61 RM	43 RM	27 RM
	M	7 RM	7 RM	12 RM
74	AF	12 RML	19 RML	12 RML
74B	R	12 RML	–	–
75	TL	25 RT	20 RT	7 RM
76	AR	11 RM, 10 XA	14 XA	9 XA
78	D	3 RT	–	–
	PM	23 RT	14 RM	10 RM
81/C	AV	6 RM	6 RM	–
81B	AV	4 RM	6 RM	3 RM
81	AV	–	–	3 RM
83	ON	24 RM	25 RM	6 RM
85	NB	3 RM	–	–
	AF	9 RM	13 RM	–
85A	AF	4 RM	2 RM	–
86	RD	11 RT	–	–
	U	15 RT	27 RT	9 RML
	AP	–	–	3 RT
88	S	19 RM	17 RM	8 RM
	SW	31 RM	13 RM	14 RM
93	AF	6 RT	7 RM	–
	A	25 RT	19 RT	14 RT
95	BN	14 RM	14 RM	–
95A	BN	–	–	7 RM
99	AM	10 RT	8 RM	–
	AW	–	–	3 RM
100	U	RML (ex 15)	RML (ex 15)	RML (ex 15)
102	AD	22 RT	15 RT	8 RM
	MH	–	–	3 RM
104	FY	13 RML	9 RML	14 RML
	HT	–	6 RM	–
104A	FY	5 RML	–	–
106	H	9 RM	19 RM	–
	PR	15 RM	7 RM	–

Route 99 had Saturday and Sunday allocations of RMs at the end of 1969, but not for much longer. The route was converted to omo using MBs in the first month of 1970. Abbey Wood's RM 637 is seen one Sunday in June 1969 in Woolwich.
Colin Stannard

106A	H	–	–	4 RM	155	AL	16 RT	12 RT	6 RT
	D	–	–	12 RM		NB	–	–	4 RM
113	AE	22 RM	11 RM	4 RM	162	U	9 RM	–	–
115A	TH	–	–	4 RM	162A	U	–	6 RML	–
116	AV	11 RT	7 RT	5 RM	165	RD	14 RML	14 RML, 1 RT	6 RML
117	AV	32 RM	22 RM	10 RM	169	BK	5 RT	5 RM	4 RT
	V	–	9 RT	–		AP	11 RT	11 RT	–
123	AD	13 RM	–	–	171	NX	15 RM	8 RM	16 RM
	WW	19 RM	15 RM	7 RM		AR	19 RM	11 RM	–
	WN	–	8 RM	4 RM	173	PM	5 RM	7 RM	3 RM
127	EM	20 RM	15 RM	–	174	NS	19 RM	10 RM	6 RM
	E	13 RM	13 RM	3 RM		BK	–	11 RT	–
	HT	–	–	10 RM	177	AW	8 RT	5 RT	8 RM
130	TC	25 RML	22 RML	10 RML		NX	14 RT	16 RT	4 RM
130A	TC	–	6 RML	–	180	AW	11 RM	10 RM	–
130B	TC	12 RML	–	–		TL	11 RM	5 RM	–
130C	TC	8 RML	8 RML	10 RML	181	SW	10 RT	7 RM	–
	TH	–	–	5 RM	183	AE	16 RT	14 RT	9 RM
131	AL	–	4 RT	–	187	ON	9 RT	5 RM	–
	NB	16 RM	15 RM	–		X	–	3 RM	4 RM
134	MH	17 RM	16 RM	9 RM	191	E	8 RT	–	–
	PB	14 RM	8 RM	4 RM		AR	–	9 RM	–
	J	–	–	4 RML	197	TC	17 RT	15 RT	5 RML
137	N	27 RM	17 RM	6 RM	207	HL	38 RML	27 RML	12 RML
	GM	31 RM	16 RM	7 RM		UX	10 RML	7 RML	10 RML
141	NX	18 RM	–	8 RM		HW	–	–	5 RML
	WN	28 RM	14 RM	6 RM	207A	HW	17 RML	13 RML	–
141A	NX	–	8 RM	–	213A	NB	–	–	4 RM
	J	–	8 RT	–		A	9 RT	9 RT	5 RT
144	WW	11 RT	12 RT	9 RM	214	HT	7 RM	9 RM	8 RM
	WN	5 RT	6 RM	1 RM	220	S	31 RM	19 RM	15 RM
147	U	13 RT	9 RM	–	221	FY	17 RM	19 RM	3 RM
149	EM	18 RM	22 RM	19 RM		WN	5 RM	6 RM	5 RM
	SF	16 RM	11 RM	4 RM	226	AC	5 RT	3 RT	3 RM

233	TC	1 XA/FRM	1 XA/FRM	–
238	WH	10 RM	8 RM	3 RM
239	CF	6 RM	–	–
240	W	5 RT	–	–
	EW	4 RT	3 RT	–
	AE	–	2 RT	3 RM
241	WH	13 RM	14 RM	3 RM
243	SF	27 RM	18 RM	–
	WN	6 RM	–	–
243A	SF	–	–	15 RM
244	MH	9 RT	5 RM	–
245	W	6 RM	–	–
253	HT	23 RM	16 RM	11 RM
	SF	26 RM	17 RM	17 RM
255	R	8 RM	4 RML	–
256	WW	8 RM	6 RM	–
259	AR	9 RM	6 RM	–
	HT	8 RM	11 RM	–
260	FY	12 RM	8 RM	5 RM
	SE	11 RM	–	–
	AC	–	8 RM	–
	AE	–	–	3 RM
261	AD	7 RT	8 RM	–
262	T	10 RML	7 RML	3 RML
	WH	10 RML	8 RML	3 RML
266	W	13 RM	16 RM	8 RM
	AC	13 RM	5 RM	–
	SE	–	–	8 RM

267	FW	20 RM	10 RM	9 RM
271	HT	14 RML	10 RML	8 RML
278	WH	11 RM	8 RM	–
279	EM	18 RM	26 RM	7 RM
279A	EM	17 RM	–	–
281	FW	17 RM	16 RM	6 RM
283	NB	3 RM	3 RM	–
285	FW	8 RM	7 RM	2 RF
	NB	6 RM	6 RM	4 RF
295	S	5 RM	–	–
Inter-Stn	NX	–	–	1 RM
N82	NX	1 RM	1 RM	1 RM
N83	SF	1 RM	1 RM	1 RM
N84	PR	1 RM	–	1 RM
N85	PM	4 RM	–	4 RM
N86	PM	3 RM	–	3 RM
N87	BN	3 RM	–	3 RM
	SW	3 RML	–	3 RML
N89	R	3 RM	–	3 RM
N90	AR	3 RM	–	3 RM
N91	AC	1 RML	–	1 RML
N92	J	2 RML	–	2 RML
N93	HT	1 RML	–	1 RML
N94	W	2 RM	1 RM	2 RM
N95	BK	2 RM	–	2 RM
N96	T	2 RML	–	2 RML
N97	V	3 RM	–	3 RM
N99	WH	1 RML	1 RML	1 RML

A

Aarhus	141
Abbey Wood	120, 133
Addlestone	12, 32, 40, 91, 94, 95
AEC	9, 10, 17, 19, 25, 28, 29, 30, 32, 37, 39, 42, 43, 52, 56, 57, 59, 60, 62, 63, 84, 85, 86, 87, 98, 99, 100, 107, 109, 122, 125, 126, 127, 133, 135, 136, 142
Airide	48, 92
Alabama	142
Albion Lowlander	84
Aldenham	11, 35, 51, 54, 83, 86, 90, 93, 100, 107, 120, 129, 130, 131, 133, 140, 141, 142, 143
Aldgate	39, 70
Aldwych	26
Alperton	79, 100, 118
Aluminium Centenary Exhibition	22
Amsterdam	142, 143
Andover	128
Anglesey	10
Antwerp	143
Ashfield, Lord	8
Associated Commercial Vehicles	42, 63
Atlantean	137, 138, 139, 143
Austria	143
Automotive Products Ltd.	18, 103

B

Baker Street	94
Baltimore	143
Barking	63, 70, 71, 142
Basle	140, 143
Battersea	41, 69, 120
Beadle, John C. (Coachbuilders) Ltd.	9
Beaton	34, 123
Beaumaris	9
Belgium	143
Bensham	123, 125
BET	10, 32, 122
Bexleyheath	68
Birkenhead	143
Blue Arrow	121
BOAC	22, 129
Bow	69, 103
Brentwood	39
Bridgemaster	37
Bridge of Weir	125
Bristol	12, 37, 57, 84, 123, 142
British European Airways (BEA)	73, 86, 87, 118, 126, 127, 128, 129
British Airways	93
British Transport Commission	13, 37, 42, 98
Brixton	76, 116
Brooke Bond Tea Ltd	143
Bruges	120, 143
Brussels	143

C

Camberwell	51, 103, 120, 121
Canada	143
Canterbury	86
Carshalton	68
Castle, Barbara	120
Catford	120
Cave-Brown-Cave	23
CAV	47, 48, 50, 51, 80, 105
Chalk Farm	28, 99, 103, 112, 115, 116, 143
Charing Cross	77
Charlotte	142
Chaul End	59
Chelsea	75
Chertsey	8
Chester-Le-Street	123, 125

Chingford Mount	73
Chiswick	8, 13, 15, 25, 27, 28, 31, 35, 38, 39, 43, 87, 93, 103, 112, 129, 131, 132, 138, 139, 140, 141, 142, 143
Chobham	23, 28, 52
Cincinatti	141
Clapton	68, 120
Clay Hall	31, 35, 69
Clayton Dewandre	34, 50, 109
Colindale	18
Commercial Motor Exhibition	15, 43, 75, 84
Commer/Harrington	22
Consett	125
Copenhagen	141
Council of Industrial Design	43
Coventry	24
Cricklewood	23, 26, 27, 63, 67, 69, 70, 75, 78, 79, 97, 98, 99, 109, 118, 119, 120
Crook	26
Croydon	63, 75, 100, 120, 139, 142
Crystal Palace	24

D

Daimler	18, 75, 84, 100, 109, 115
Dalston	98, 101, 116, 142
Darlington	123
Dartford	9
Deans	38, 85, 123
Delaware	141
Denmark	141, 143
Dennis	84
Dorking	67
Dunlop	31, 48
Dunton Green	94, 106, 107
Durham	123
Durrant, A.A.M.	8, 9, 10, 15, 59, 62, 132
Dusseldorf	141

E

Ealing	120
Earl's Court	15, 22, 43, 68, 75, 80, 84, 122, 123, 135, 136
Eastern Coachworks Ltd	13, 35, 37
East Grinstead	94, 95, 112, 115
East Ham	60
East Kent	43, 36, 122
Edgware	97
Edgware Road	35
Edmonton	59, 76, 77, 96, 133
Egham	79
Elmdon	10
Elmers End	75, 79
Enfield	120
Epping	40, 91
Esbjerg	143

F

Felixstowe	143
Fighting Vehicle Proving Ground	23
Finchley	67, 77, 78, 79, 83, 97, 104, 115, 141
Finland	140
Firestone	31, 48, 92
Firths	125
Flamstead End	76
Forest Gate	73
France	140, 142
Fulwell	42, 67, 68, 78, 79

G

Garston	91, 94, 114, 116
Gateshead	122, 125
Geneva	141
Glacier	37
GLC	115, 121

Godstone	106, 112, 114
Golders Green	24
Grays	94, 95, 104, 105, 106, 107
Greater Manchester Transport Society	98
Green Line	34, 36, 37, 38, 39, 40, 48, 51, 70, 88, 90, 91, 92, 93, 94, 95, 104, 105, 112, 117
Grove Park	78
Guildford	39, 90, 94
Gütersloh	125
Guy Arab	84, 122

H

Hackney	69, 70, 100, 103, 118, 119, 120, 142
Hague, The	140, 143
Halifax	87, 122
Hallam, Sleigh & Cheston	19
Hamburg	143
Hammersmith	73, 87
Hanwell	59, 63, 67, 75, 97, 98, 103, 114, 119, 120, 140, 143
Harlow	91, 93, 116, 121
Harrow Weald	97
Hartlepool	123
Hatfield	93, 94, 95
Heath, Edward	141
Heathrow	86, 87, 98, 107, 127, 129
Hemel Hempstead	94, 95, 116
Hendon	97, 101, 118
Hertford	39, 90, 91, 93, 94, 105, 106
Highgate	65, 67, 73, 75, 76, 77, 82, 83, 99, 112, 115, 116, 120
High Wycombe	39, 116
Hitchin	40, 95
Holborn	78
Holdsworth	19
Holland	140, 143
Holloway	63, 75, 83, 97, 99, 100, 101, 118, 119, 133
Houston	141
Hornchurch	118, 120
Hounslow	67, 79, 87, 97, 98, 121

I

Imperial Chemical Industries Ltd (I.C.I.)	9
Ilford	72
International Union of Public Transport	15
Isleworth	42, 68, 78, 79
Italy	142

J

Japan	103, 142, 143
Jensen	22

K

Kingston	31, 79, 120

L

Lancashire	62
Lansing Bagnall	128
Latham, Lord	10
Lea Bridge	68
Leamington Spa	18, 103
Leavesden	9
Leipzig	143
Leyland Motors Ltd	9, 13, 34, 35, 37, 43, 52, 61, 62, 63, 84, 85, 87, 88, 97, 98, 99, 100, 106, 108, 109, 112, 118, 122, 123, 125, 129, 130, 132, 133, 136, 141, 142, 143
Leyton	118, 120
Lille	143
Lincoln	34
Liverpool	64, 86, 122, 141

Liverpool Street 71, 77
Lockheed 18, 25, 34, 47, 50, 80, 90, 105, 109
Locomotors Ltd 128
Lodekka 37, 84, 123
Loline 84
London Aircraft Production 9
London Bridge 79
London Country Bus Services Ltd 95, 121
London County Council 111
London General Omnibus Company 130
London Passenger Transport Board 8, 98
London Transport Board 98, 121
London Transport Executive 96, 98, 121
Lord Mayor's Show, The 26
Lower Clapton 71
Lowestoft 13, 37
Lunghi, Phil 8

M

Manchester 98, 122
Marples, Ernest 132
Marsh, Richard 120
Marshall of Cambridge (Engineering) Ltd 128
Maudslay 57
MCW 8, 13, 32, 37, 129
Memphis 141
Mercury 29
Metalastik 61
Metrobus 109
Metro-Cammell 13
Middle Row 59, 79, 100, 112, 119
Middlesbrough 123
Midland Red 18
Milan 142
Ministry of Defence 9
Ministry of Supply 23
Montreal 143
Moorgate 77, 78
Morden 61
Mortlake 63, 67, 97, 98, 99, 114, 119, 141
Motor Industry Research Association 22, 23, 28
Mulley, Fred 121
Munich 15, 141
Muswell Hill 99, 101

N

National Bus Company 95, 121
National Freight Corporation 121
Nebraska 142
New Addington 101, 120
New Barnet 95
Newcastle 123
New Cross 67, 78, 79, 119, 120
New Jersey 141
New Orleans 141, 142
New York 142, 143
Nixon, C.B. 13
Noise Abatement Society 132
Norbiton 79, 99
Northern General Transport Company Ltd 87, 122, 123, 128
Northfleet 114, 121
Northolt 22, 28, 29
Northumberland Park 77
Norway 142
Norwood 103, 118
Nuneaton 22, 28, 30

O

Olympian 109
Omaha 141
Omnibus Society 135
Orion 32
Oslo 109, 142

P

Palmers Green 121
Panama Canal 141
Paris 143
Park Royal 8, 13, 28, 32, 37, 42, 43, 56, 57, 78, 82, 84, 86, 87, 88, 96, 100, 103, 106, 108, 112, 122, 123, 126, 127, 135, 136, 137
Peckham 63, 75, 98, 99, 120, 121, 139
Phelps-Brown, Professor Henry 100
Philadelphia 141
Plummer, Desmond 121
Plumstead 119
Pneuride 48
Poplar 48, 60, 67, 68, 69, 70, 71, 72, 103, 116, 118, 120, 131, 142
Potters Bar 94, 100
Princes Street 138
Putney 35, 97, 99, 100, 101, 112, 116, 118, 119, 120, 143

R

Ranko 60
Red Arrow 116, 137
Redhill 31
Reids 125
Reigate 31, 39, 112
Reliance 29, 100
Ricardo & Co, Engineers (1927) Ltd 132, 133
Richmond, Virginia 142
Riverside 69, 70, 72, 94, 103, 112, 116, 119, 142
Road Haulage Association 132
Robbins, R.M. 135
Romford 37, 39, 94, 104, 105, 106, 107, 118
Rotterdam 140, 142, 143
Roundshaw 139
Royal Victoria Dock 142
Rubery Owen 128
Rye Lane 63, 67, 97, 98, 99, 121

S

Sainsbury, Arthur 8, 13, 23
San Francisco 141
St Lawrence Seaway 142
Saunders Engineering & Shipyard Ltd 9, 21
Scotland Yard 28
Scott, Douglas 8, 17, 19
Scottish Transport Group 121
Self Changing Gears Ltd 18, 31, 38, 62, 136
Shave, K.G. 132, 135
Sheffield 135
Shepherds Bush 53, 67, 73, 118
Shoreham-by-Sea 132
Short Bros. Ltd 9
'Silver Lady' 65
Simms 47, 51, 90, 105, 109
Singapore 142
Slough 116, 119, 121
Southall 53, 57, 60, 98, 114, 120
Spurrier, Henry 13, 62
Spain 78
Staines 79
Stamford Brook 87, 129
Stamford Hill 77, 112, 114, 116
Stevenage 40, 91, 94, 121
Stockholm 140
Stockton 123, 137
Stockwell 63, 97, 116, 118, 119
Stoke Newington 77
Stokes, Donald 62
Stonebridge 67, 75, 78, 79, 97, 109
Strachans 137
Stratford 72, 73
Sunderland 125
Surrey 31
Surrey Docks 26, 142
Swanley 93, 94
Switzerland 140, 141, 143

T

Team Valley 123
Tees 125
Thompson Pressings 59
Thornton Heath 79, 120
Tilbury 142
Tilling 9, 37, 122
Titan 109
Titsey Hill 22, 28
Tokyo 142, 143
Toledo 142
Toronto 143
Tottenham 41, 63, 70, 72, 76, 77, 79, 97, 100, 112, 114, 116, 120, 138, 139, 141
Transport and General Workers Union (TGWU) 10, 15, 82, 96
Transport Holding Company 120, 121
Tunbridge Wells 39, 106
Turnham Green 18, 31, 70, 114, 120
Tynemouth 125
Tyneside 87, 125

U

Underground 90, 93, 121
United Automobile Services Ltd 122
Upton Park 27, 35, 63, 69, 83, 100, 103, 114, 118, 119, 120, 121, 143
USA 140, 142
Uxbridge 98, 119, 121

V

Valentine, A.B.B. 10, 17
Vauxhall Motors 59
Verdon-Roe, G. 9
Vickers 126
Victoria 76, 77, 93, 103, 136
Vienna 143
Vitafoam 54
Vybac 34

W

Waltham Cross 76
Walthamstow 67, 71, 72, 97, 116, 120, 121
Walworth 114, 118, 142
Washington 125
Waterloo 26
Welwyn Garden City 93, 94
West Croydon 75
West Germany 125
West Green 76
West Ham 47, 48, 68, 69, 70, 71, 72, 73, 75, 115, 116, 130, 131
Westinghouse 91
West London Air Terminal 86, 127
Weymann's Ltd 13, 32, 35
Whipsnade Zoo 107
'White Lady' 65
Wicks, J.W. 8
Willesden 35, 41, 68, 69, 70, 72, 83, 97, 103, 114, 116, 118, 120, 121, 143
Wilson 18, 34
Wimbledon Stadium 75
Winchmore Hill 77
Windsor 39, 91, 99, 106, 107, 116, 119, 121
Woodford 72
Wood Green 76, 77, 78, 79, 120
Worldmaster 35
Wrotham 93, 94
Wulfrunian, Guy 75, 84

Y

Yokohama 142

Z

Zurich 141